PENGUIN BOOKS

BLESSINGS IN DISGUISE

'Charming, enjoyable and extremely well written' – John Mortimer in
the *Sunday Times*

'[He is] an excellent raconteur ... The revised version still contains
highly enjoyable chapters on Gielgud, Guthrie, Ralph Richardson,
Ernest Milton, Martita Hunt, the Sitwells and Sir Sydney Cockrell. To
these, Guinness has added a new one, which culminates in a curious
luncheon with the late Freya Stark. It was clearly unwise of him to
offend a strong-willed lady who had just shown two bottles of snake
venom to her assembled guests' – Benedict Nightingale in *The Times
Literary Supplement*

'Such a joy ... so wise, so humorous, so tolerant of human failings and
foibles' – Francis King in the *Sunday Telegraph*

'Entirely original' – Simon Callow in *Books and Bookmen*

'He shows himself as charming and accomplished with words as he is in
his best performances' – Jonathan Cecil in the *Spectator*, Books of
the Year

ALEC GUINNESS

Blessings in Disguise

Mel

Hope you like it!

Thanks for everything in 2001

LOL
Mick
x x x ,

PENGUIN BOOKS

PENGUIN BOOKS

Published by the Penguin Group
Penguin Books Ltd, 27 Wrights Lane, London W8 5TZ, England
Penguin Putnam Inc., 375 Hudson Street, New York, New York 10014, USA
Penguin Books Australia Ltd, Ringwood, Victoria, Australia
Penguin Books Canada Ltd, 10 Alcorn Avenue, Toronto, Ontario, Canada M4V 3B2
Penguin Books (NZ) Ltd, Private Bag 102902, NSMC, Auckland, New Zealand

Penguin Books Ltd, Registered Offices: Harmondsworth, Middlesex, England

First published by Hamish Hamilton 1985
Reissued with a new chapter, 'Ophidia and Others', 1996
Published in Penguin Books 1997
7

Acknowledgement is due to Faber & Faber for
permission to quote from T. S. Eliot's *Four Quartets*;
and to David Higham Associates for Edith Sitwell's *Façade*

The moral right of the author has been asserted

Printed in England by Clays Ltd, St Ives plc

Contents

Illustrations

1a, 1b, 6, 8b, 9b, 11a, 11b, 12a, 12b, 12c, 12d, 13, 16a and 16b are from the author's collection; 2a, 2b, 3a, 3b and 5a are from the Mander and Mitchenson Theatre Collection; 4a, 7b, 8a, 15a and 15b are from the BBC Hulton Picture Library; 4b is the property of L. A. Holder; 5b is reproduced by courtesy of the Public Archives of Canada, photo by Walter Curtin RCA; and 9c by courtesy of the National Film Archive Stills Collection and of Columbia (UK) Ltd.

PUBLISHER'S NOTE:
For this reissue of *Blessings in Disguise*, a new chapter, 'Ophidia and Others', has been added and a few minor amendments made to the 1985 edition; the text is otherwise unchanged.

Stage Directions

This is a book of casual memoirs and not an autobiography, although it contains much autobiographical material.

Enter EGO from the wings, pursued by fiends. Exit EGO.

Ego, as a very young person, with no professional experience, assumes that his natural place in the scheme of things is up-stage centre but quickly learns that, for a long time to come, he must be down-stage, very much to the side, and with his back half turned to the audience. With the passing of years he grows to like this position and in later life, when he has a little say in some theatre productions, he often expresses the wish to sidle into a play rather than take the bull by the horns. The bold statement is never likely to be his: he is well aware he is not in the same class as Olivier, Richardson, Gielgud or the other greats. His pleasure is in putting little bits of things together, as if playing with a jig-saw puzzle.

The fiends which chase or jostle him are Impatience, Fretfulness, Hurt-Pride, Frivolity, Laziness, Impetuosity, Fear-of-the-Future and, lurking nearby, Lack-of-Commonsense. ('Don't underestimate commonsense' was written across a report at his drama school.) He knows their fiendish characters well enough and despises them, but is constantly caught off guard. In youth his fuse leading to explosion was very short; perhaps with age it has lengthened and burns more slowly. He is not at all proud of himself or his achievements and is equally attracted and repelled by the limelight, as if never quite sure how to present himself, or who he is or what he would really like to be. Deep in his heart he hankers to be an artist of some sort, but he is only an actor. To be an actor was his adolescent dream and has been his means of livelihood for fifty years or more; but although he has no complaints about that (indeed it would be ungrateful of him to make any) he knows that an actor is usually no more than an assortment of odds and ends which barely add up to a whole man. An actor is an interpreter of other men's words, often a soul which wishes to reveal itself to the world but dare not, a craftsman, a bag of tricks, a vanity bag, a cool observer of mankind, a child, and at his best a kind of unfrocked priest who, for an hour or two, can call on heaven and hell to mesmerise a group of innocents.

When Hamish Hamilton suggested I should attempt to write an autobiography Ego was immensely flattered and *I* was appalled. My chief objection was that so many autobiographies reveal, on almost every page, rivulets of I's, and that in amateur hands such as mine this would be the case yet again, reaching perhaps almost torrential proportions. Also, that theatrical autobiographies often read like first- or last-night speeches – fulsome thanks to playwright, management, director, fellow actors, electricians, and the wardrobe mistress without whom the show couldn't have been got on. Eventually Ego and I reached some sort of compromise; I would try to write of some of the people or events that have influenced me, or have at least stayed firmly enough in my memory, and Ego could make his entrances and exits as often as he chose (almost continually, I am ashamed to say) if they had some bearing on the subject. The result is not so much a patch-work quilt of memoirs as a cat's cradle of reminiscences, all tangled round myself.

It would be impossible to define in what way, exactly, I have been influenced by John Gielgud, for instance, or Guthrie, Komisarjevsky, Basil Dean, Michel St Denis or a host of others. They have all left an indelible mark and I count myself lucky in having crossed their paths. Perhaps Edith Evans, Leon Quartermain, Ernest Milton and Ralph Richardson were the performers to whose lightest word, professionally, I paid most attention. Then I have been blessed in knowing well Eileen Atkins and Anthony Quayle, and something of Cyril Cusack (who ranks alongside Pierre Fresnay as one of my two favourite actors), and Albert Finney, Tom Courtenay and others too numerous to mention. They all have my gratitude, not only for the intense pleasure they have given, but for just being themselves. My gratitude is not confined to actors of course; there have been poets, authors, and people from other walks of life with an equal claim to my love.

Ego seems to have disappeared. But not for long, I know. I can hear his lightest tread.

This is the moment when Ego, now heavily disguised as a small, reddish-haired and very freckled child, makes his fearful entrance; upstage; centre; pursued by his infantile demons but greatly comforted by his good angels.

CHAPTER ONE

The Lady in the Ground Floor Front

Many actors, when they have made a name for themselves, are endlessly recounting in the public prints how they don't know who they are, why they are, or, indeed, where they are. Poor, rich, exceptionally brilliant Peter Sellers never seemed to get himself sorted out in spite of the fact that, apart from some upset marriages, there didn't appear to be much confusion in his life. I, on the other hand, was born to confusion and totally immersed in it for several years, owning three different names until the age of fourteen and living in about thirty different hotels, lodgings and flats, each of which was hailed as 'home' until such time as my mother and I flitted, leaving behind, like a paper-chase, a wake of unpaid bills.

My birth certificate registers me as Alec Guinness de Cuffe, born in Marylebone, London, 2nd April 1914. My mother at the time was a Miss Agnes Cuffe; my father's name is left an intriguing, speculative blank. When I was five years old my mother married an army Captain, a Scot named David Stiven, and from then until I left my preparatory school I was known as Alec Stiven (a name I rather liked, although I hated and dreaded my stepfather). At fourteen I was told, quite casually, that my real name was Guinness and that de Cuffe and Stiven were obliterated. So it was as a very small Alec Stiven, shortly after the start of my mother's violently unhappy marriage, which only lasted three years, that I entered yet another new 'home' – a very depressing three-roomed flat at the top of a gloomy house in St John's Wood.

The basement of the house was occupied by a caretaker and his wife, whom I cannot remember, and the ground floor front room was lived in by a mysterious old lady whom I didn't encounter for several weeks. An echoing, stone staircase twisted up the house past three deserted floors. The whole place was chilly and spooky, and to pass the empty flats, with their locked doors of peeling black paint, I found terrifying even if my hand was held. To this day I can still be apprehensive, on a grey day, when passing the shut door of a room I know to be empty; it is always just possible that the room

holds an unknown presence – a snake, a corpse or the wraith of an
old lady who might skim over the floor and disappear through a
wall.

In the middle of the night, shortly after we had moved in, I woke
and called out, 'There's a man in my room!' And indeed there was;
it was Captain Stiven, crouched on the floor, fumbling in the bottom
drawer of a creaky wardrobe, which was usually locked, for his
service revolver. The bullets were kept in a small, soft leather bag
slung over a door-handle. 'It's only me,' he whispered, and crept out
of the room in his striped pyjamas, fully armed and ready for action.
For once his voice was reassuring and as there were no further sounds
I fell asleep again. In the morning I overheard my mother talking in
a low voice to the caretaker's wife, who had come up to do a little
dusting. 'The Captain,' my mother was saying, in a tone which
might have implied Field-Marshal, 'heard someone up here in the
night and I thought I saw someone standing at the foot of the bed.
Whoever or whatever it was slipped downstairs quickly when the
Captain said, "Where's my gun?". He always has his gun with him,
in case the Sinn Fein come after him.' 'Ah!' said the other voice. My
mother went on, 'It disturbed the boy. But I think he thought it was
a dream. But it wasn't a dream. This house is haunted. We may have
to leave.' Later in the day I said, 'What's haunted mean?' 'Ask no
questions and you'll hear no tales. It means silliness.' I wasn't satisfied,
but left it at that.

The following afternoon, the Captain not at home, my mother,
looking fetching in a cloche hat, told me she was going out 'for just
a few minutes'. I grew accustomed, later on, to interpreting 'just a
few minutes' as two or three hours. 'You stay in here and draw me
a nice picture. I'll be back before you've even started.' I settled down
happily in the sitting-room and drew a huge fleet of dreadnoughts.
As smoke and shells bulged out of every gun I provided an appropriate
'boom'; until it struck me that it was getting dusky, I needed lights,
and the house was exceptionally quiet. Could I hear breathing somewhere? I began to panic. 'This house is haunted.' I still didn't know
what that could possibly mean but I felt something unpleasant was
beginning to happen. I went on to the landing and peered down the
well of the stone staircase, wondering if I could get safely to the
basement and the indifferent comfort of the caretaker's. Not a sound
anywhere. I tiptoed down the first flight of stairs, holding my breath
as much as I could, and waited by the black door of the next flat to
see if it moved. Nothing. I took the next flight at greater speed,

paused in terror at the second door, and then plunged down the last flight with an uncontrollable clatter and stood panting in the hall where, to my horror, the door to the Ground Floor Front stood ajar.

'Who's that?' asked an old voice, neither male nor female.

I began to back towards the basement stairs.

'Who *is* that?' the voice demanded, very imperiously.

'Me,' I said. There was a short pause.

'Who is me?'

In my anxiety I forgot my name.

'Me.'

'Come here, Me! Don't be afraid, Me! Come in.'

I edged to the door and gave it a little push which opened it a few more inches.

After some reflection I decided the voice was not unfriendly, and I made my entrance. The room was a large bed-sitter, cluttered, untidy and musty-smelling; but it was safer than the staircase, more interesting than the basement and had a happier atmosphere than the flat at the top of the building. It was strange, like its occupant, but not sinister.

She was old, shrivelled, big-nosed and very white, and she lay, propped up by pillows, under a frayed coverlet on a brass bed. Her head was turned towards me, a long, welcoming arm extended and she had an almost twisted smile on her face.

'So you are the little boy at the top of the castle. I hear your footsteps on the stairs. Why do you always run? A young gentleman should *walk*, not run.'

She eased herself a little higher in the bed before continuing. 'Deportment! De-port-ment! Walk with a book on your head, stretch your neck up, up, up; down with your shoulders; keep your b-t-m in, flat. That's what it means, deportment.'

I was more interested in a brass knob on the bedstead, which wobbled as she spoke, than in what she was saying. She was an impoverished Miss Havisham who had lived in a different social world. There was no cobwebbed wedding-cake but under her bed she did have a partially-eaten rice pudding, which she presently asked for.

'Under the bed, Me, you will find my pudding.'

It was in a small, chipped, green, enamel dish, burnt at the edges.

'You've got a lot of fluff under your bed,' I said, handing her the pudding and a bent spoon.

'You must excuse me, Me. I'm an old woman now, dear, and it

isn't often I take a broom to things. There was a time – ah! Bright lights! Bouquets! Admirers! *Then* things were more ship-shape.'

She made an attempt to straighten the spoon. She gave me a confidential look and lowered her voice.

'I had to pop the silver, dear; you know what I mean.'

I returned to the subject of bed-fluff.

'*We've* got a bizzle,' I told her.

'Then you are very lucky. You actually *own* a bizzle?'

'My mummy bought it. In a shop. *We* don't have *any* bed-fluff.'

'Lucky again,' she said, and pushed her pudding aside.

'Do you play games?' she asked. 'Cricket? Football?'

'No, not yet. When I am six. I am nearly six. My new daddy wants me to play games when I am six.'

Her face came closer to mine and her eyes widened in an extraordinary way.

'We are going to be *great friends*, aren't we?'

I nodded.

'You don't find it too dark in here?'

It was fairly dark and I peered round the room; at the standard-lamp with its fringed shade, the shawls draped over chairs, the photographs decorated with artificial flowers, the china objects on the black marble fireplace and the unlit gas-fire. Then I tried to count the wrinkles on her face, but that was a hopeless task and I knew I couldn't count high enough.

'Not *too* dark,' I said, rather bravely.

'It's cosy in the dark,' she said, 'and you can whisper secrets. Will you come and see me again tomorrow? And remember, don't run down the stairs; walk down like a proper gentleman. And when you reach my door knock hard on it and call out in a loud voice, "Overture and beginners, please." Then I shall know it is you. Now, before you go, I'm going to give you a little present.'

She dragged open the drawer of a bedside table, took out a small candle and lit it. The room sprang into life with a hundred jumping shadows.

'That's to light you upstairs. You must leave me now. Goodnight, Me.'

Holding the candle well in front of me I stepped into the hall.

'Close the door!' she called out, and when I did the candle guttered alarmingly. I forgot to go to the basement and, concentrating on the candle flame, I tried not to notice my looming shadow behind or the unsteady darkness above. Having got upstairs I didn't know what to do with the candle. I stood in the kitchen for a long time before throwing it in the sink, where it sputtered itself out. Then I lay on the floor, too frightened to move. When my mother returned I pretended to be dead.

Sometime the following morning I slipped out of the flat carrying the bizzle, which I clumped down to the hall. I knocked at the old lady's door but couldn't remember the secret pass, if such it was. In answer to her muffled query from inside I said, in an attempt at a gruff voice, 'It's the man with the bizzle.'

'Oh, come in, bizzle man,' she called. Flinging open the door I rushed in, bizzling as I went. I crashed round the furniture pretending I was a train but managed to get rid of the fluff from under the bed; after which I rested from my labours on the handle of the machine, well satisfied with myself.

'How much do I owe you?' the old lady asked from her bed.

'One hundred pounds, Miss.'

'I shall have to pay you tomorrow, as I don't think I have a hundred pounds by me just now.'

'Very good, Miss,' I said, and dragged the bizzle up to the flat.

The next afternoon I found another opportunity to slip downstairs again. When my mother asked where I was going I told her I wanted to listen to the goblins who burbled to each other in the water tank in the basement – a frightening fiction of the caretaker's wife. For some reason I wished to keep my friendship with the lady in the Ground Floor Front a secret.

This time when I knocked the door was opened from the inside immediately; she stood there in a flowered dressing-gown, fluffy slippers and a large embroidered shawl round her shoulders. She clapped her hands in welcome. 'Sit down, I am going to dance for you.'

I curled up on the old squashy sofa with a lot of dusty cushions.

'You will have to imagine the music. We are in a big theatre. Drury Lane.'

She picked up a waste-paper basket, put it on her head, raised her arms high and started to hum. Her arms began to undulate slowly.

'Do you hear the fiddles?'

'No.'

'Use your imagination, boy! Hark at the cymbals! And the tinkling bells. And here come the drums! You must applaud, boy. Clap your hands!'

I clapped dutifully and vigorously. She took a few stately steps, raising first one slippered foot, then another, and revolved.

'I am a Persian Princess,' she explained, 'dancing in the Harem to please my husband the Prince. That's you. I am carrying a basket of pomegranates.'

She took the basket from her head and pretended to throw fruit from it as she dipped, curtseying around the room. She came to an abrupt stop, a little puffed.

'I am not as young as I was,' she said. 'I would like you to have seen me in my prime. At Drury Lane. When you are grown up you will be able to tell your children you saw The Great Deva dance "The Persian Princess". Did you like it?'

'Yes,' I replied, 'but I would have liked it more with music.' But I remembered to clap, which pleased her.

Upstairs again, I picked up a waste-paper basket and whirled round the sitting-room. The Captain scowled. 'What do you think you are doing?' my mother asked.

'I am a Persian Princess,' I said. 'I am dancing in a big theatre. I am in my prime.'

'The boy's touched,' the Captain said.

'Oh, he's only being a boy,' my mother said.

'Then why the blazes is he pretending to be a girl? Stop it this instant!' he shouted.

I put down the basket of pomegranates and withdrew to a table where my drawing paper was. I drew a very big gun, scribbled a violent explosion and pointed the whole thing towards the Captain. 'Bang, bang, bang!' I muttered and burst into tears.

Not until the day we left the flat for good did I see the old lady again. A taxi was outside the house to take us to the station, and from there we would go by train to Bexhill, where I was to be a boarder at a small prep school called Normandale, which was run by a friend of my step-father. I was just six years old, but quite cheerful at the idea of starting school properly. As we stood in the bleak hall the old lady opened her door.

'They tell me you are going away, Me, and I don't expect we shall meet again. I would like you to have this; it's a little Russian bear.' She handed me a brightly-painted wooden bear, a few inches high, but the Captain snatched it out of my hand and gave it back to her.

'It's very kind of you but he doesn't accept presents. And he wouldn't want a toy, would he, at school? He's going to learn to play cricket and keep a straight bat, not play with wooden dolls. He may be another Jack Hobbs.' (David Stiven was a friend of Jack Hobbs and that summer had dragged me out to the pitch at Lord's cricket ground to shake the great man's hand; he was kindly, but smelled of damp flannel, I remember.)

'I'm sorry,' the old lady said; and she went back to her room.

As we drove away I expected her to look through the window of the Ground Floor Front to wave me good-bye, but she didn't.

'Poor old thing,' my mother said. 'I believe she used to be an actress.'

'Did you pay the bill at the newsagent's?' the Captain asked.

'Oh, I'm sure I did,' my mother replied. It didn't seem to matter. We would be sixty miles away in no time.

CHAPTER TWO

Button Boots

My second term at Normandale, at Bexhill-on-Sea, proved to be my last there. I had been sent there as a boarder, at the age of six, shortly after my mother had married David Stiven; and I was blissfully happy, being by far the youngest boy in the school and, consequently, much fussed over. But when the summer term ended I found myself spending a dreary, lonely August holiday confined to a rather gloomy London hotel in the Cromwell Road; a place of unlit Turkey-carpeted passageways, loos of great flowered bowls set in wide mahogany seats with pull-up brass handles for flushing, tinted windows of tulip designs and dusty, green brocaded curtains. Very little air found its way into the hotel; the ferns, in their brass tubs, gave out a fetid smell like dying jungle vegetation. Now and then someone took me for a boring walk in Kensington Gardens, and once I was treated to a visit to the Natural History Museum, but for the most part I was left to my own devices – filling a bath to float a little, lopsided sailing-boat; drawing fierce battle scenes; teasing a tired old maid or building card-houses on the floor of the 'Residents' Lounge'. The only positive enjoyment I discovered was being allowed, occasionally, to work the hotel's water-lift – a slow and stately machine which gurgled its way up and down when you pulled on a greasy rope. Into this contraption, on a morning when I was operating it, there lightly stepped a large foreign lady of advanced years, dressed in threadbare black.

I had doubts whether the water could replace her immense weight; I eyed her like a hangman and then hauled on the rope manfully and successfully. When eventually we reached her floor, after a little upping and downing, she complimented me on my skill; so we became instant friends. She told me, among other interesting things, that she used to be a champion pole-punter in Russia, oh, long before the Revolution; that she had once given a gymnastic display before the Tsar and that as a small girl she walked the tight-rope. A vision filled my head of this new and welcome friend high in the air, wearing a sort of spangled bathing-costume, balancing on a rope with the aid of her punt-pole, while, way down below, crowned heads rose in tumultuous applause. She asked me if I had ever been to the circus. The answer was 'No'. Had I, perhaps, ever been taken to the theatre? Well, I had seen *Chu-Chin-Chow*, which I had enjoyed very much; and I gave her half a verse of 'The Cobbler's Song'. I had also seen *Puss in Boots* but had hated it. 'This must be remedied,' she said, and instantly proposed taking me the following week to a matinée at the Coliseum, where there was a Variety show. She was as good as her word. She bought seats for the two of us in the Dress Circle. I hate to think, now, what economic heart-searching she must have gone through, rummaging in her vast black bag to see if she had sufficient funds, and wondering, perhaps, if she would have to draw on her meagre savings.

The Coliseum offered jugglers; clowns; maidens in flimsy frocks who danced in flickering lights, attempting to look like flames; a man, with his hands and feet shackled, in a glass tank of water, from which he just managed to escape in a flurry of bubbles; some funnyish men in squashed hats and baggy trousers; acrobats, of course, of whom my hostess was sternly critical; some boring singers; and then – and then – the Top of the Bill, Nellie Wallace.

I don't believe I laughed at Miss Wallace on her first appearance. Truth to tell, I was a little scared, she looked so witch-like with her parrot-beak nose and shiny black hair screwed tightly into a little hard bun. She wore a loud tweed jacket and skirt, an Alpine hat with an enormous, bent pheasant's feather, and dark woollen stockings which ended in neat, absurd, twinkling button boots. Her voice was hoarse and scratchy, her walk swift and aggressive; she appeared to be always bent forward from the waist, as if looking for someone to punch. She was very small. Having reached centre stage she plunged into a stream of patter, not one word of which did I understand, but I am sure it was full of outrageous innuendoes. The audience fell about laughing but no laughter came from me. I was in love with her.

Later in the afternoon she turned up in a bright green, shiny and much too tight evening gown. She kept dropping things – bag, fan, handkerchief, a hairbrush – and every time she bent to retrieve them the orchestra made rude sounds on their wind instruments, as if she had ripped her dress or farted. Her look of frozen indignation at this pleased me enormously, but my companion clearly thought the whole act very vulgar and something which would not have been tolerated by the crowned heads of Russia. I laughed a lot but didn't fall out of my seat until Nellie's next act, in which she appeared in a nurse's uniform ready to assist a surgeon at an operation. The patient, covered with a sheet, was wheeled on stage and the surgeon immediately set about him with a huge carving-knife. Nellie stood by, looking very prim, but every now and then would dive under the sheet and extract with glee and a shout of triumph quite impossible articles – a hotwater bottle, a live chicken, a flat-iron, and so on. Finally, she inserted, with many wicked looks, a long rubber tube which she blew down. The body inflated rapidly to huge proportions and then, covered in its sheet, slowly took to the air. Nellie made desperate attempts to catch it, twinkling her boots as she hopped surprisingly high, but all in vain. The orchestra gave a tremendous blast as she made her last leap; and that is when I fell off my plush seat and felt faintly sick.

I left the theatre in a daze, trying to walk like her, catching imaginary corpses in the air, glaring with wildly shocked eyes at innocent passers-by and generally misbehaving myself. My kind friend cannot have been very put out, as she offered me an ice-cream soda at Lyons. I liked the idea but asked the price. She said it would cost about two shillings, but that was all right as personally she only needed a cup of strong tea. I asked if I might please spend the two shillings on something else. 'On what?' Without any hesitation I said I would like to buy some flowers for Nellie Wallace. Those were days when flower-women could be found almost anywhere in London, so somewhere near Trafalgar Square we bought a small bunch of yellow roses which I proudly carried to the stage door of the Coliseum, where a note was written by my hostess and signed in a scrawl by me. The flowers were sent up straight away – I stood around to make sure of that – to my dotty new heroine. 'You shall have the ice-cream all the same,' I was told. It was proving a far more expensive outing than had been intended, I fear. At Lyons I slowly got through an enormous ice, giggling from time to time with blissful memories of the afternoon in the theatre and then thinking, with reverence, of those button boots and the impertinent feather in Nellie's hat.

Perhaps the ice-cream was a mistake; the whole experience had been too much for me. By the time we got back to Cromwell Road I was feverish and put straight to bed. By night-fall I had a temperature of 104° (which impressed me no end) and my mother, in a panic, called for a doctor. I was kept in bed in the gloomy hotel for a month and was fairly ill, on and off, for a year.

That might have been the end of my over-excited matinée, but it wasn't quite. After I had been in bed a week I received a great bunch of yellow roses together with a note which read, 'I hope the little boy who sent me flowers gets better soon. Love, Nellie Wallace.' The kind Russian lady had gone to the theatre, explained my passion and asked Miss Wallace to send me a postcard. The flowers came instead. I can remember protesting loudly when the water was changed in the vase; I was under the impression that Nellie had provided not only the roses but the vase and water as well. And perhaps she had fired an ambition in me as well. I was determined that one day I also should have a hat with a broken feather. I never met her. Later in life I saw her a few times, but it was never quite so magical as when I was seven. No doubt, with the years, her vitality had diminished, her hoarse voice grown feebler and her brand of vulgarity become too familiar. Yet the boots seemed to live on. I would like to think they are well cared for in some eccentric museum and, when darkness falls, that they shed their primness, take up idiotic positions and tap out some old, raucous, ribald music-hall song.

CHAPTER THREE

The Rain Machine

It must have been in the winter of 1930 when I first saw Sybil
Thorndike; in the little old theatre at Bournemouth. She and Lewis
Casson were there for a week, acting in a melodrama called *The Squall*
and in Ibsen's *Ghosts*. The so-called squall was really a reach-me-down
storm, in a Spanish setting, with undertones of smouldering sex.
Lewis Casson wore a Cordoba hat, I remember, and carried a menacing whip with which he frequently tapped his high shiny boots. Sybil
wore a gigantic glossy black wig, which supported a huge Spanish
comb. Apart from that she appeared to be motherly, warm-hearted,
understanding, and occasionally gravely distressed. I can't remember
what it was all about but I found it fairly exciting. Castanets were
clicked from time to time, copper pans were polished and the ingénue,
who was greatly given to pouting and sulky airs, at one moment
slowly lifted her skirt to expose a knee. But it was really the stage
effects I had gone to see, attracted by the title rather than Sybil's
name and guessing, rightly as it turned out, that there would be
thunder and lightning. At the end of the week the company had a
change of pace and décor, substituting a fusty Norwegian parlour
for an Andalusian farmhouse. Sybil appeared as Mrs Alving (in a
grey wig now) and Lewis, looking remarkably like himself – but
with side-whiskers, was Pastor Manders.

As it was the last week of my school holidays and pocket-money
was very low I decided I could only afford to see one of the plays.
Ghosts would have to go by the board; so it was to a mid-week
matinée of *The Squall* that I treated myself. Mid-week matinées were
not much more rewarding to managements then than they are now,
unless a great success was being shown, and I found the theatre
almost empty. It didn't occur to me, at that age, that empty stalls
were depressing; after all the actors were getting my two shillings
and I was well content with the bargain. The thunder, lightning and,
above all, the visible rattling rain in the last act were very much to
my liking. I longed to know how it was all done; largely with a view
to reproducing it in a school play when I returned to Eastbourne. I

knew it was unsuitable for *The Pirates of Penzance* or *Silas Marner*, both of which I had directed – 'produced' we used to say – but perhaps a good storm could be worked into Barrie's *Shall We Join The Ladies*, which was in the offing.

When I got back to my mean holiday digs that evening I decided to write to Sybil. My letter went something like this:

Dear Miss Thorndike [this was about a year before she was made a Dame],

I saw you in the play this afternoon and I quite liked you. I did like the storm scene though. Would you please tell me how you made the rain? And do you have a thunder-sheet? It is important for me to know as I want to be an actor. I am sixteen and a half.

Yours sincerely,
Alec Guinness

I posted it immediately. Two mornings later I received a hastily-scrawled note which just said, 'Come to the matinée of *Ghosts* on Saturday and my husband will show you how we make the storm. Ask for me at the stage-door after the performance. Do you like poetry? I do hope so. Yrs Srly, Sbl Thorndike.'

Well, that meant asking for more pocket-money. I said I needed it because Miss Thorndike had invited me to see *Ghosts*. Objections, of a mild nature, were raised; Sybil was widely known to be a Socialist, a friend of that firebrand Bernard Shaw and a pacifist; and surely *Ghosts* was reputed to be a disgusting play about an unmentionable disease. It was also said to be very gloomy. I would find it very boring. My obstinacy held out; I said a great actress like Miss Thorndike couldn't be let down; it would be shameful not to accept what was practically a royal command; and finally I was handed a few shillings.

The next thing was for me to brush up some poetry in case the Cassons invited me to recite. I knew some Ella Wheeler Wilcox, which I found hysterically funny; also some Keats, Tennyson, Chesterton and quite a few yards of Shakespeare. After much fussing and lip-biting I decided to re-learn a musical-monologue called 'Dangerous Dan McGrew'. It began, if I remember rightly:

A bunch of the boys were whooping it up
In the Maamut saloon.

This had proved a great success at school (Roborough, Eastbourne), a year or so back, when I had painted a thin black moustache on my upper lip and wore a slouch hat belonging to one of the masters. (I had once seen a man recite it at the London Pavilion, standing in a green spotlight and thoroughly quelling his audience.) It seemed to me now just the right stuff as a curtain-raiser for a play called *Ghosts*. Surely I can't have entertained any idea that I was going to be engaged, on the spot, as an actor? I think not; but I may have day-dreamed of such a thing.

I sat through *Ghosts* without understanding much of the dialogue but disliking Pastor Manders heartily. I rather warmed to the feckless, handsome Oswald. (Ten years later, at the Old Vic, the Oswald played, quite excellently, the enigmatic, priggish Tibetan Abbot in Auden/Isherwood's *Ascent of F.6.*, in which I acted the even more priggish hero, Ransom.) The set was very claustrophobic; full of heavy furniture, a round table covered with a dark green velvet cloth, heavy red curtains to the windows. It was not unlike gloomy digs I had experienced in Bournemouth, Brighton or St John's Wood. I admired the oil-lamps they used (electric of course) and the way the actors pretended to light them and adjust their brightness. The play left me chilled and rather disturbed and when, after the performance, I found myself in Sybil's presence I was tongue-tied. She was wearing a blue and white flowered dressing-gown; was sweetly welcoming, and there wasn't the least condescension in her manner or conversation. To her statements, though, about the greatness of Ibsen – how he cleared the air, got rid of all the bed-fluff, gave women their proper due, and so on – I could only nod in a way which I hoped looked intelligent. 'You did like this better than *The Squall*, didn't you?' she asked, rather suspiciously. I nodded again vigorously, but it was a lying nod; and yet, today, I retain a far more vivid impression of that production of *Ghosts* than I have of the foolish melodrama. Except for the storm scene.

Lewis Casson came into her dressing-room, sporting a baggy pair of grey flannel trousers and an old crumpled jacket. His bright, little, blue Welsh eyes twinkled at me. 'Ah, the young man who wants to know about the thunder-sheet!' Then they both took me to the stage. Two things amazed me: the heat that still hung in the air although the lighting had been switched off, and the solid reality of the set. They allowed me to go round fingering everything – the tassels and bobs on the curtains, the books and oil-lamps. I opened and shut doors, sat on the chairs; and a foolish, awe-inspired grin spread over my face. Sybil and Lewis watched, amused, I expect, but probably wondering how long they were going to be saddled with this oddity with large outstanding ears. They had another performance to give in two hours' time. Would this be the moment for me to suggest, modestly, 'Dangerous Dan McGrew'? Fortunately Lewis interrupted my reverie, 'Now, the thunder.' He led me to the back of the stage where he belaboured a great iron sheet, suspended from the flies. 'But it's the rain he wants,' Sybil bawled over the din. So they both went to a long wooden trough, over which they crouched while vigorously turning a couple of large handles – rather like those to be seen on old-fashioned mangles. This operated a sausage-shaped metal colander, high above us, which revolved and released streams of small grey air-gun pellets. Even in the dim light they looked uncommonly like heavy drops of rain. With proper theatrical lighting the effect, I knew, was magical. The two of them worked hard at their rain-making for a few minutes. I was merciless and never asked them to stop. Finally they straightened up and Lewis, quite puffed, said abruptly, 'That's all we can show you.'

'Now tell me,' said Sybil, taking me to her room, 'do you like poetry?' I nodded. Lewis followed us, in case she needed protection. 'Do you know *The Cenci*?' Sybil asked. I shook my head in a non-committal way. Sybil continued, 'You must read lots and lots of poetry. I learn a sonnet every day. What sort of poetry do you like?' Was this going to be my opportunity? Dan McGrew again loomed dangerously in the forefront of my mind but I suppressed him; somehow the atmosphere didn't seem right for a drunken saloon bar in the Wild West. I volunteered, in sheer panic, 'Thou still unravish'd bride of quietness.' Neither of them asked me to continue so I ceased as suddenly as I had begun. 'Well, that's a lovely, lovely, lovely poem, isn't it? And now we must have our tea. Ooh, boiled eggs! Thank you for coming to see us. Come again one day.' And I was shown the door with great kindness.

I stood outside the theatre in a daze, oblivious of the drizzle that was seeping down, wanting only to stop any passer-by who might come along with, 'I've met Sybil Thorndike!' But there was nobody in that damp little side-street. Only Oswald, who emerged from the stage door in a camel-hair coat and full make-up – Leichner sticks numbers 5 and 9, a red dot in the corner of each eye and a lot of mascara. In my puritanical way I was rather shocked; also perhaps a little alarmed. There was something ambivalent about him which I couldn't grasp, but which also glamourised me. I did not ask him for his autograph in spite of the searching look he gave me. If it hadn't been for the mascara I would have done.

There was never anything remotely ambivalent, in any sense, about the Cassons. Their 'yea' was 'yea' and 'nay' was 'nay'. They were straighter and clearer in their personalities than most people outside the life of the theatre.

The next time I saw Sybil was in the spring of 1931, when she appeared in the revival of *St Joan* at His Majesty's. There was a measure of disappointment for me because I had to acknowledge that she was a little too old for the part; besides, her delivery had become rather richly vibrato – a habit she dropped later in life. The opening scene of *St Joan* is embarrassing in itself and Sybil's enthusiastic, hoydenish attack didn't help. (The only actress I have seen deal successfully with that opening was Eileen Atkins in 1977.) There were memorable moments in the 1931 production: particularly Sybil's delivery of the great speech which contains – 'France is alone; and God is alone; and what is my loneliness before the loneliness of my country and my God?' Ernest Thesiger, the most superb Dauphin we have had in our time, was exquisitely droll; Robert Donat a wildly romantic Dunois; and I think it was H. R. Hignett who compelled total attention delivering the Inquisitor's seemingly interminable speech. I didn't go round to see Sybil, but the following winter, when she and Lewis were with Ralph Richardson in *The Knight of the Burning Pestle* at the Old Vic, I spent ninepence on a pit-stall for a matinée. Afterwards I presented myself at the stage door, announcing myself as a friend of Miss Thorndike's. I was wiser in my own conceit by then, twirling my school cap as if it was a topper instead of crumpling it in damp hands. Although Sybil greeted me warmly I am sure that for a moment or two she was non-plussed, not recognising me. Then a light dawned or a penny dropped, and pointing a finger at me she said, 'Thou still unravish'd bride of quietness, hast thou read *The Cenci* yet?' I hadn't. And I still haven't.

If she had forgotten me, momentarily, it was a rare occurrence, for her memory was phenomenal. Names, faces, lines from plays – were all recalled instantly. She only met my wife once, and briefly, in 1939, I think, and yet she would always ask after her, not with, 'And how is your wife?' but 'How's Merula? And Matthew?' – our son, whom she had never seen.

The last time I saw Sybil to talk to was at a small private lunch party at the Garrick Club. She was an old lady by then, suffering acutely from arthritis but remarkably gallant and cheerful. I asked her if she still managed to learn a few lines of verse each day, which had been her life-long custom. 'Yes,' she said, 'but only a very few. I've given up the Greeks. But the real sadness is my silly old hands, which don't allow me to play Bach any more. Sometimes I try to bang out something with one hand but it is not very satisfactory.' She was wearing a white woollen coat and skirt: she always wore white, in public at any rate, after Lewis's death; a mourning in reverse; her religion was all-important to her. I imagine it to have been a broad-minded high Anglicanism, both serious and gay. While she was still able to get about with comparative ease she was a daily communicant, setting off to church early in the morning, returning to make a family breakfast and do the household chores before getting down to the work of the day. There were letters to be answered, the piano to be practised, a script to be studied and then, as likely as not, a rehearsal to attend or a sick friend to be visited in hospital. One day I said to her, 'Aldous Huxley writes somewhere that no actor can be good, because no actor can develop his own personality and know reality. What do you say to that?' She made one of her impatient 'P'shaw!' sounds and then added, in a strong, indignant voice, 'Rubbish! Actors are *good* people. I know there are some silly ones. Perhaps there are some nasty ones, but I don't know them. Our people are *good*.' Her own goodness was deep inside herself: it appeared to cost her no effort; and yet to say that is, perhaps, unintentionally to diminish her.

Tyrone and Judy Guthrie, who were close friends, had a tremendous regard for Sybil as a person, and indeed for the entire Casson family. They shared simple tastes and total indifference to worldly success, money or luxuries; but there was mocking glee in Tony's description of a late supper chez Casson after a gruelling dress-rehearsal – 'Steaming cocoa with sausage and mash.' I remember him telling me of a morning call on Sybil to discuss a play. He found 'The Great Dame', crouched on hands and knees, half under a high, old-fashioned bed, busy with dustpan and brush. Her plangent voice rang among the bed-springs, 'Lovely, lovely bed-fluff.'

Lewis nearly always made himself agreeable to me although I was aware that he disapproved of my acting and thoroughly disliked my way of phrasing speeches. He believed passionately in what he called 'the tune': I could only believe in what I considered credible, combined with my own idiosyncratic rhythm. In 1938 I was contracted, at £12 a week, under Guthrie's management at the Old Vic to play, among other parts, the juvenile in *Man and Superman*, which

Lewis was to direct with Anthony Quayle in the lead. I only attended one rehearsal. It was on the morning after the opening of Guthrie's modern dress *Hamlet*; a full-length version which lasted over four hours. (It is a much better play in its entirety, 'little eye-asses' and all.) Perhaps I was seeking praise or sympathy (the notices had not been good) or, at any rate, appreciation of the fact that I might be exhausted, but Lewis pounced the moment I opened my mouth as Octavius Robinson. 'No! No! No! You must *sing* it! Di-da-di-diddi! That's what is wrong with your Hamlet. You don't *sing* it.' Acting Hamlet six nights a week plus a Saturday matinée, which started at lunchtime, seemed about as much as my vocal equipment could stand. I couldn't face up to the di-da-di-diddies as well, so in mid-morning I asked to be released from *Man and Superman* immediately. Guthrie concurred and Lewis was probably relieved by my departure. In long retrospect I regret having left the play, as I might have learned from Lewis something useful about Shavian acting, of which I have had minimal experience.

In January 1939 the Old Vic company, partly re-composed and about twenty-strong, set off on a tour of Egypt and Europe, sponsored by the British Council. Lewis was to be a sort of father-figure in charge of the company and the admirable Esmé Church a sensible mother-cum-matron. Among the plays we took were *Hamlet*, in which Lewis replaced O. B. Clarence as Polonius and Cathleen Nesbitt followed, Niobe-like, in Veronica Turleigh's footsteps as Gertrude; *Henry V*, with Tony Quayle as the King and me replacing Marius Goring as Chorus; *The Rivals*, with Tony and Lewis as the Absolutes, and *Man and Superman*. Andrew Cruickshank with his wife Curigwen Lewis; Tony's first wife, Hermione Hannen; André Morell and Cathleen's husband, Cecil Ramage, were the more experienced members of the company. We embarked, with our scenery, costumes and props in the *Alcantara*, a handsome liner of 24,000 tons, which didn't stop her being thrown about like a cork in the Bay of Biscay.

Lewis had a cabin not far above the Plimsoll line. Needing some more air on our first night out, he rashly unscrewed his porthole. A large wave sloshed in, swamped him, ruining his clothes, and chased him down the passage before dispersing. He made light of it the next morning but was quiet and pensive for the remainder of the voyage.

We docked at Lisbon on the morning of the 23rd and watched with horror as all our scenery was carefully lowered into the Tagus. It disappeared and then emerged streaked, grimy, battered and fairly useless. It was probably a genuine error on the part of the crane workers but the British were far from popular in Portugal. The Spanish Civil War was dragging to its close and the fall of Barcelona to Franco's troops was imminent. When, three days later, Barcelona finally fell to the Nationalists Lisbon went mad with joy. We found it very depressing. Even more depressing was the sight of the grander makes of British cars displaying the Union Jack flanked by the Swastika, the Rising Sun of Japan, as well as the flags of Nationalist Spain and Portugal. Most of us, I think, felt small, alien, lonely and threatened; and not a little suspicious of our fellow countrymen in Lisbon. September 1939 was not all that far off.

That first evening in Lisbon I went down to the theatre – a lovely building which still had the same boards on its stage which Macready had trod a century before. Esmé Church and Lewis, stripped to their underwear, were helping the stage-management and carpenters to repaint and refurbish Roger Furse's admirable sets. The two old things (well, old to us, who were mostly in our early or middle twenties) were dishevelled and filthy but as happy as could be. Half-heartedly I offered to help. Lewis, paintbrush in hand, waved me aside, with, 'Go away. You must be rested and fresh for *Hamlet*.' I needed no rest but I detected no sarcasm in Lewis's voice. I felt a little ashamed. As I had been married little more than seven months and Merula was accompanying me (but not acting) perhaps Lewis felt, as we certainly did, that this tour was our proper honeymoon.

Apart from deferring to him or seeking his advice about social occasions, Lewis and I didn't have much to say to each other. With the indifference of the young, I failed to pick his brains, even if only to reject what I might have gleaned. To me his acting was costive, his manner often a little peremptory; while he felt, I am sure, that I was undisciplined and my personality flippant and self-centred. He was quite right, of course. Eventually, however, when we were acting in Rome, at the Valle Theatre, he suddenly congratulated me, quite unexpectedly. It was at the conclusion of the first night there of *Hamlet*. The Pope, Pius XI, had died a few days previously, while we were in Florence, and all Rome was in mourning. Mussolini, who had sent an invitation to me to take tea with him in his box, at a matinée, cancelled his appearance. It was a curious sensation playing Hamlet, in conventional 'nighted colours' in spite of the modern dress, before an audience entirely swathed in black. When the curtain fell on that performance there was some cheering from out front and a few red roses were thrown on the stage. I ignored the roses, not knowing for whom they were meant. Perhaps one of the cast had an ardent admirer or lover in the stalls. Lewis whispered, 'Pick them up. It's your night.' I did so and I only hope I didn't hug them to myself, but had the manners to divide them between Hermione Hannen, who was playing a cool Ophelia, and Cathleen. When all was over Lewis wrung my hand, muttering, 'Well done! Keep it that way!' I was unaware that I had performed any differently, but perhaps the black audience had triggered in me some new emotion or, at least, a sense of occasion.

*

Richard II was played by the Old Vic company at the New Theatre for two consecutive seasons after the war. It was a performance of which I am still ashamed – a partly plagiarised, third-rate imitation of Gielgud's definitive Richard, at the same theatre, in 1937. Beverley Baxter, the drama critic of the *Evening Standard*, headed his scornful column, 'Open the door, Richard.' One critic complained that I had no music in my speaking (Ah, Lewis!) but yet another said it was like listening to Bach (Ah, Sybil!). Since then I have rarely read the critics, except for amusement. Ralph Richardson directed the play, on very spare lines. His only piece of advice to me, before we went into rehearsal, was to hold up a beautifully-sharpened Venus pencil and say, 'Play it like this pencil, old cock.' I wasn't greatly illuminated. He himself acted John of Gaunt. He wouldn't wear the collar of his fourteenth-century costume up, as designed by Michael Warre, insisting it should lie flat on his shoulders. It differentiated him from the rest of us, of course, but made him look like a large, bearded Peter Pan. 'Never come within six feet of me on stage, old cock.' This meant that, as the King, I was often huddled with Bushy, Bagot and Green in a rather undignified way, while Ralph could free-wheel in plenty of space and air. Ralph was cannily aware of all the old actors' tricks (he worked as a young man with Charles Doran) and delightfully jealous of his stage-craft. He was a great and good man, a loving friend, and probably the most imaginative and interesting English actor of our day; but it was wise to be aware of his dodges. No counter-action was of much avail. (Anyone interested in such things should look at the brilliant exercise in upstaging between him and Noël Coward in the last scene of the film of *Our Man in Havana*.)

When *Richard II* was re-rehearsed, for its 1949 showing, Lewis Casson replaced George Relph, that beautiful actor, as Duke of York. One morning, doing the deposition scene, I found Lewis, who had

little to do in it other than wring his hands, occupy͏ ͏ ͏ ͏
confidence the centre of the stage. The self-uncrow͏ ͏ ͏
to be impossible in such circumstances. I didn't like͏ ͏
Lewis that he was standing where I expected to be, s͏ ͏ ͏
Ralph for help. Ralph was in the stalls, puffing away ͏ ͏
Charatan pipe, oblivious of my difficulty. Finally, when͏ ͏ ͏ ͏ ͏nd
I had collided, I stopped and said, 'Ralph, there's somethi͏ ͏g wrong
here.' 'What's the trouble?' Puff, puff, on the pipe. 'Well, it's difficult
to say, actually.' I winked vigorously but there was no response;
only more smoke drifting up from the stalls. Then Lewis spoke up,
with charming diffidence. 'I think I see the difficulty,' he said, and I
heaped mental blessings on his head. He went on, 'What is wrong,
if I may say so, is that you are saying Di-do-dee, di-do-dee, when it
should be didi-do-dee, didi-do-dee. That's the tune. Try singing it.'
I thanked him, naturally; he stood his ground, and I left the problem
to be solved another day.

When it came to the dress-rehearsal Lewis appeared in a most
individual make-up; well, it wasn't really a make-up at all, as he wore
no foundation but had drawn a large, carmine, equilateral triangle
on each cheek. I don't know what effect he was striving for, but to
the rest of us he looked like a Russian doll. 'Perhaps the cheeks are a
little too red,' Ralph suggested, but Lewis didn't agree so he continued
with his triangles. He always wore his socks under his tights –
clearly visible from the front of the house – but mercifully without
suspenders. It was very much a custom for actors of a previous
generation to keep their socks on in costume parts; it enabled them
to make a quick get-away at the end of the evening to catch their
public transport. I suppose Lewis must have used taxis many times
in his life, but somehow I always imagine him on a bus or tube.

*

St Paul's Church, in Covent Garden, has the sobriquet of the Actors'
Church. Sybil was to be seen there at almost all the innumerable
memorial services for dead performers. In recent years there has
developed a tiresome custom of referring to these services as 'Cele-
brations' – a cosy euphemism, such as 'industrial action' to explain
the cessation of work. Those of us who sometimes attend these
memorials eye each other, I think, with the unspoken query, 'Who
is to be celebrated next?' Yet Sybil managed by her presence to bring
a certain gaiety and spiritual confidence to the proceedings. Often,
in old age, she would read a sonnet with heart-rending clarity. She

d always arrive, in white wool, with clockwork punctuality and be led by the presiding priest to a front pew. She would be the last to arrive and the first to leave; a sort of gravely smiling Alpha and Omega, acknowledging all and sundry, genuinely looking forward to the resurrection of the dead. In spite of her rheumatic pains she really did believe the body would rise again, whatever that may mean. When, eventually, she could no longer manage to get to Covent Garden her place was often taken, I believe, by Dame Flora Robson, who also sported white from top to toe. Unfortunately the only time I saw Dame Flora at St Paul's – I can't remember whom we were celebrating – she had met with a nasty mishap. She arrived twenty minutes late, looking rather battered. Her white hat was dreadfully squashed and her walk up the aisle was somewhat erratic. At the end of the service I asked her if she was feeling all right or needed any help. She graciously declined my offer, in the most beautiful female voice the theatre has known in my time:

> The melting voice through mazes running;
> Untwisting all the chains that tie
> The hidden soul of harmony.

'So sorry I was late,' she said. 'My train from Brighton. And at Victoria Station a plank fell on my head. Is my hat in good shape?' I reassured her: I wasn't quite sure what the shape should be.

Now that Sybil and Lewis are dead I would be quite happy to see a return of black for mourning, and to hear no more electric guitars in church. Perhaps we could return to resounding hymns, such as 'Onward, Christian Soldiers'. After all, Lewis would certainly recognise the 'tune', and Sybil's voice would rise, unfailingly, above all.

CHAPTER FOUR

Quintessence of Dust

At the age of sixteen, one early summer day, I arose from under the hands of the Bishop of Lewes a confirmed atheist. Holy Trinity Church, Eastbourne, was crammed with Confirmation candidates, their parents, friends, schoolteachers and sponsors. The girls, mostly in grey uniforms, filed up to kneel at the Bishop's left hand and the boys, in blue serge, to his right. It was intriguing to watch who might get spliced to whom. I remember white episcopal hands and shaggy black eyebrows, but little else until I returned to my pew. A pale greenish light filtered through the window-panes, giving a subaqueous hue to the perspiring congregation, and my mind turned away from a benevolent God to the horror of the ichneumon-fly. No one had been able to satisfy me about the necessity, in creation, for the ichneumon-fly; and they still haven't. It is an unpleasant little creature which pierces the body of the charming, rotund, prettily-decorated puss-moth caterpillar, depositing its unwelcome eggs which, when hatched, eat their way out through their living host. (I have come across one or two humans with similar habits.) Back in my place, clearly not aflame with the Holy Spirit, I gazed at a nasty little boil on the neck of the boy in front of me, remembering what an attractive young animal he had been before he took to shaving. Now he was solemnly at his prayers. I flicked a look round at other school-fellows, wondering if any were as disillusioned as myself; they all looked deadly serious and self-absorbed. Alas, I must have been the odd man out; a thought which made me feel a little sick. With a flash I realised I had never really believed what I had been taught, anyway.

Canon Warner, of Holy Trinity, a worthy, white-haired man carrying a load of solid flesh towards the General Resurrection, was a fundamentalist at heart. He believed, among other Biblical fables, that the serpent who tempted Eve was still alive in the world, sloughing its skin and waiting, presumably with some anxiety, for a lady to crush its head with her heel. Who the lady was or when this might happen, Canon Warner didn't inform us. In flippant mood,

a few of us proposed that a zoological expedition should be mounted
to seek out the beast and put an end to its crawling life of misery. Each
Monday evening, during the previous few weeks, Canon Warner had
invited a handful of confirmation candidates to the vicarage for a
'chat', weak cocoa and banana sandwiches. He was a kindly, if
boring, man and our few fumbling questions soon came up against
a brick wall. Did we have to believe the sun stood still for Joshua?
'Oh, yes. It's in the Bible.' Did he really think Jonah could live inside
a whale? 'Well, our Lord Jesus thought so.' In my pew, lonely,
dispirited, and confirmed, I reflected on the unintelligible evenings
at the vicarage and the implausibility of so much of holy writ. It
seemed to me that the Bible, or at any rate the Old Testament, on
which they were all so keen, was an unreliable history of a bronze-age
tribe who had an unhealthy passion for collecting the foreskins of
Philistines. A year or two of necessary, though intermittent, hypocrisy lay ahead of me. Certain incidents or sayings in the New
Testament would pluck me back, from time to time, to something
approaching belief; and I retained a constant interest in religious
matters while being ignorant of any theology, but for the most part
gave in to adolescent cynicism, which was self-encouraged by reading
the witty works of Dean Inge. (Why on earth was he labelled 'The
Gloomy Dean'?) Clergymen were either funny curates who couldn't
find their galoshes, or rather sinister missionaries back from the
African bush, with unappealing lantern-slides of themselves – in solar
topees – sitting smugly on folding chairs, surrounded by poor,
squatting, hideous, heathen folk.

We sang with vigour our hymns of twilight or geography – 'Abide
with Me', 'From Greenland's Icy Mountains' (do the spicy breezes
still blow soft o'er Sri Lanka's Isle, I wonder?) – and even more
vociferously hymns of Christian hope and the Church Militant. The
enthusiasm was suspect. Perhaps Canon Warner had greater spiritual
success with other candidates.

Presbyterianism was tolerated – two or three boys at Roborough
attended Eastbourne's Presbyterian Church, which was ministered
to by the remarkable, near-blind Rev. Reid, who preached brilliantly
– and by the age of seventeen I was permitted, with a few others, to
attend the evening services there instead of at Holy Trinity. The
headmaster, ever a kindly, liberal-minded, understanding man, was
perplexed. 'But, Guinness, the *language* of The Book of Common
Prayer! How can you sacrifice that for a lot of talk from the pulpit
and extempore prayer?' It was true I missed the Magnificat, the Nunc

Dimittis and the Prayer of St Chrysostom; but I did not miss the Tables of Kindred and Affinity, with which I had over-familiarised myself, like the dates of English kings, during Canon Warner's hair-splitting sermons. Mr Reid was more stimulating and opened up, unintentionally, avenues of escape. I don't think I was aware of Aldous Huxley's novels until I heard them denounced, as the work of the devil, in that red-brick Presbyterian church. Although I was seeking a way out from the Established Religion (unconsciously) during the days I was not fluttering an atheistical or agnostic flag, it would never have crossed my mind even to step inside a Roman Catholic Church. Tolerance of Catholics, unless one personally knew them, was limited to the sympathetic, although condescending, pages of *Barnaby Rudge*. But one day I did casually visit a high-Anglican church in the town, was amazed by the elaborate décor and, believing I was somehow on spooky Roman property, hastily withdrew.

At my preparatory school near Bournemouth, Pembroke Lodge, there was universal horror when it was rumoured that a sweet woman who taught drawing and botany in the lower house had left to become a nun. There was partial relief when it was learned that she hadn't Poped but had merely joined an Anglican sisterhood. Relief, but not Reunion All Round. From the grim reading of psalms at bedtime, in the presence of staff, boys, butler and maid-servants within the gates, I gleaned no sense of religion at all – only a vague fear of a future life. Dying of whooping-cough or the dreaded appendicitis seemed preferable to living for ever in a cavernous, unknown world, but Christianity held more immediate fears than eternity. In the junior school I had dreaded the headmaster's random visits to take Biblical classes which consisted usually in acting out, very heartily, skirmishes between Israelites, Ammonites and Amalekites, with Mr Meakin – his large yellow teeth bared – roaring, 'Smite them! Smite them, Israel!' Until I was about ten I had a slight difficulty in pronouncing my th's and often, through laziness or fear, would substitute an f. One day I was landed with reading aloud in class a few verses of the Passion of Our Lord, with disastrous results. 'I thirst' came out of my mouth as 'I first'. Mr Meakin gave a yelp of horror, smacked me across the ear, seized me by the hair and shook my head until I was dizzy. The vengeance of the Lord satisfied, the hair that had been wrenched from my head was sprinkled away with disgust by bony hands. Many sparrows must have fallen that day and the auditing department in heaven kept busy. And yet, in some ways, Meakin was a kindly man (he showed generosity to me after

I left school and occasionally wrote) but he was horribly impatient, except with handsome boys who were good cricketers.

Sundays, ordinarily pleasurable, were made uncomfortable by the necessity of reciting the Collect of the Day, together with half a dozen verses from the Old Testament, learned the previous evening. One single mistake was likely to land us with a further set of verses to be conned by nightfall. On Saturday evenings in summer, boys who were not in the 'nets' would climb trees and, slung along the branches, clutching their prayer books, could be heard piping among the leaves, 'Keep us, we beseech thee, under the protection of thy good providence, and make us to have a perpetual fear and love of thy holy Name,' or, from the very top of a tree, blasphemously, would come, 'Exalt us unto the same place whither our Saviour Christ is gone before.' In winter, our bottoms parked on sizzling radiators, we might shout, 'To order myself lowly and reverently to all my betters' – until a paper dart, or pellet shot from a catapult, finding its mark, an unholy pandemonium would break out.

Most of our Bibles were ink-stained, well-thumbed where the word 'piss' could be found, but treated as quasi-holy things, largely because they had 'With Love from Mummy', or some such connection with home-life, written on the fly-leaf. One boy received a severe tanning for scribbling in another fellow's Bible, after the inscription 'From Father and Mother', 'and the Holy Ghost'. The forgery had been spotted by Matron, when admiring the Morocco binding and heavy gilt. 'Not that I care a damn,' the rather languid owner said to me. 'Father is a rotter and Mother wouldn't care a damn either. She's not all that keen on The Good Book. We *never* go to church in the holidays. Father has his golf and she always has a headache.' He was a tall, charming, clever boy, more sophisticated than most of us, with an outrageous habit of calling everyone 'My dear' and closing his eyes with mock boredom. He had invited me out to tea with his parents when they visited him one half-term and I think I was even more impressed by their elegance than by the shiny Hispano-Suiza which zoomed us to a rich hotel. Afterwards he said to me, 'Did you find the pater too dreadfully gloomy? Frankly, my dear, I think we may have a DIVORCE on our hands.' Divorce was a word which was almost taboo, and always whispered, as something too painful to contemplate; but my friend appeared to be not in the least put out by the idea. The one or two boys who were known to have separated parents were treated as if they were convalescing after illness. I remained a mystery to all of them; known to have a mother but never a mention made of any father. My mother visited me once, arriving in an old, throbbing taxi and mysteriously had left her handbag behind somewhere. The loan of a fiver from the Maths master saved the day but I wondered whether it would save it for me; my school-fellows were very car conscious. Boys whose parents arrived in a Daimler or Bentley were treated with special respect, particularly by the masters. No one mentioned the taxi and the loan was never referred to. They could be desperately polite at times. (And dear Jack Hawkins, in later years, was too polite to mention the tenner he forked out in a Brighton pub when he came across my mother, again without her bag.)

Accident, it seemed to me in those early years, was the chaotic rule of the universe; nothing was certain and promises were made only to be broken. School life, religion apart, provided a dimension of security, a stable routine, and a happy freedom from the domestic dramas of holiday-time, with their financial and emotional upsets. At the age of twelve a real religious appreciation might have provided a sure, safe background to my life, but somehow I didn't grasp whatever I may have been taught; my mind only carried a series of prohibitions which, if broken, threatened dire punishment and, like most children, an acute awareness of the hypocrisy of grown-ups. Moral precepts, such as honesty, courage, fair-play and cleanliness had an exclusively English, rather than Christian, emphasis: they went hand in hand with middle-class shibboleths about not wearing the collar of your cricket-shirt outside your blazer, avoiding words like 'nice' and, being the sons of gentlemen, always calling masters by their proper names and never 'Sir'. You never 'sucked up' to those from whom you could benefit, you gave the hand of friendship to avowed enemies and, above all, you never sneaked. Blubbing was treated with contempt, but allowable in the loss of a mother or grandmother. Sex, of which we were basically ignorant – we would be enlightened, it was hinted, by some grave talk about butterflies before leaving school – was never mentioned, of course; except perhaps when hiding in the bushes, or in furtive, queried whispers in the dormitories after lights were out. After the headmaster had made one of his occasional visits to a dormitory – usually to tickle the Captain of the First XI – and darkness and silence surrounded us, then sometimes an enquiry would begin as to the nature of the 'seed' a chap had to be so careful about. One boy, with a very knowledgeable manner, assured me it was a black pip which popped out of your penis unexpectedly, and you should be ready to catch it every time you relieved yourself. He had lost his pip months ago and feared that, as a result, he would never become a father. 'But what should you *do* with your pip, if you're lucky enough to catch it?' 'You keep it safely in your locker and then one day give it to some woman you want to marry.' I was doubtful of all this so I asked my sophisticated friend what he thought. 'My dear, my mother says it's all too disgusting for words and not to be thought of. Besides,' he said, with closed eyes, 'only girls talk dirt.'

I thought about the pip for some time. Then I suddenly remembered that when I was seven years old I possessed a small hazel-nut which I kept in a tuckbox. It had, for me, magical properties and was a great personal secret. Sometimes I would sing the National Anthem to it, and each day I would look to see if it had grown. In my imagination it was destined to grow until the day it would open up and a small manikin, dressed in blue, step out. He would be about a foot tall, wearing a blue velvet jerkin and breeches, and round his middle there would be a leather belt bearing a tiny cutlass. His hair would be light brown, his face ruddy and smiling, and he would be my 'best friend' for always. As a twelve-year-old I could afford to be amused at my fantasy of five years earlier, knowing it was foolishness and that the hazel-nut had long been lost – probably now nothing more than a little scattered dust, unless it was a tree. And yet was that absolutely so? A hazel-nut (though not a real one) came into my life again some forty years later.

In my early forties I read, for the first time, Julian of Norwich's *Revelations of Divine Love*. In that extraordinary book I found a passage which astonished and delighted me: it also slightly disturbed me by reviving the memory of the tuckbox-nut. 'Our Lord . . . showed me a little thing, the quantity of a hazel-nut, in the palm of my hand; and it was as round as a ball. I thought there upon with the eye of my understanding, and thought, what may this be? And it was generally answered thus: It is all that is made. – I marvelled how it might last, for methought it might suddenly have fallen to nought, for littleness. And I was answered: It lasteth, and ever shall last, for God loveth it. God made it; God loveth it; God keepeth it. – But what is to me soothly the Maker, the Keeper, the Lover, I cannot tell.' In Julian of Norwich I also found the comforting refrain, 'All shall be well and all manner of thing shall be well', used by T. S. Eliot in the *Four Quartets*.

In a vague way there seemed to be some connection between my tuckbox secret, the desire for a perpetual friend (whom I could conjure up when wanted, manipulate as I chose, but to whom I would listen), and the anchorite of Norwich.

Discussing the peripheries of Roman Catholicism with the late Honor Svejdar (Honor Guinness) a few years after my conversion, I showed her the hazel-nut passage. When she herself was reconciled with the Church, a year or two later, she presented me with a hazel-nut – but it was of rare gold, to be worn in a buttonhole or as a tie-pin, of exquisite workmanship, which she had commissioned from Wartski's. It is unlikely to fall to dust, for although I never made it I loveth it and keepeth it. Something had come full circle, as I have often found in life, giving the lie to my earlier concept of accident, meaninglessness and chaos.

When I finished with schooldays, at the age of eighteen, and was given a job (through kindly string-pulling by my recent headmaster, Douglas Gilbert) as a copywriter in Ark's Publicity, advertising agents in Lincoln's Inn Fields, I found myself in a very different milieu from anything I had experienced. For weeks I felt lost, nervous and acutely self-conscious, but gradually made friends who were wonderfully helpful. There was no more talk of religion, which was dismissed as so much rubbish, a wicked scheme of the Establishment to keep the working-man in his place – though I must admit I was not aware that the average worker was much of a church-goer; but the magazine *U.S.S.R. Today* was passed from hand to hand, greatly admired for its photographs of factory chimneys. Also doing the office rounds was an illicit (then) copy of *Lady Chatterley's Lover*, not for its literary merits but for the passages of sexual explicitness, which were as thumb-marked as any preparatory-school Bible. How many of those office typists, I wonder, retain the image of violets twined in pubic hair? I formed a casual friendship with a commercial artist, a young woman whose sister was studying drama at RADA, which was a greater thrill than D. H. Lawrence could provide. I was paid a pound a week, later rising to thirty shillings, for generally making a hash of my job; but my spare time was happy enough. Once a week I went to the theatre (usually the Old Vic, where you could get in for sixpence) and weekends I often spent with a good young man from the office, Adolf Deys, and his wife Daisy, at their small flat in Gray's Inn Road where I was not only fed but permitted to read aloud to them nearly all Shakespeare's plays and a good deal of Shaw. At other times I occasionally assisted a Communist friend to distribute Marxist/Leninist literature under cover of darkness, believing I was doing something very clandestine and illegal. A few

times I visited Quaker meetings, but I soon got the impression that
the Spirit usually 'moved' the most garrulous and boring person
present and I lost interest. But I had begun to recognise, before a
meeting commenced, the types most likely to get to their feet – and
in this the Spirit and I were at one. In fact, I began to look at people
with greater observation; I was quickly storing away, for possible
future use, an odd assortment of habits, idiosyncrasies and personalities.

My good fortune at this time was to be given an introduction
(again through the Gilberts) to a group of young people, about a
dozen of them, who called themselves The Thirty-Nine Club and met
each Thursday evening to read aloud, talk, discuss and occasionally go
on a modest pub-crawl. They were mostly a few years older than
me; a couple of medical students, a solicitor, a cellist, a designer
of furniture, a schoolmistress, an accountant and assorted wives,
husbands or girl-friends. They had nearly all been to university and
it was through this group that my tardy education really began. Their
political attitudes were largely Liberal and I began to slough off my
ill-digested Marxism, which was given a final tug by the horrendous
Moscow Trials of the early thirties, in the same way as the savage
suppression of the Hungarian uprising in 1956 led to many defections
from the Party in this country. We were mostly agnostic and our
one venture into the religious field was when we were persuaded to
go to a Buchmanite meeting in a rich household – an embarrassing
affair at which an hysterical woman talked about being raped, when
it was obvious that nothing of the sort had happened to her but
she harboured hopes. We decided, mistakenly perhaps, that Moral
Rearmament was no more desirable than any other rearmament.

Later I presented myself to some Singhalese Buddhists; Buddhism
sounded an admirable philosophy, but I was dismayed by the superior
airs of a Buddhist monk with a streaming cold. Then one Sunday
evening, in my casual search for a meaning to life, I spotted a board
outside a building in Regent Street which advertised, 'Mazdaznans.
All Welcome.' I wandered upstairs and found myself in a hall filled
with gilded chairs, a small platform at one end, a grand piano and
several potted palms. The sparse congregation consisted of rather
well-dressed elderly ladies. There was a large metal symbol of the
sun mounted on the wall behind the platform, and in front of it stood
a tall young Canadian, with a black moustache and wearing a white
priest-like robe. At the piano sat a large lady, singing some mystical
hymn about her ship coming home. When she had finished, the

Canadian talked at length about San Francisco (apparently in need of funds), the Golden Gates, the Wise Men of Persia, his sexual prowess since he had embraced Mazdaism, and how that wonderful Mr Hitler in Germany was sympathetic to their cause. As I started to slip away he made a dive at me and, with a brilliant smile, demanded any piece of silver I had on me. Reluctantly I parted with a shilling, for which he gave me in return a small bottle, saying, 'Very few people are aware of the benefits of eucalyptus oil. May the Sun God always guide you.' I ceased my spiritual enquiries for several years.

One more stab at seeking enlightenment from the Buddha took me, at the start of the war, to a run-down house near Regent's Park. I rang the bell several times before the door was unchained, but only partially opened, by a young Indian muffled in woollen scarves. 'I'd like to speak to the Guru, or whoever is in charge,' I said. 'Guru not here. Gone away.' 'When will he be back?' 'Guru will come back when no war and no bombs.' The door was firmly closed and chained again. No bombs had fallen, anyway. I turned homeward, knowing that pacifism – if it was in my mind – was not for me. And it was falling bombs, curiously enough, that led to a re-awakened interest in Christianity.

When I was playing Hamlet at the Old Vic, in 1938, a small white-haired man came to my dressing-room after an evening performance. He was dressed in mufti but introduced himself as an Anglican priest, the Rev. Cyril Tomkinson, Vicar of All Saints, Margaret Street, which was very much the centre of West End Anglo-Catholicism. (Laurence Olivier's father had been at one time, I believe, Curate of All Saints, and I suspect Larry's sense of ritual stems from that source.) Mr Tomkinson eyed me sternly. 'I have just come to tell you,' he said, 'that you cross yourself incorrectly in the play. You should do it like this – forehead to chest, then left to right.' He crossed himself in illustration and departed. Two weeks later he turned up again, saying, 'You are still doing it incorrectly. It offends me. It spoils an otherwise admirable performance. Do please get it right.' Later, hearing that the company was leaving for Portugal, Italy, Egypt and Greece, he sent me a selection of Baedeker guides, together with an invitation to lunch at the Oxford and Cambridge Club. I found him entertaining, witty, eccentric, rather old-maidish in a naughty way, and with an absorbing passion for Jane Austen and Dr Johnson. I didn't see him again until the night of the blitz on Bristol, when bombs and I arrived at the same time.

The city was devastated; fires climbing everywhere, water-mains

broken, streets cordoned off, and I walked from the station, dragging
a suitcase, not knowing where to go for food or shelter. I felt I had
walked for miles, hiding in doorways from shrapnel, trying for a bed
in 'guest houses' which were already full, before I spotted a police-
man. I asked him if he knew anywhere I might find a place to sleep.
'No, mate, you won't find much sleep tonight; but you might try
the Vicarage up the road, just by the church.' It was a large, red-brick,
Victorian house, with neo-Gothic windows of stained glass. The
door-bell clanged. 'Come in! Come in out of that dreadful noise!' a
voice called. Both Cyril Tomkinson and I were equally surprised to
see each other. He had left Margaret Street a year previously to take
over this parish. He was most welcoming, told me I could stay as
long as I wanted but did hope I had my ration-card with me: I spent
four days at the Vicarage, unable to get back to Merula and Matthew,
who were in a rented cottage at Stratford-upon-Avon. Bristol was
cut off. Water had to be collected in buckets from a hose at the street
corner but wine flowed in the Vicarage, for the Rev. Tomkinson
kept a good cellar. 'We shall have a splendid claret tonight,' he would
say, 'so I do hope you won't object to Algerian for lunch. I find that
a bottle of Algerian, with a glass of port mixed in with it, can be
passed off quite successfully as a reasonable Burgundy. It is almost
impressive with a dried-egg omelette.'

He showed me over the church, sprinkled holy water at me in a
rather flippant way, gave me a copy of St Francis de Sales's *The
Devout Life*, told me, with mock horror, that many of his lady
parishioners had Lesbian tendencies, expressed the hope that I would
attend all the services, and instructed me always to genuflect towards
the altar. 'I do believe in The Real Presence, you see.' I didn't know
what he was talking about.

One morning, sipping our pre-lunch sherries in his study, standing
with our backs to a small smoky fire and a large print of Leonardo
da Vinci's 'Last Supper', he suddenly said, 'Do you not think,
with all these bombs about, you should make your confession?' I
demurred, saying I wasn't at all sure what I believed; that I didn't
quite understand his brand of Anglicanism; that I had no idea how
or what to confess; that I would be embarrassed. 'It's very simple,'
he said, toying with his glass. 'Just kneel at my feet and tell me
everything that is on your conscience. I assure you I will have heard
it all before. You are unlikely to surprise me.' 'No!' I said firmly.
There was a pause while he put his sherry on the over-mantel. 'How
sad! I apologise. But I shall bless you.' And he waved a sign of the

Cross at me before he picked up his sherry again. We remained somewhat silent as we ate our tinned pilchards, but he regained his spirits and good humour after he had visited the church for ten minutes, and by the evening he was chatting merrily, and interestingly, of Jane Austen, Dr Johnson and the letters of St Teresa of Avila.

He had a brilliant mind and was a good friend; very perceptive, very snobbish, delighting in the famous, the rich, the beautiful or talented; and very intolerant of bad manners and all solecisms. He was authoritarian and Laudian in ecclesiastical matters but my gratitude to him is enormous, in spite of his foibles, for he opened up for me a new world – the world of Hooker, William Law, Bishop Gore, Archbishop Temple; and the wide world of St Augustine and Newman. He was polite, though distressed, when years later I became a Catholic. 'Oh, dear! They will teach you to think me a heretic,' he said. 'Surely not,' I replied. 'Only schismatic.' 'Schismatic! It sounds like something to do with motor-cars.'

The last years of his life were spent in Cambridge; lonely, infirm in body and melancholy in mind. He brightened up on a day I visited him, saying, 'Lady Someone-or-Other was good enough to ask me where I lived now. She used to be a penitent of mine, but mum's the word. I gave her the address. "Oh," she said, disapprovingly, "one of those nasty little villas on the main road." Well, it suits me.' When he died he left me in his will a magnificent edition of Jane Austen, of which he was justly proud. A year after his death his surviving brother wrote asking if the family could have it back. I complied promptly, reluctantly and a little crossly. I still have, though, the tattered St Francis de Sales he gave me in Bristol.

There was a brief period, at the beginning of the war, during which I got up in the early hours of winter mornings to bicycle in the dark to Holy Communion at a country church; but my habitual sloth soon prevailed and my enthusiasm for Anglo-Catholicism declined. All was much the same as before, but in the very early fifties – particularly when I was tired and also when preparing my notoriously disastrous *Hamlet* of 1951 – I went through odd, almost mad, phases of near-psychic experience. Two of them are, perhaps, worth recounting.

Merula and I had bought a painting by Meninsky which we fancied and hung it in our bedroom. It was called, I think, 'Two Irish Girls', and there was no mistaking that the picture showed two solid-looking females in shawls, confronting each other in some place of bright green bushes and withered hedgerows. And yet there was something enigmatic about it. One night, on entering the room, I was seized by an obsessional chapter and verse dinning in my head – Luke, Chapter XXIII, Verse 31. At first I couldn't think where in the house to lay hands on a Bible but, having found one and looked up the passage, I read, 'For if they do these things in a green tree what shall be done in a dry?' It was obvious that the words could be applied to the painting, which I was staring at with fascination. For the first time I noticed that the green bushes were loosely painted, round, self-satisfied faces and the twigs agonised, screaming, figures. I hurriedly took it off the wall, put it in another room and replaced it with a picture of the same size. When Merula entered the bedroom I noticed that she didn't even glance at the wall but she said immediately, 'What has happened to this room? It has regained its innocence.' A day or two later we learned it was the anniversary of Meninsky's suicide.

In the autumn of 1955 I went to Los Angeles to make my first Hollywood film, *The Swan*, with Grace Kelly and Louis Jourdan. I arrived, tired and crumpled, after a sixteen-hour flight from Copenhagen. Thelma Moss, who had written the film script of *Father Brown* (*The Detective* in the USA), had said she wished to take me out to dinner my first night in town. We arrived at three restaurants of repute at each of which we were refused admission because she was wearing slacks (ah, far-off days), and finally settled for a delightful little Italian bistro, where she was confident of a welcome. When we got there – Los Angeles is an endless city to drive through – there was no table available. As we walked disconsolately away I said, 'I don't care where we eat or what. Just something, somewhere.' I became aware of running, sneakered feet behind us and turned to face a fair young man in sweat-shirt and blue-jeans. 'You want a table?' he asked. 'Join me. My name is James Dean.' We followed him gratefully, but on the way back to the restaurant he turned into a car-park, saying, 'I'd like to show you something.' Among the other cars there was what looked like a large, shiny, silver parcel wrapped in cellophane and tied with ribbon. 'It's just been delivered,' he said, with bursting pride. 'I haven't even driven it yet.' The sports-car looked sinister to me, although it had a large bunch of red carnations resting on the bonnet. 'How fast is it?' I asked. 'She'll do a hundred and fifty,' he replied. Exhausted, hungry, feeling a little ill-tempered in spite of Dean's kindness, I heard myself saying in a voice I could hardly recognise as my own, 'Please, never get in it.' I looked at my watch. 'It is now ten o'clock, Friday the 23rd of

September, 1955. If you get in that car you will be found dead in it
by this time next week.' He laughed. 'Oh, shucks! Don't be so mean!'
I apologised for what I had said, explaining it was lack of sleep and
food. Thelma Moss and I joined him at his table and he proved an
agreeable, generous host, and was very funny about Lee Strasberg,
the Actors' Studio and the Method. We parted an hour later, full of
smiles. No further reference was made to the wrapped-up car. Thelma
was relieved by the outcome of the evening and rather impressed. In
my heart I was uneasy – with myself. At four o'clock in the afternoon
of the following Friday James Dean was dead, killed while driving
the car.

For six months I was absorbed in the Tarot. Wherever I went
Tarot cards or Tarot symbols caught my eye. Peter Bull and I took
a short holiday together to Tangiers having intended to go to Fez,
but the road was washed away by torrential rain, and more rain,
driven by a bitter wind, lashed Tangiers. On our first evening,
splashing through a dark, narrow street, in search of food and
entertainment, I spotted a single dim light in a shop window; when
we reached it we found nothing behind the glass except a pack of
Tarot cards, illuminated by a flickering bulb. The next day I bought
the cards and sat in my damp bedroom trying to learn something
from them. Peter was mildly embarrassed by my obsession and, a
few days later, admitting boredom, we agreed to part company – or,
rather, we said we would go to Gibraltar and when we arrived there
Peter, Freud coming to his aid, found he had left his passport behind
in Tangiers. So he returned there to have a jolly time with some new
friends, and I set off, walking much of the way, for Malaga. My
Tarot cards were safe in my pocket.

Back home I found out all I could about them: I was told
(erroneously, for sure) that they were part of the ancient Book of
Wisdom, scattered when the Library of Alexandria was sacked at the
end of the fourth century, and re-assembled as playing cards not long
after in Southern Europe. James Laver, a very well-informed friend
at the Victoria and Albert Museum, pointed out that the basic Tarot
symbols – chalice, spear, tree and spiky crown – corresponded to
hearts, spades, clubs and diamonds and represented the Crucifixion.
The Tarot symbols can be found, I believe, carved on a pillar of
Chartres Cathedral. I was hooked until an evening when I got the
horrors about them and impetuously threw cards and books on a
blazing log fire. When Merula saw what I had done she expressed
gratitude that I had returned to my senses. The Tarot card depicting

a wolf barking at a crab at the edge of a moonlit pool no longer
haunted my dreams; nor the Hanged Man; nor the Drowned Phoeni-
cian Sailor. They all went up in smoke, leaving only ash.

*

My friendship with Cyril Tomkinson had reduced my anti-clericism
considerably but not my anti-Romanism. Then came the film of
Father Brown, directed by my very good friend Robert Hamer (who
had been responsible for *Kind Hearts and Coronets*) and on location in
Burgundy I had a small experience the memory of which always
gives me pleasure. Even the fact that, having done insufficient homework and taken instructions in the script for granted, I was incorrectly
dressed for a Catholic priest didn't seem to matter.

Night shooting had been arranged to take place in a little hill-top
village a few miles from Macon. Scaffolding, the rigging of lights
and the general air of bustle caused some excitement among the
villagers and children gathered from all round. A room had been put
at my disposal in the little station hotel three kilometres away. By
the time dusk fell I was bored and, dressed in my priestly black, I
climbed the gritty winding road to the village. In the square children
were squealing, having mock battles with sticks for swords and
dustbin lids for shields; and in a café Peter Finch, Bernard Lee and
Robert Hamer were sampling their first Pernod of the evening. I
joined them for a modest Kir, then discovering I wouldn't be needed
for at least four hours turned back towards the station. By now it
was dark. I hadn't gone far when I heard scampering footsteps and
a piping voice calling, 'Mon père!' My hand was seized by a boy of
seven or eight, who clutched it tightly, swung it and kept up a
non-stop prattle. He was full of excitement, hops, skips and jumps,
but never let go of me. I didn't dare speak in case my excruciating
French should scare him. Although I was a total stranger he obviously
took me for a priest and so to be trusted. Suddenly with a 'Bonsoir,
mon père', and a hurried sideways sort of bow, he disappeared
through a hole in a hedge. He had had a happy, reassuring walk
home, and I was left with an odd calm sense of elation. Continuing
my walk I reflected that a Church which could inspire such confidence
in a child, making its priests, even when unknown, so easily approach-
able could not be as scheming and creepy as so often made out. I
began to shake off my long-taught, long-absorbed prejudices.

A few weeks before starting *Father Brown*, Matthew, then aged
eleven, was stricken with polio and paralysed from the waist down.

It was a worrying summer, with the burden of his illness falling heavily on Merula. For his part he seemed to remain philosophically cheerful, whatever turmoil reigned within. The film, after its French location, was made at Riverside Studios in Hammersmith and at the end of each day's work I would walk back to St Peter's Square along the river. The future for Matthew, for all the medical reassurances, looked doubtful; and in my anxiety I formed the habit of dropping in at a rather tawdry little Catholic church which lay on my route home. I didn't go to pray, to plead or to worship – just to sit quietly for ten minutes and gather what peace of spirit I could. There was never anyone else about. After I had done this several times I struck a negative bargain with God. 'Let him recover,' I said, 'and I will never put an obstacle in his way should he ever wish to become a Catholic.' It sounded to me like a supreme sacrifice on my part. About three months later he was able to walk in a stilted way. By Christmas he could play football. And not long afterwards I was taken up on my side of the bargain. Matthew had been put down to enter Westminster School but we decided we wanted to move out of London to the country; it seemed ridiculous for the boy to spend his time in a city while his mother and I enjoyed fresh air and the countryside. So another public school had to be found, and quickly. I discussed the matter with various friends but no suitable school had a vacancy. Finally, Peter Glenville, who was a very close friend, who had been educated at Stonyhurst and had a high regard for the Jesuits, suggested Beaumont, near Windsor. 'But it is Catholic!' I said; then remembered my promise in the little Hammersmith church.

The Rector, the Rev. Sir Lewis Clifford, greeted us affably when we arrived for an interview. From under his shabby soutane could be glimpsed an old army sweater and scuffed cricket boots, which we found comforting. 'We only have three non-Catholic boys,' he explained, 'and if he comes here I have no doubt that by the time he is sixteen he will wish to conform. They all do. No pressure will be put on him, I assure you, but it is most likely he will express the wish to be received. Would you object?' I hesitated, and then said, 'No.' The Rector looked relieved and invited us to see the school play that evening. We declined but I asked what the play was. 'Bernard Shaw's *St Joan*.' My eyebrows must have shot up for he continued, 'It's a great play. And if any boy leaves here without good answers for Mr Shaw, well, we will have failed in our job.' Matthew went to Beaumont (Peter Bull a firm Wykehamist was outraged) and

at the age of fifteen announced that he was going to submit himself
to the Holy Roman Catholic and Apostolic Church. What impressed
him most, I think, was the breakfast feast provided in his honour the
day he was received.

The summer of 1955 proved a happy one for me. All days were
idyllic, with a sense of expectancy in the air which I couldn't account
for. Then, one Saturday afternoon, I got on my bicycle and, almost
aimlessly, pedalled the two miles down to Petersfield and stopped
outside the Church of St Lawrence. It is a quite pleasing red-brick
building with a green copper dome. I had never been inside before
and was surprised by the simplicity of its white interior and the
absence of hideous plaster statues. Half-formed at the back of my
mind was the idea that if I caught a glimpse of the parish priest, and
liked the look of him, I might ask for instruction in the Faith. In fact,
I would be asking him to give of his time and effort while I just
picked over the goods for sale; I would let him know later if I intended
to buy. On the other hand, if the priest looked as if he might say,
'Top o' th' mornin',' or 'Ah, 'tis th' luck of th' Irish,' or appeared in
any way blinkered or narrow, then I would hastily back-pedal. Fr
Henry Clarke came round a corner: a tall, gentle, civilized-looking
man. The church was empty except for the two of us and he asked
if I was waiting to go to confession. I explained I was an ex-Anglican
who thought he wished instruction. He was kindly, un-pushy and
sympathetic, saying he was an ex-Anglican himself. Later on I
discovered that he had received Group-Captain Cheshire, VC into
the Church. We arranged for meetings over the following weeks.

In some ways I was troubled at how easily everything fell into
place; all was so natural apart from Indulgences (now greatly played
down) and Papal Infallibility, that I began to suspect Fr Clarke must
have missed out some essential which would turn out to be a major
stumbling-block. Finding no obstacle at St Lawrence's I determined
to seek the worst further afield. I wanted to see Catholicism at its
grimmest and least sympathetic. Accordingly, after a few enquiries,
I arranged to go for a few days as a guest to a Trappist monastery,
where life was mostly silent and reputed to be bleak. I excused myself
from visits to Fr Clarke for a time and took myself to Mount St
Bernard Abbey, a grey cluster of buildings surrounded by farmland
in the shaggy stony landscape not far from Leicester.

Mount St Bernard, apart from its gardens, is not very prepossess-
ing, having a flat-faced utilitarian look. My heart sank when I
approached the gates; and I was nonplussed by the elderly, red-

Alec Guinness, aged 13

A.G., aged 22

Nellie Wallace

Sybil Thorndike in *St. Joan*, 1924

Ernest Milton as Hamlet, 1925

John Gielgud as Hamlet, 1929

Edith Sitwell, photographed by
Baron in 1956

Sydney Cockerell, photographed
by Dorothy Hawksley, *c.* 1930

bearded Lay Brother who emerged from a wooden hut making wild but genial gestures towards me. He kept tapping his ear, pulling his nose and indulging in an extravagant deaf-and-dumb sort of language which I couldn't even guess at, let alone decipher. However, I must have caught the essentials of his gestures for when I repeated them, later in the day, to another monk he laughed and said, 'Oh, he was only saying, "Don't go down to the quarry today, they are about to make an explosion." ' The warning, it seemed to me, might just as well have been, 'The bears are having a picnic.'

I was given a large bedroom furnished with Victorian junk, dominated by a huge crucifix. The adjacent lavatory had an unpleasant smell. I was taxi-less, lost and felt unable to escape. 'This is it,' I thought, 'Mother Church testing the catechumens.' Worse was to come; firstly in the shape of baked beans and flabby bacon on wet toast (I had been looking forward to having the same simple, wholesome, vegetarian fare as the monks) and, secondly, the jollity of some of my fellow guests although one of these, a very serious young man, exuded extreme gloom. He stopped me on the stairs. 'You are in films, aren't you?' he asked, almost malevolently. 'Sort of,' I replied. 'I don't go to films,' he hissed. I sensed rising hysteria. Then he screeched, 'And I NEVER will; not until they do away with SEX!' He clattered down the stairs leaving me dumbfounded by his 'holier than thou' thought-for-the-day. I longed for something nasty to happen to him in the woodshed; which was a poor start for a monastic retreat.

Wandering in the Abbey grounds I saw what I took to be a young man, in white cowl and habit, silently hand a rose to another similar young man, for him to smell. They smiled at each other, bowed and parted. From their looks I would have guessed them to be in their early twenties; I was to find out later that they were well into their forties. The youthful appearance of almost all the monks was very deceptive. After I had been presented to the Abbot, on my first night, I was asked to guess his age and, knowing he was a Mitred Abbot, I added a few years to my estimate. 'Thirty-four,' I suggested. 'No,' I was told with glee. 'Seventy!' Before going to bed I looked at my own haggard, lined, pudgy face in a cracked mirror and reflected on an ill-spent life.

Although the Cistercians of the Strict Observance (they are not keen on being called Trappists, I discovered) keep a formidable silence, except in the case of absolute necessity, a monk was allocated to chat to me whenever I wanted. Father Robert Hodge, OCSO, had

been an Anglican priest at Dartmouth; he was in his fifties, I imagine,
and not in very good health. He had great charm and proved to be
almost garrulous – relief, I suppose, at being temporarily let off the
silent string – and it was I who mostly refrained from talking, except
to ask questions. He gave me a run-down on many of his fellow
monks and their past professions; told me proudly that Hore-Belisha
had been a frequent guest (I had a vision of yellow traffic beacons
and zebra crossings flowing from the Abbey precincts) and asked me
what I thought the most difficult part of being a monk might be.
'Other monks,' I replied promptly. He gave me a long quizzical look,
of the kind Edith Sitwell was so expert at giving, and said, with some
solemnity, 'Yes!' I felt I had gone to the top of the class.

Nothing was required of me other than the courtesy of attending
morning Mass and evening Compline. After my first Compline (a
beautiful short service), shuffling off to bed along a dark corridor,
the Abbot sloshed me in the face with holy water from a bowl he
was holding. I didn't know whether to acknowledge the wetting
with, 'Thanks a lot,' or ignore it. I settled for pious indifference but
from then on I slightly winced every time I saw the holy man, never
sure what ecclesiastical tricks he might have in store. My first morning
I was awakened at about 4.30 by a chatty Irish Lay Brother bringing
me a cup of strong sweet tea and a chocolate biscuit. He eyed the
biscuit enviously, but no doubt offered it up to God. Arriving at the
large, draughty, austere, white chapel I was amazed at the sights and
sounds that greeted me. The great doors to the East were wide open
and the sun, a fiery red ball, was rising over the distant farmland; at
each of the dozen or so side-altars a monk, finely vested but wearing
heavy farmer's boots to which cow dung still adhered, was saying
his private Mass. Voices were low, almost whispers, but each Mass
was at a different stage of development, so that the Sanctus would
tinkle from one altar to be followed half a minute later by other
tinkles from far away. For perhaps five minutes little bells sounded
from all over and the sun grew whiter as it steadily rose. There was
an awe-inspiring sense of God expanding, as if to fill every corner of
the church and the whole world. After being transfixed by the
unexpected beauty of it all I wasn't sure what to do; it seemed best
just to remain there until the last monk had gathered up his props
and left. Later in the day Fr Hodge told me that some of the monks
had commented (with what signs? I wondered) on my devotion at
having remained for all the Masses. Clearly I was marked out as quite
exceptionally pious. I wish I had blurted out that the truth was I had

merely dreaded a greasy breakfast and my fellow laymen; all I managed was the statement that I wasn't yet a Catholic.

'Brother so-and-so,' Fr Hodge informed me, as we strolled through a very anonymous graveyard, 'was a Customs Official. A very holy man, God rest his soul. Father What's-it was a Major in a Rifle Corps.' His eye fell on two monks clipping a hedge. He said, sotto voce, 'Brother John, now he was in the Metropolitan Police until a year ago; and Brother Timothy – you will have noticed, I expect, he is black – well, he comes from Abyssinia and is a wonderful farmer. He came here just for a few weeks, oh – twenty years ago. I don't know what we would do without him. *Very* cheerful.' We rounded a corner and nearly collided with a very tall monk who was in great haste. We passed without greeting. 'That was Brother-You-Know-Who. He is in charge of the aviary. Budgerigars.' There was a slight pause. 'He hates them.' When, about three years later, I returned to Mount St Bernard for a short visit I enquired after the budgerigars. 'Poor Brother-You-Know-Who! He got very cross with them one day; wrung all their necks. Much happier since then.'

The regularity of life at the Abbey, the happy faces that shone through whatever they had suffered, the strong yet delicate singing, the early hours and hard work – for the monks are self-supporting – all made a deep impression on me; the atmosphere was one of prayer without frills; it was easy to imagine oneself at the centre of some spiritual power-house, or at least being privileged to look over the rails, so to speak, at the working of a great turbine. If this was the worst that Rome had to offer, it was pretty good. Perhaps the rot, if it existed, lay further afield, under moiré silken robes, or in the political hands of some Eminence Grise.

On my last day there (of my first visit), my mentor, guide, gossip and new friend, for whom I felt a warm affection and great respect, took me to the Library and Scriptorium. There was no sound, other than the buzzing of a bee and pens writing. I would like to say they were writing with quills on parchment but it was all too modern and practical for that. My memory provided me with a line recorded by Robert Louis Stevenson's nurse, when he was four years old, 'Lou dreamed he heard the noise of pens writing.' I stood still to listen and Fr Hodge suddenly looked as if he had gone into a trance. After a moment he turned to me and whispered, 'You know an actor called X?' 'Well,' I told him. 'And he has a wife who was a Y?' I confirmed it. 'Could you get a message to her?' I was expecting to see Y that evening, when I was to collect her son, still a schoolboy, to take him to Petersfield for the week-end. 'Of course,' I said. 'Will you please tell her not to worry about her father? All is very well with him.' Until that moment there had been no mention between us of X or Y or indeed any other actors. Then I recalled that Y's father, who had died some years previously, had been headmaster at Dartmouth and must have been known by Fr Hodge. When I passed the message on – with some puzzlement and a little embarrassment – Y said, with great emotion, that it was what she had been longing to hear for a long time. I gathered she had been instrumental in dissuading her father from changing his Anglican allegiance.

The film of *The Swan* cropped up and I flew to California, over-weight with mostly tedious theological books, to do four months' work for MGM. Before leaving England, I had promised Fr Henry Clarke to do my best to attend Mass each Sunday. I came unstuck very quickly. The flesh-pots of Los Angeles sang their siren songs; and on the first Sunday that I went to morning Mass, accompanying Grace Kelly, I heard a ghastly young priest say from the pulpit, 'We are the only people in the world who rise early to worship the Lord.' If I had had a prayer-mat or a fez with me I would have hurled them at him, or even the Book of Common Prayer. I was greatly put off and remained on a see-saw of indecision until my return home. On March 24, 1956, Fr Clarke accepted my reconciliation with the Church, with tact and kindness, at St Lawrence's, Petersfield. Like countless converts before and after me, I felt I had come home – 'and known the place for the first time.'

Merula was sympathetic and pleased but probably felt a little out of things. It was a beautiful sunny day. After the ceremony, which was attended by only two or three friends, we returned to Kettlebrook Meadows and I took myself upstairs. For a long time I stood looking at the lovely line of gentle hills which surround us on three sides; the Hangers to the north-west; Butser Hill to the south and Harting Down in the east. Some phrase of Newman, in garbled form, ran in my head – something about the line of the hills being the skirts of the Angels of God. Checking it up I find, 'I say of the Angels, – every breath of air and ray of light and heat, every beautiful prospect is, as it were, the skirts of their garments, the waving robes of those whose faces see God.' Such was my mood that day and I was more than content: now the trees we planted thirty years ago have grown tall, obscuring much of the view in summer-time. In these latter days, like Roy Campbell, 'I love to see, when leaves depart, the clear anatomy arrive'. The winter hills nourish my faith. There had been no emotional upheaval, no great insight, certainly no proper grasp of theological issues; just a sense of history and the fittingness of things. Something impossible to explain. Père Teilhard de Chardin says, 'The incommunicable part of us is the pasture of God.' I must leave it at that.

On the whole the press left me well alone. A young man from the *Daily Express* turned up at the house on Good Friday, a few days after my reception, just as I was about to leave for a service. I welcomed him with a certain amount of dismay, I suspect, but politely. Anyway, I gave him a drink. I was rather amazed to see his article, when it appeared, saying he had found me leaning against a life-size Buddha drinking a tumbler of gin. I *do* possess a carved, wooden, Chinese lamp, which stands about two feet, six inches high (the Buddha must surely have been taller) and I am confident the tumbler of gin was a glass of water. Actors should learn to get used to such things, I know. Only one abusive letter reached me – anonymous of course – and written on the Royal Automobile Club's notepaper. The hundreds of other letters, from people of various persuasions, were pleasing and touching. The only irritation I felt was on reading an article, in a French Catholic paper, saying that the Virgin Mary had appeared to me over a garden wall. (Why over a wall? I wondered. If she was about, why couldn't she have come right on over and played?) I soon got used to the absurdities of some Catholic journalism, the rumours of alleged miracles that didn't bear inspection and the fine crop of anti-Popes (the present number standing, I believe, at sixteen), but nothing of the sort ever emanated from as sober and rational a place as St Lawrence's.

Archbishop Henry King, Bishop of Portsmouth, lived in Winchester; he confirmed me privately, in an attic in his residence. Peter Glenville acted as my sponsor and, in the ritual of those days, was required to stand with one of his feet on one of mine. Our faces remained solemn but I fear we were shaken by silent giggles, which became almost uncontrollable when the Archbishop put on an abnormally low mitre which looked like a paper hat from a Christmas cracker. His Chaplain, an elegant young man, straightened it for him saying, 'Excuse me, Grace.' Peter had to hold his foot down very hard. It was all but full circle to Holy Trinity, Eastbourne, and the Anglican Bishop of Lewes; except that this time I was no longer obsessed with the ichneumon-fly or filled with adolescent rancour. I loved the Archbishop-King and was as happy as a Fool.

Some months later, while I was in Ceylon making *The Bridge on the River Kwai*, Merula, without informing me until after the event, made her submission to Rome. When she joined me for a few weeks we were able to celebrate our first Christmas together as Catholics – in a little church, open at the sides to palm trees and the sound of surf breaking on a hot, white, sandy beach, with tropical birds flitting over the heads of the congregation, who squatted on the earth floor in colourful saris in deep devotion. The whole world, however poverty-stricken, seemed a wide-open bright and sunlit place, 'where all contraries are reconciled'.

Back in London I was walking up Kingsway in the middle of an afternoon when an impulse compelled me to start running. With joy in my heart, and in a state of almost sexual excitement, I ran until I reached the little Catholic church there (St Anselm and St Cecilia) which I had never entered before; I knelt; caught my breath, and for ten minutes was lost to the world. Coming out into the glare of day, mingling with sensible citizens on their lawful occasions, I wondered what on earth had possessed me and if I had become momentarily deranged. I decided that I was still fairly sane; that it had just been an unexpected, rather nonsensical gesture of love. My friend, Richard Leech, when I told him about it, was rather distressed, thinking my tiresome, convert enthusiasm had gone too far; but I argued that if a religion meant anything at all it meant that the whole man worshipped, mind, and body alike; that it was a totality and indivisible. There was some reassurance when I discovered that the good, brilliant, acutely sane Ronald Knox had found himself running, on several occasions, to visit the Blessed Sacrament. Time has slipped by and I don't run anywhere; I am passed by joggers of all shapes and ages, while for me the fat accumulates. And yet I do not feel myself a slave, whatever bad habits I may nourish and treasure, having given, at any rate, part of myself to something which spans the centuries. One of Chesterton's most penetrating statements was: 'The Church is the one thing that saves a man from the degrading servitude of being a child of his own time.' Just a *little* more effort, I hope, and I may deny myself that extra pat of butter, the third glass of wine, one lascivious thought, and achieve a moment when irascibility is controlled, one bitchy remark left unsaid; and, more positively, find a way to make some small generous gesture without forethought, and direct a genuine prayer of good-will towards someone I dislike. It is a fairly pitiful ambition after a quarter of a century of genuflexion.

There have been moments when I have wished to tug myself away from Roman Catholicism, but they have only been moments of personal dejection and accidia and soon disposed of. Much water has flown under Tiber's bridges, carrying away splendour and mystery from Rome, since the pontificate of Pius XII. The essentials, I know, remain firmly entrenched and I find the post-Conciliar Mass simpler and generally better than the Tridentine; but the banality and vulgarity of the translations which have ousted the sonorous Latin and little Greek are of a supermarket quality which is quite unacceptable. Hand-shaking and embarrassed smiles or smirks have replaced the older courtesies; kneeling is out, queueing is in, and the general tone is rather like a BBC radio broadcast for tiny tots (so however will they learn to put away childish things?). The clouds of incense have dispersed, together with many hidebound, blinkered and repressive attitudes, and we are left with social messages of an almost over-whelming progressiveness. The Church has proved she is not mori-bund. 'All shall be well,' I feel, 'and all manner of things shall be well,' so long as the God who is worshipped is the God of all ages, past and to come, and not the Idol of Modernity, so venerated by some of our bishops, priests and mini-skirted nuns.

Pope Pius XII died, racked by hiccups, in 1958. Four days before his death Merula and I were presented to him as plastic surgeons. The Pope's astronomer, the saintly Fr O'Connell SJ, who lived alongside his observatory at Castel Gandolfo, suggested that as we were holidaying in Rome we might like to attend an audience the Pope was to give, in his summer palace, to a small group of plastic surgeons. We sat on gilded chairs facing His Holiness, who looked pale and drawn. At his feet, crouched on the steps of the throne, sat the future Pope Paul VI, shredding a handkerchief to ribbons each time the Pope hiccuped. Fr O'Connell whispered to me that the lecture being read was not only brilliant but in beautiful Italian. When it was over a dozen or so plastic surgeons, including ourselves, were lined up to be presented; we stood near the end of the line next to a middle-aged American couple. I didn't grasp what the Pope said to me (I was desperately anxious for him to say nothing and get back to bed) but I assumed it was about surgical alterations to the face and not about theatrical make-up; but I did catch every word said by the Americans. They both kneeled to kiss the Fisherman's Ring, and then the man burst into loud sobs, the tears coursing down his face. The Pope patted him, took his hand, saying the Italian equivalent of 'There! There!' and the man grasped his white cassock. The wife explained her husband away with a motherly smile. I imagined her to be a woman who would not have permitted him to buy his own shirts, socks or underpants. 'He's so moved, Your Holiness,' she said. 'It is such an honour to meet you. Isn't it, dear? He's always like this on great occasions. Aren't you, dear? Oh, he's very moved! And just think, Your Holiness – we've come all the way from Michigan!' The Pope mastered a hiccup. 'Michigan?' 'Sure, Michigan.' 'I know Michigan,' the Pope said, and managing to free himself from the plastic surgeon's grip he raised a hand in blessing: 'A special blessing on Michigan!' Those were probably the last words of English he spoke. The entourage sped him away from the audience chamber. His private doctor followed, glowering at each of us in turn as he passed. The look he gave me was so suspicious, if not downright sinister, that if it hadn't been for the presence of Fr O'Connell I might have responded with some gesture to ward off the evil eye.

We were in Rome again, for a week, the Christmas of the following year and given tickets for the Pontifical High Mass to be celebrated by Pope John on Christmas morning. We were a party of five and, as the tickets were not for a particularly good position – which didn't trouble us at all – and it was lashing with rain, we went in grubby raincoats over old clothes. Jostled and bruised by violent nuns we eventually squeezed into our seats, surrounded by animated lady tourists loudly discussing the shoes they had bought in the Via Condotti. I told them, peremptorily, to shut up. An uneasy, astonished silence prevailed – only to be broken by a major-domo, a tiny, withered man in black satin breeches, who stamped down the length of St Peter's waving a black wand and calling out, 'Sir Guinness! Sir Guinness!' When he got near us we cowered in our raincoats but he spotted me, or at any rate realised the face was English and would do as a substitute. He was triumphant. 'Please to come!' he shouted. I shook my head. He looked cross; he waved his wand. 'Come, please.' In a hoarse whisper I pointed out that there were five of us, and mimed we were unsuitably dressed. There was no way of thwarting his determination so, apologising to the shoe-fetishist ladies for disturbing them, we clambered after him. Banging his staff of office he led us towards the High Altar and placed us in the great red velvet chairs reserved for royalty. Then he disappeared. Cardinals knelt on the hard marble at our feet, no cushions to ease their old knees. God knows who they thought we were. Fr Philip Caraman, who was our host, was in some trepidation as apparently he was incorrectly dressed, looking rather like some crumpled curate from an impoverished English vicarage. Pope John appeared, to thunderous applause, carried aloft on his Sedia Gestatoria, wearing his red velvet bonnet pulled well down over his ears, looking small, round, very serious and somewhat queasy. As soon as Mass started he got everything slightly wrong, having to be prompted frequently. It was the first Christmas Mass in St Peter's with vernacular responses; I had the impression that it was the thrilling vigour of the responses from the vast congregation which made him lose his place. We were within fifteen feet of him and I was grateful that he never once looked our way – he could well have thought some ghastly revolution had erupted during the night. When all appeared to be over the major-domo reemerged, exposing us to shame once more, clucking, 'Sir Guinness,' and making us walk the full length of the Basilica behind the Pope's chair, which swayed perilously on high. We were rushed to the roof to witness the Papal Blessing, Fr Caraman insisting we should kneel in a lead gutter of trickling water.

My only glimpse of Pope Paul VI was through a barrage of Mickey Mouse and Donald Duck balloons in the vast piazza one Easter.

The great Benedictine monastery near Subiaco (home town of Gina Lollobrigida) is perched on a steep hillside thirty odd miles east of Rome. I took myself there for a four-day retreat and was given the Pope's bedroom: a fair-sized, white-washed room with dusty-red brocade curtains, a tall, narrow brass bedstead, and a dozen high, straight-backed, plush-seated chairs ranged Italian style along the walls. The Abbot, a cultured, urbane man of about fifty, amused by life and tolerant of his few guests, invited me early each morning to trudge up the road with him and a garrulous American painter to attend Mass in the little chapel which had been frequented by St Francis of Assisi. It was on the site of St Benedict's original hermitage. They were magical mornings, bright and crisp; to one side the thickly-wooded precipitous mountainside in blue shade, to the other green and gold rolling hills. The Abbot asked me what I felt about the white marble statue of St Benedict which stood in the chapel; I was obliged to admit I didn't like it, finding it sentimental, effeminate and sugary. 'Oh, but it is not meant to be a likeness of the Saint as a man,' he said, 'it is a portrait of his soul.' The painter nodded in sycophantic agreement. 'Well,' I said, 'if he had a soul like that I doubt if he would have climbed this far; he would have had the vapours on the way. I would prefer to see in its place something like Bernini's "David" fiercely flinging a stone at any unwelcome visitor.' I apologised, the Abbot laughed and the painter winced.

In the entrance to the monastery there is a fresco of 'King James the Third of England' – the Old Pretender – riddled with bullet holes. The

Abbot shrugged sadly at it. 'One day,' he said, 'we will repair it. The Germans broke in and thinking he really had been the King of England opened fire on the fresco with machine-guns. War!' he added in a voice of contempt. He had been at one time, I gathered, a soldier.

On the morning of the day I left, thinking it right that I should make some contribution towards my keep but being rather hard pressed for lire, I put about £30's worth in an envelope and had it delivered to the Abbot. Ten minutes later there was a pounding at my door and he plunged in, flushed with excitement, saying, 'You will please stay for lunch. We will have a Festa with your kind gift.' He immediately dispatched a lay-brother to Subiaco, in a rattling old car, to buy hampers of the local fish. It was like the miracle of the feeding of the five thousand in reverse. During lunch there was much smiling towards me, with gestures of appreciation, as we tucked into the muddiest, boniest, most evil-smelling fish I have felt forced to eat. The monks were gleeful; except perhaps for half a dozen who were not Italian and who picked their way as cautiously as I did through the revolting carcasses.

Outside the monastery gates when I left, two or three press reporters had gathered, together with a small batch of 'paparazzi' with their cameras and motor scooters. The Abbot was outraged, did his best to shoo them away, and then, seeing the Cadillac which had come to collect me, and its burly chauffeur, said, 'You should have no difficulty shaking them off.' He sketched a valedictory blessing on the afternoon air and withdrew inside his spiritual fortress. The reporters jumped forward and the 'paparazzi' zip-clicked.

'Do you know Gina Lollobrigida?'

'I have met her, briefly.'

'Which do you like the most, Gina or Sophia Loren?'

'Impossible to say.'

'Who . . .' making extravagant circular gestures, 'has the bigger boobs? Gina? Sophia?'

'I haven't thought about it.'

'What penances did they give you inside for your terrible sins?' They obviously looked on the monastery as prison.

'Eating fish from Subiaco,' I replied, rashly.

'You don't like Subiaco? You hate Subiaco?'

'No, no. I like Subiaco but I do not like the fish.'

'Why they give you this fish penance?'

I was once again in what people refer to, approvingly, as 'the real world'.

'Excuse me,' I said, 'I think I am going to be sick.' Not feeling at all sick I acted nausea and dragged myself into the car. Carlo, or Luigi or Stefano drove me away as if from the Gates of Hell, shooting most traffic lights until we were in the centre of Rome.

My friend Bridget Boland, who lived in Rome for several years, had kindly lent me for a month her delightful small apartment high up in the Torre del Grillo, overlooking the Forum of Trajan, and adjacent to the palace of the Knights of Malta. Hot and sticky from my drive from Subiaco, I stepped into the shuttered cool of her sitting-room, floored with tiles of a white, blue and yellow pattern, and flung open the French windows. The hot late afternoon air took possession of the whole apartment. I stepped on to the balcony, where Bridget's precious pot-plants were withering for lack of water, and looked thoughtfully at the view. The Forum Romanum couldn't quite be seen from there nor, happily, the Victor Emmanuel monument, but below me were broken columns, red brick walls which had been excavated, slabs of paving stones, and several stray cats. A workman, wearing a triangular hat made of newspaper, such as we used to make as children, was mixing cement on a board.

> Imperial Caesar, dead and turned to clay,
> Might stop a hole to keep the wind away.
> Oh, that that earth, which kept the world in awe,
> Should patch a wall, t'expell the winter's flaw.

Refusing to let my mind be drawn to 'The Last Four Things' (which it has never been willing to entertain) I fetched water for Bridget's dying plants; this trickled over the balcony, splashing on the cobbles below. There was a shout from the workman. I looked down and made signs of contrition, he accepted them with a ravishing smile, unfolded his paper hat and held it over his head, mockingly, as a makeshift umbrella. 'The beauty of the world; the paragon of animals; and yet, to me, what is this quintessence of dust?' Caesar is dead, Leonardo and the great medieval Popes, Garibaldi and Mussolini, but the warm charm of the Italian peasant and workman lives on, determinedly. And perhaps the scrubby little herbs and pot-plants would survive. I was content and not afraid of death.

'Oh, you are lucky to be a Catholic,' people sometimes say, as if my Premium Bonds had paid a handsome dividend. Well, yes; but the constant failures are painful, when not just laughable, and boringly repetitive. A few years ago, on an Ash Wednesday, standing in line to be smudged on the forehead with ashes, as is the custom, a small boy of about seven was immediately in front of me. In front of him shambled a man probably in his late eighties. Behind me stood a very pretty young woman. Each of us, as the ashes were imposed, would hear the words, 'Remember man, you are dust, and to dust you will return.' Caesar, the Pope, the small boy, one's friends and oneself, all destined to be blown away, recycled or reconstituted: I cannot see much to grumble at. Others coming after us will love much of what we have loved and many new beauties besides. The ashes imposed on our heads are the burned, pulverised and blessed palm branches left over from the previous year's Passion Tide; and another Easter is always on the way.

The longevity of the Holy Roman Catholic and Apostolic Church, her wisdom and kindness, can well embrace the naive strugglings of an adolescent English schoolboy kicking, so to speak, against the pricks. She has books to read aloud, pictures to show, consolations to offer, strength to give and some marvellous people, from all ages, to hold up for the world's admiration; not many in high places, perhaps, but thousands in the market square, hospital ward, back pew, desert and jungle. And in recent years, when she has been swift (at last) to acknowledge her human failings, they have been found occupying the Chair of St Peter.

The fear I mostly entertain is that my personal religion is notional rather than real; but I can say, with the nineteenth-century New England Transcendentalist Margaret Fuller, 'I accept the universe'; and, with Carlyle, his rejoinder, 'Gad! She'd better.'

CHAPTER FIVE

Sportin' Instincts

Martita Hunt was born in 1901, brought up in the Argentine and sent to England in her early teens to be educated at Eastbourne, where she was horrified by the English climate and her first bite at an apple, which her father had cracked up to be the finest fruit in the world. She avoided apples for the rest of her life and escaped to France at any opportunity. Her early years as an actress were spent playing rather drab mackintoshed parts (except when she was at the Old Vic opposite John Gielgud) but there came a day when, after a holiday in Provence and Paris, she decided to alter her life-style. From flat shoes she took to high-heeled golden sandals, expensive sheer stockings – she had long, thin, elegant legs – and a generally French wardrobe. She also developed a taste for expensive food and the best wines. By the time I first met her, late in 1933, her habitat was a smart little flat in Knightsbridge; she was also to be seen frequently at Prunier's restaurant (not yet within reach of my pocket) in St James's Street. She had become a bird of rare plumage and was the first woman I had ever met who wore silk trousers and painted her toe-nails. Her work by now was mostly in the West End theatres, playing eccentric princesses, duchesses and other high-flying creatures, diversified with small parts in films. She said to me one day, in a tone of disgust, 'It's no use them trying to cast me as a woman of the people,' and yet one of her most memorable performances was as a Belgian peasant woman, hair scraped back, black-shawled and clogged, in the film of *Nurse Cavell*.

In 1933, working in a very minor capacity in an advertising agency for thirty shillings a week but determined to get into the theatre somehow, I applied for an audition at the Royal Academy of Dramatic Art, where I hoped to obtain the Leverhulme Scholarship. This, if achieved, would provide me with free training for two years and something like £5 a week. It was a shot in the dark from a blinkered and ignorant youth; so I paid my £1 audition fee and was given a list of short pieces to be learned from various plays; these included a Chorus from *Henry V*, speeches from *The Three Sisters* and *St Joan*, and something of my own choice. The audition was to be held in January, in four months' time, and it dawned on me, as I held the list in my hand, that I hadn't a clue as to how to start work on it or, indeed, what would be required of me or how to comport myself at an audition. A wild idea struck me; perhaps John Gielgud would take me through my pieces or at any rate advise me. He lived then in a flat in St Martin's Lane and I found out his telephone number and had the nerve to call him. We were, of course, total strangers. He was kind on the telephone but in effect only said, 'You might try Martita Hunt. She'll love the money.' Because of my surname John must have assumed that I was one of the rich Guinnesses. And when I called Martita she undoubtedly thought the same, cooing and being formally respectful at the same time. When she saw me in her flat the following evening – a thin twenty-year-old in a well-worn suit I was gangling out of – she was visibly appalled and crestfallen. I had polished my shoes, cleaned my nails, brushed my dry, dark mouse-coloured hair and straightened my tie but the message was clear – no money.

Up and down the stairs to Martita's flat there plodded an assortment of ladies to minister to her; a French manicurist (and toe-nail painter), a French seamstress for mending gloves and hemlines, a French maid and a very English lady, known as Watty, with her higher-irrigation apparatus. All were called 'chérie'. The evening I arrived the door was opened by a dark-haired little soubrette. She explained that Mis' 'Unt was in her bath. The bathroom door was ajar and bubbling sounds, steam and exotic perfumes filled the air. 'Forgive me, dear Mr Guinness,' she cooed, 'I am in my bath. I think perhaps you are a little early.' (I was; I always am.) There was a sound as if she had submerged, followed by, 'Go into the sitting-room, there's a good fellow, and make us dry martinis.'

I was horrified and wished only to sink through the rich, deep pale-grey pile of the carpet. Being a very unsophisticated lad I wasn't even sure what a dry martini was composed of – gin and vermouth, I guessed, but I had no idea in what proportions, and why the heck it should be called dry. Stepping gingerly into the room, fearing to soil the carpet, I looked around with apprehension and a certain aesthetic pleasure. It was quite a small room but very elegant, with pale Regency-striped curtains, a sofa covered in a summery yellow silk, a handsome Louis Quinze desk, a Sickert painting above the over-mantel, bowls of exotic flowers, a huge gramophone and, horror of horrors, a glossy cabinet which had been converted for drinks. Staring at me, indeed, were bottles of vermouth, gin, sherry and whisky, beautiful crystal glasses and a jug with ice. The gin bottle in particular caught my attention; it was empty. 'Can't make cocktails without gin,' I thought and got as far away from the cabinet as possible. Bubbling in the bathroom ceased, water gurgled and then I heard Martita's voice call, 'Goodnight, chérie.' The front door closed. After a long dramatic pause Martita made her entrance.

She was tall, lean, and dressed in a blue-and-white striped silk blouse, royal-blue silk trousers, cut like a sailor's, with gilded sandals and scarlet toe-nails. She entered the room with a long arm extended, all smiles. It was a fine entrance for Act I. Then she saw me and the curtain almost fell; the glittering almond-shaped eyes darkened and dulled, the welcoming hand dropped to her side.

'You're not exactly an athlete,' she said.

'No. I'm sorry. It's an actor I want to be.'

'Where are the martinis?'

'There's no gin,' I said.

'I need a drink. Whisky.'

She sat down, and with a thin, trembling hand groped for a cigarette from an elaborate crystal box while I mentally struggled with the whisky. One inch? Two?

'There doesn't appear to be any soda,' I said, fumbling around.

'Neat!' she said. 'My God, I need it.'

She looked me up and down suspiciously.

'Your shoes are clean, I hope.'

I peered at the uppers, worn but polished.

'No,' she said, 'show me the soles.'

I turned up my feet, hopping and terrified they might reveal dog dirt. Clean enough. She seemed reassured. Not until later did I learn that Martita always put down druggets over her carpeting except when she was expecting important guests, fearing what lesser mortals might tread into her flat. In me she had been expecting an important visitor; seeing what she had got she was almost kicking herself. I gave her a tumbler half full of whisky and she told me to sit down, so I perched carefully on the edge of a Georgian chair. Later I would know that every time a guest departed, important or not, she, or chérie, would wipe where he had sat with some cleansing fluid.

After I had explained my ambition to try for the Leverhulme Scholarship she asked me to read something to her, so I unfolded the RADA audition syllabus and burst forth. 'O, for a Muse of Fire,' I wailed.

Martita buried her face in her hands, muttering 'Oh, my God!' while the smoke from her cigarette drifted through her hair.

'Think, when we speak of horses, that you see them . . .'

'I see nothing!' she said. 'Nothing! My dear boy, I see nothing.'

She got up suddenly and seizing me by the upper lip, tried to drag me across the room by it. It slipped from her fingers and lolled for a moment or two before returning to its proper position.

'Flab!' she said, contemptuously. 'No muscle. If you want to be an actor you must have muscle in your upper lip. Like mine!' She bared her teeth, wrinkling her nose rather unattractively. I had to admit there was plenty of muscle there and asked her if she would be prepared to take me through my audition pieces. She downed her whisky and stared at me.

'You are working in an office. What is your pay?'

'Thirty shillings a week.'

'Have you a private income?'

'About twenty-seven shillings a week but it won't last much longer.'

She exhaled a cloud of smoke, sighed a little, examined her finger-nails and then said, 'I will give you ten one-hour lessons at a pound a time. Once a week. We will start tomorrow. And now you must go; I am expecting someone important.'

She showed me the door. No 'chéri' for me as yet. I borrowed the ten pounds from an ex-schoolmaster and managed to repay him two years later.

Have I guyed Martita? I don't think so: it was all as I recall it. Have I made her appear a dragon? Well, although only thirteen years older than me, she could appear dragonish and had a sharp tongue and a quick South American temper. With time I grew to love her and appreciate her sterling qualities as a friend, her warmth and extravagant generosity; there were occasions when I was astonished by her ordinary human concern and her willingness to sacrifice her comfort or interests, particularly during the war years, for the sake of a young married couple.

For four or five of the lessons, always in the evening, after my office hours, she tried to teach me the rudiments of voice production, a subject in which I don't think she was expert; but when it came to dealing with the texts of the plays she was much more on home ground. She put a swift stop to my amateur, cliché-ridden attitudes, my frequent false emphasis, and helped me to think, as an actor, what I was speaking. (Very rarely do I rely on any rule of thumb but

Martita gave me one, at that time, which has stood me in good stead. Unless there is reason to the contrary, she taught me that, in speaking, the verb, which is the driving force of a sentence, should have first importance, then the noun, and that the adjectives and adverbs would take care of themselves and that personal pronouns should never be emphasised except in special circumstances.) More importantly, perhaps, her personality, surroundings, conversation and interests awakened in me a feeling for the arts and awareness of a more sophisticated world than I had encountered among schoolmasters and advertising agents. She talked well about literature and was a perceptive critic of drama. In later years I always found going to the theatre with her both instructive and stimulating, although I had to make allowances for her prejudices against certain actresses. Once, when I had expressed admiration for Diana Wynyard, she countered my enthusiasm with, 'Good English loaf, without any crust.' She had to doff her hat to Edith Evans, whom I worshipped, but it rankled, so she commented on Edith's legs: 'She has the legs of a farm woman' – which wasn't strictly true.

My sixth lesson with Martita was to be on a Sunday morning and when I arrived I found her flat door ajar and her in bed, talking on the telephone. 'Is that you, Mr Guinness? No, chérie, I'm talking to someone who has just arrived. Hang on a moment. Mr Guinness, come in here.' She was sitting up in bed, her head bound in pink chiffon, holding the receiver to her ear and her hand over the mouth-piece. Her eyes flashed at me and indicated a side-table.

'Your money is over there, dear boy,' she said. 'All ten pounds of it. Take it and go away, there's a good fellow. I can't teach you. Try some little amateur group. Stick to your advertising. Forget all about the professional theatre.' I was flabbergasted and promptly sat down on the edge of the bed. 'Chérie,' she said to the telephone, 'I'll ring you back in five minutes. Difficulties.' The receiver went down with a plonk and we stared at each other.

'I can't forget the theatre,' I said. 'I want you to go on teaching me.'

'You're wasting your time, and mine. And your money.'

'I don't care,' I said.

She reached for a cigarette and made a great act of slowly waving out the match and blowing smoke. 'Very well,' she said at last. 'But not today, dear boy; I haven't the energy or the spirit. This poor old envelope' – she indicated her body – 'needs rest and quiet. Come tomorrow evening.' As I left her room, angry and perplexed, I could hear her dialling busily.

Martita was better than her word. When I had completed the agreed ten lessons she suggested I should continue with her for a few more weeks, and when I said I had insufficient money she replied that that was of no consequence, the lessons would be free. She seemed to see a glimmer of hope for me at last and I must have had another dozen hourly visits right up to the time of the audition.

Having got the day off from the office (no easy thing to arrange in those days, except in an emergency) I took myself, in a highly nervous state, to the Royal Academy of Dramatic Art at the appointed hour. I was met at the entrance in Gower Street by a lady in a green dress and long drop-earrings.

'You must be Mr Guinness,' she said. 'I tried to reach you, but here you are. We are not giving the Leverhulme Scholarship this year after all. What a good thing you haven't come all the way down from Scotland. So sorry!'

I turned away and felt despair. My friends at the advertising agency had been kind but I knew that, behind my back, they must have been ridiculing my ambition. The idea of facing them the next day was appalling and as I walked slowly along Gower Street I thought that perhaps I just wouldn't show up at the office again. I turned a corner and came face to face with a girl I was sure I recognised. She passed me and then turned round. She was a girl I had been friendly with when we were both about fourteen and staying in the same hotel in Eastbourne. She had always been attractive and bright and now she was an elegant young woman and recently married. I told her my lamentable tale about RADA and she listened with sympathy. She, at least, believed me. As children she and her two sisters were dragged into playlets I devised and which we performed, with storms of giggles, to anyone in the hotel who could be persuaded to sit still for twenty minutes. It had been agreed among us at that time that I was to be an actor. Standing on the street corner she suddenly looked at her watch and then said, 'You'd better hurry along to Baker Street. I happen to know, through a friend, that they are holding auditions at the Fay Compton Studio of Dramatic Art this afternoon or evening. And they give a scholarship too.' She gave me the address and, barely stopping to thank her or say goodbye, I ran. I arrived after the audition had started but was admitted and was the last of about twenty aspiring young actors and actresses to be heard. I trundled out my RADA audition pieces and threw in an impersonation of

George Arliss as Disraeli for good measure. After a brief interview – there were I think five judges, one of whom, Mollie Hartley-Milburn, was to become a good friend for life – I was awarded the scholarship: free training for a two-year course but no money attached. I telephoned Martita, who invited me round for a glass of wine, and almost everyone else I knew. Martita wasn't too keen on Fay Compton I gathered (though she couldn't fault her perfect diction or the marvellously controlled way she moved) but she was obviously relieved that her tuition had had some result. From that night on Martita and I became friends, our relationship suddenly on a different footing. At the office next day I was able to hold my head unmodestly high while I received astonished congratulations, and I gave a month's notice. How I was to live was another matter. Micawber-like I assumed I would manage somehow.

The Fay Compton Studio, a rather ramshackle small drill-hall with a stage at one end, together with changing rooms and offices, provided voice production classes in the morning, followed by tap-dancing or fencing or movement, and rehearsals of scenes from musical comedy. The afternoons were devoted to Shakespeare, modern comedy and, occasionally, to some dismal Greek Tragedy choral speaking. Shakespeare was in the hands of Charles Hickman, hot from the Old Vic, and at that time married to Mollie Milburn, who was responsible for the modern work and encouraged me enormously. Diana King, Richard Hearne (later to be Mr Pastry) and his future wife and sister-in-law and others provided me almost daily with sandwiches and fruit when they found out my circumstances. The most distinguished of my fellow students was John Le Mesurier, whose brilliant comic timing was evident even then. I kept Martita informed of progress and sometimes she gave me a chic little meal. Immediately after the summer show of 1934 my allowance finally failed and I hadn't enough money left to pay the ten shillings a week for my squalid room; I knew I had to leave the Studio and find work within a few days. How good fortune came my way I tell in what I have written about John Gielgud.

With my early jobs as a professional actor Martita continued to take an interest but decided I had got above myself; she took every opportunity to point out, rather sharply, any solecism I committed and generally expressed disapproval of my flippant character. 'Take care you don't fall in with a wrong set,' she said to me one day, rather ominously. But when you are young how do you know when you are falling or where? You jump at what seems congenial company and people who talk the same language. Somewhat huffily I told her I could take care of myself, although perhaps her warning was wise. Young actors today seem to me a generally nicer lot than we were fifty years ago.

In the late summer of 1939, temporarily out of work, I made an adaptation of *Great Expectations* and showed it, almost casually, to George and Sophie Devine. There was talk, with the outbreak of war, of forming a small theatre company with George, Martita, Marius Goring, Vera Poliakoff and one or two others. None of us had any money, except Marius, who was able to provide £50. George and the others decided, to my genuine surprise, that my adaptation would make a suitable first play for the company, which was then formed. It was to be followed, if successful, by *King John, All's Well* and a Molière. Martita was to play Miss Havisham, which was almost hand-tailored for her, Marius was to be Pip and George was to direct. London was blacked out; we rehearsed at any old pub room we could find and we opened at the Rudolf Steiner Hall, which suited us admirably once we had managed tactfully to disguise its anthroposophical atmosphere. And it was there that we closed six weeks later. The Shaftesbury Theatre, where we hoped we might transfer, was bombed and, in spite of good business after a splendid notice from James Agate, we simply couldn't make ends meet; not helped by the fact that the scenery cost almost twice as much as expected. It so happened that David Lean and Ronald Neame saw the production and decided to make a film of the book as soon as the war was ended, and they used Martita as Miss Havisham and me in my old part of Herbert Pocket; but we were not to know, in 1939, what the future held for any of us. It looked grim.

Some time in the mid-thirties Martita had moved from her Knightsbridge flat to a rather more spacious one, which she made even more elegant, in Wimpole Street, and during the war years she entertained there lavishly on gleanings from the Black Market. Butter, eggs, saddles of lamb and French cheeses seemed to provide no problems for her. 'I know a little man, dear heart,' she would say, shrugging away raised eyebrows. Or, 'George the taxi-man is very good to me.' She had a fleet of taxi-men at her call and from time to time I have come across one or the other and they always mention her with affection but manage to get the name wrong. 'Remember Marsha Hunt?' they say. 'She was a one. Fond of the horses too.'

At the start of the war good French wines were always served in Upper Wimpole Street but as time dragged on they were replaced with Algerian, and, as the bombs fell increasingly, wine gave way to gin and water. Omelettes fines herbes never failed. Often, when passing through London in my naval uniform, on the way to catch a train to Glasgow or Newcastle, I would drop in on her for an hour or two, after which she would summon George or Harry or Les to drive me to the station; and she would accompany me, feeling that it was her patriotic duty to be at the side of the forces when possible. Invariably she would press into my hands, at Euston or St Pancras or wherever, a little parcel she had prepared, which when opened on the train was found to contain a half bottle of champagne, a peach and smoked salmon sandwiches or other delicacies. When Matthew was a few months old and he and Merula were to join me for a short while she insisted on the three of us staying a night at her flat. Never before or after can it have seen nappies on a line in the kitchen or a baby crawling across the carpet, but precautions had been taken – there were druggets everywhere. She must have had an uncomfortable night, interrupted by sirens and baby-squeals, but she treated it all very light-heartedly; the only serious note she struck was when she advised us to have Watty for higher irrigation, an offer we firmly declined. She wrote to me regularly, if not often, during my service years, in her long, angular, speedy and almost illegible hand – short letters but always full of affection and always welcome. When she died I was moved and almost distressed to find that she had kept, in the Louis Quinze desk, all my scribbles to her.

I was still in uniform, but about to be demobbed, when I did a screen test for David Lean's film of *Great Expectations*. Having got the part I did a further test, for make-up, wig and clothes, at Denham Studios, and David invited me to sit next to him to see the 'rushes' of the previous day's work, which was the scene of Miss Havisham showing the young Estella her ancient wedding-cake, covered in cobwebs and nibbled by mice. I watched it fascinated but was troubled, at the back of my mind, about something in Martita's performance; and when David turned to me happily, saying 'Well?', I could only mutter, 'It's marvellous; but I didn't realise you put the sound on afterwards.' 'What do you mean?' he asked, suddenly worried. 'It's in perfect sync!' I had no knowledge at all of filming and didn't want to make a fool of myself so I just said, 'It's just that I couldn't see Martita's mouth move when she was speaking. It looked as if she had a stiff upper lip.' He obviously thought I was

mad. Then it dawned on me; a week or two earlier, when I had told
Martita I was going to play Herbert Pocket, she had said, 'My
darling, I have at last found the secret of acting on the screen, it is
never to move the upper lip.' What price all that lip muscle, I had
thought. It was great nonsense, of course, and typical of her to be
always pinning her faith on some new theory, of breathing, speaking,
meditating, tooth-brushing, bowel movement or just living. She was
always seeking new knowledge. On one occasion I discovered her
near tears with the great tome of *Mathematics for the Million* open on
her lap. 'Darling,' she said, looking up sorrowfully, 'I wanted to
learn how to work out twelve percent and now I'm lost in logarithms.'

In 1951 my wife and I bought a ten-acre field near Petersfield in
Hampshire, and built a modest house which we intended to use as a
weekend cottage but which eventually became our permanent home.
One of the first people we invited down for a couple of nights was
Martita, in spite of the fact that Merula said the prospect of cooking
for her was too alarming. The answer to that was to suggest that
Martita should be asked to cook dinner, something she always
enjoyed doing, and accordingly a splendid chicken was bought and
everything we thought she might need. A Rolls-Royce arrived –
loaned by a friend of hers complete with chauffeur – and Martita
descended in leopard-skin coat, chic hat, with white hide luggage
and a flurry of little parcels of expensive luxuries none of which she
could possibly afford. I had explained the house was small and simple
but that at least she would have her own bathroom. One look and
she knew she was in for a weekend of slumming, but she rallied at
the idea of cooking dinner. The chicken was pinched and prodded
with an approving, greedy smile. 'Darlings,' she informed us, 'I
think it would be good to do it in a French way I am sure you will
like very much.' Pans and apron and all the equipment for a special
operation were put on display; seasonings and spice ready to hand,
the oven explained, and she all ready to go when, quite casually, she
said, 'Chéri, all I need now is six pounds of butter.' There were only
four pounds in the house, Sunday to get through and the shops shut.
I explained the butter situation, which until that moment I hadn't
looked on as a shortage. She flew into a rage, picked up the chicken
and threw it on the kitchen floor, tore off her apron and rushed
into the living-room, where she flung herself full length along a
window-seat. Merula and I were aghast. 'Fools! Fools! Where's the
telephone?' She dialled for her friend's Rolls to collect her as soon as
possible – which it wasn't able to do until the following morning. I

can't remember the rest of the evening except for the fact that it was extremely uncomfortable and Merula turned out a perfectly respectable roast chicken and I poured out several whiskies and uncorked quite a lot of wine. It took Merula years to recover from the shock of knowing you *could* require six pounds of butter to cook a chicken and I don't think she or Martita ever saw eye to eye again.

Wimpole Street was exchanged for a ground-floor studio flat in a quiet little corner of Primrose Hill. Quite a lot of film work came her way, largely due to the great kindness and generosity of Jimmy Woolf, who ran Romulus Films, and had become a close friend, and life continued in much the same old way, with manicures, expensive hair-dos and higher irrigation. Jimmy saw to it that she was supplied with the little luxuries that were so essential to her and when her flat was badly burned – she and the curtains went up in the flames of a guttering candle, not unlike Miss Havisham – he arranged and paid for redecoration while she was recovering in hospital. When filming she took to having a little mid-morning tea tray provided for her on the set, which led to difficulties. The tea wasn't hot; what came down the spout of the elegant pot was a neat Highland brew. 'No, chérie! No milk. No lemon. Just a little tea; that's all the stimulant I need.' It was a sad habit which deceived no one; brought on, I think, by the wartime air raids, when she was so often alone and frightened in her Wimpole Street eyrie, and it was a habit which was intensifying with the years.

A mild flutter on the horses became one of her major pleasures. She studied form, in an amateur way, and had a few horsy friends who advised her on bets and accepted, too often I suspect, 'surefire' tips from George or Harry or whoever the current favourite taxi-driver might be. Not that I disapproved in any way, but she never took me in her confidence where racing was concerned. Watching her wield a pencil over a tipster's column in an evening paper I couldn't resist a wry smile which she caught. 'You, my darling, have no sportin' instincts,' she said: which was true; except for my periodic passion for roulette.

We were together in Peter Glenville's marvellous production of Feydeau's *Hotel Paradiso* at the Winter Garden Theatre and had adjacent dressing-rooms. Every evening, while making up, I could hear her doing her vocal exercises, 'Ho! Ho! Ho-ho! Hi! Hum, um, oom. Aha! A-a-h-h!' (Larry Olivier does a brilliant imitation of this.) One night I was aware that no exercises were being done and I could hear the quiet hum of a long conversation with someone. I heard her door close and footsteps retreat; then a tap at my door. Martita stepped into my room in Edwardian wig and her dressing-gown, looking very serious.

'He's got no balls,' she announced.

'Who hasn't?' I asked in some alarm.

'Mr So-and-so.' She kept to the formalities all right.

'How do you know?'

'He told me. He came for a chat about sex.'

Martita was quite keen to chat about sex.

'Did you verify?' I asked her.

'Of course not, chéri. One doesn't ask to see a gentleman's private parts. Not unless you are Miss B.' She named a notorious man-eating actress.

'What's happened to his balls?' I asked.

'It's very sad, not a laughing matter. Apparently they simply *never came down.*'

Her tone implied that Nature was an untrustworthy Dame and life full of disappointments.

'Do you think I should put him on to Watty?'

'Well, she would bring down almost anything,' I said.

Leaving me rather haughtily she threw over her shoulder, 'Sometimes you are disgusting. And unfeeling.' We met again on stage and as Mr So-and-so made his entrance our eyes met and we both had barely controlled giggles. By the interval she was reconciled to the poor man's plight and whispered, 'Anyway, I think Mr So-and-so is a bugger, so it probably doesn't matter much.'

The Mad Woman of Chaillot was a great personal success for Martita in New York; less so in London. I saw her in the play in Philadelphia when she was on tour. The day I arrived she had locked herself in her hotel suite. I don't recall the reason for this but it was probably the result of some quarrel with the management, with her agent and with Miss Estelle Winwood – who also had made a success and who insisted on her small dog taking a curtain call with the rest of the cast. Martita objected to Estelle, her dog, the leading man and Philadelphia. She wouldn't answer the telephone or a knock at her door. Information was passed on slips of paper pushed under the door and food left outside it, but I called out my name boldly and the door flung open. She hugged me emotionally and I accompanied her down to the theatre. The whole episode of locked rooms was over. Martita should have been, had the gods been kinder, what she yearned to be: a great actress and a great star. Unfortunately, although talented, she was neither; but she was certainly a big personality and could cause hell to break loose if the mood was on her. Curiously enough she was adored by the people on whom she most depended, dressers, maids, waiters, and workmen, whom she sometimes treated abominably. On the first night of *Hotel Paradiso*, unable to find her property wedding ring she told her old, sweet-natured dresser to lend hers. The old girl refused, saying, 'Miss Hunt, my wedding ring has never left my finger. It's been there over fifty years and that's where it's staying.' Martita screamed at her, 'Margaret, you are a silly old cow! Give it to me at once!' She dived at Margaret's hand; there was a fierce tussle; the theatre resounded with their shouts and screams. Martita got the ring and her dresser collapsed in hysterics. The next day they were loving friends again, the proper ring was found and all was as if nothing untoward had happened.

One Christmas Eve I gave supper to Albert Finney, not yet a great star, in a small, chic, and excellent Soho restaurant which has now had to make way for Chinese junk. We found ourselves seated at a table opposite Martita and her constant drinking companion. I crossed the room to kiss her, whereupon she flung out her arms and brought her hands together with great force over both my ears by way of greeting. I was stunned and deafened by the blow. Back at my own table I said to Albie, 'It's no use talking – I can't hear a thing.' Three days later, my ears still ringing and feeling off-balance, I went to see a specialist. 'Lucky the blow was uneven,' he told me, 'or you'd be totally deaf for life. As things are, only the left ear is dented.' He blew the eardrum straight with an old-fashioned motor horn but I am still weak in that ear and deaf to certain registers. The specialist asked who had struck me so violently and when I told him he said, 'I have always suspected she was a dangerous woman.' I had disliked the man on meeting him but now I loathed him. 'Actually,' I said, 'she is kind, highly intelligent and very special. What is the fee for your treatment and uncalled-for comment?' I stumbled from his consulting room and erased his name from my memory. Yes, perhaps she was dangerous; but then she was always so easy to forgive.

After the first fire in her flat she managed to do it again, although not so badly. One of the last times I went to see her she had arranged for oysters and a crab dish to be sent from Prunier's for lunch. George or Harry or Les delivered them. She was sitting up in bed; her hair singed, cigarette burns the size of saucers all over the blanket, wire springs spiralling through the seats of chairs, a table with only two legs propped against a wall and a very good French clock lay face down on the stained carpet. A few books were scattered around on the bed and the whole place looked grubby but was probably fairly clean. 'Oysters or crab?' she asked. I settled for the crab. She smiled at the oysters and paid small endearments to each one before gobbling it. 'You're a fat little fellow, aren't you, darling? And you taste very fresh and good. You *were* a good fellow. Now, who else is plump and pretty and ready for Marti?' I could have wept, except that she was cheerful. She suddenly referred to the maid she employed for a few hours each week and the maid's husband.

'Isn't it disgraceful? The poor girl! Her husband doesn't take off his pyjamas when they have sex. Now that's not sportin'.' She rambled on, lit a fresh cigarette while she had one still alight and only half-smoked in her hand, pushed some books off the bed impatiently and said she needed to sleep. I took my leave, but before kissing her goodbye carried the Prunier's remains to the kitchen, removed her lit cigarette and stumped it out, and then drew the curtains against the strong daylight. She was very sweet; like a small girl being tucked up for the night.

Some time after her death a plaque was unveiled to her in St Paul's, Covent Garden; her sister and half a dozen of her friends were present. It was a sunny, summery noon and a few very brief prayers were read. The Vicar kept looking anxiously at his watch, as did Martita's good friend Caroline Ramsden (greatly given to the race track) as two expected friends looked like being too late for the little ceremony.

'I think we must consider ourselves under starter's orders,' said Miss Ramsden.

'I am the Resurrection . . .' the Vicar commenced, but Caroline Ramsden halted him.

'Hold it, Vicar!' She had peered through the plate glass door of the church and saw the expected couple arriving. 'They're round the bend! They're coming up the straight! Neck and neck! Well done, well done.'

The church clock struck.

'You're off!' she said to the Vicar. If she had had a pistol I believe she would have fired it. A nice, jolly woman.

'I am the Resurrection . . .' the Vicar started again. Soon he was reading a splendid passage which included the words 'death is but an horizon' and it alerted that marvellous actress Gwen Ffrangcon-Davies, who had been silent until then.

'I like that,' Gwen said. 'Death is but an horizon. Where does that come from?'

The Vicar ploughed on without enlightening her, so Gwen wandered across to the plaque, which she studied and then read aloud to us, 'Martita Hunt – Actress – 1901–1969.' The Vicar did his best.

I had invited Martita's sister, Gwen, Caroline, Stanley Hall and McGregor (both of Wig Creations) to lunch and when the service ended a vast, black limousine was waiting for us at the church entrance. We all piled in and drove in slow and stately style round St James's Park, to admire the blossom, past Buckingham Palace and up St James's Street to Prunier's. Any other restaurant would have been unthinkable; Martita had entertained all of us there, no doubt, so lavishly over the years. Menus were gazed at silently and then each one of my guests said, 'Oysters.' When the platters of oysters arrived Gwen, who is very short-sighted, looked at hers intently, murmuring, 'Death is but an horizon.' The oysters were washed down with a fine, dry Sancerre which Martita had introduced me to the first time she took me to Prunier's, and it had made a deep impression on me: cool, elegant, sophisticated and delightful. It was, I hope, a fitting remembrance, if not an epitaph.

CHAPTER SIX

The Readiness Is All

'Come on from the left. No! No! The *other* left! – Oh, someone make him understand! – Why are you so stiff? Why don't you make me laugh?' The superb tenor voice, like a silver trumpet muffled in silk, kept up a rapid stream of commentary together with wildly contradictory instructions from the stalls while I fumbled with my little Temple edition of Shakespeare on the bare stage of the New Theatre (now the Albery). It took a whole morning to set a single page of the text. Gielgud's directions to the actors were interrupted frequently, in full flight, by his calling out to the designers, Sophie and Margaret Harris and Elizabeth Montgomery, the firm of 'Motley': 'Motleys! Motleys! Would it be pretty to have it painted gold? Perhaps not. Oh, don't fidget, Frith Banbury! Alec Guinness, you are gabbling. Banbury, your spear is crooked. Now turn up stage. No, not you. You! Turn the other way. Oh, why can't you all *act*? Get someone to teach you to *act*!' And so the dreadful morning wore on, with me, at the vulnerable age of twenty, on the verge of tears and acutely aware of other members of the cast of *Hamlet* (Jack Hawkins, Jessica Tandy, Frank Vosper, George Howe, Laura Cowie, William Devlin and George Devine) sitting on benches at the side of the stage, pretending to read their newspapers to hide their embarrassment or perhaps just quaking in their shoes. Later that day George Devine came in for a Gielgud lashing with, 'Oh, why is your voice so harsh? It really is quite ugly. Do *do* something about it.' It was my first experience of being 'produced' – as we used to call direction in the early thirties – by my actor-hero, benefactor, patron and later good friend, who gave me my first proper chance in the theatre, cherished my barely visible talent and kept me solidly employed for two years.

In the summer of 1934 while a student at the Fay Compton School of Dramatic Art, I had been awarded, at the annual show, the school prize: a double-columned, minutely-printed volume of Shakespeare's 'Collected Works', bound in leatherette and inscribed, in enormous writing, by Fay. The judges at the school performance had been Gielgud, Jessie Matthews and Ronald Adam. I had been at the Fay

Compton for about seven months, on a scholarship which carried no money, and I was kept from starvation by the gift of jam sandwiches and fruit generously provided by fellow students and a weekly blow-out, given by an old advertising copy-writer friend at the Charing Cross Lyons Corner House. I lived on less than thirty shillings a week in a squalid little room off Westbourne Road, allowing myself sixpence a week for a gallery seat at the Old Vic. Walking everywhere, often carrying my shoes to save the leather, I was remarkably healthy and looked uncomfortably thin.

That summer my tiny savings and meagre allowance came to an abrupt end. As the summer holiday started I found myself with only the proverbial half-crown in my pocket, indeed in the world, and it was obvious that the drama school would have to be abandoned and a job of some sort found immediately. With some temerity I took myself to Wyndham's Theatre, where Gielgud was appearing in *The Maitlands*. I had never met him, was far from sure he would remember my name after the two or three weeks since the public show, but sent in my card. (In those days most drama students carried cheaply-printed visiting cards, as a means of getting free tickets at some London theatres.) It was after a mid-week matinée that I called and I was shown immediately to his dressing-room. Quite clearly he recognised me; and although he wasn't exactly welcoming – no doubt being used to calls from young aspiring actors – he was affable enough and very polite. I explained the necessity of obtaining work but didn't mention money. 'They are holding auditions tomorrow morning,' he said, 'for understudies for a new play by Clemence Dane. With Gertie Lawrence. It's called *Moonlight is Silver*.' He gave me a rather sly amused look. 'You might try for the understudy of Douglas Fairbanks Jr.' (*That* was going to be no go for a start.) 'Go there and say I sent you. And let me know tomorrow evening how you've got on.' Well, I went as instructed and was barely looked at – clearly I didn't fit the bill for understudying someone as tall, handsome and glamorous as Doug Fairbanks. I reported back to John and he sent me to see Bronson Albery about a small part in *Queen of Scots*, which was being re-cast. Bronnie Albery was charming but my luck was out; casting had been completed a few hours earlier. The following day John advised me to go down to the Old Vic, where auditions were being held for bits and pieces in a forthcoming production of *Antony and Cleopatra*. I started my audition piece and after a couple of lines was greeted with howls of derision from the director in the darkened stalls. 'You're no actor!' he shouted. 'Get off the fucking stage!' (Some years later he was to direct me in Priestley's film *Last Holiday*. I didn't remind him of the Old Vic audition.)

When I went back to Wyndham's that evening I had only fourpence left in the world and during the last two days had eaten two buns, two apples and had a couple of glasses of milk. John looked at me gravely when I told him of my Old Vic experience and then said, '*I* believe in you. But you are far too thin. You're not eating enough.' On his make-up table was a pile of crisp pound notes. 'Here's twenty pounds,' he said, 'until I can give you a job.' He must have had the gesture in mind and tried to hand me the money. Perhaps I was just too proud to accept, and rather light-headed from want of food, but twenty pounds was quite a sum in those days and I was terrified of getting into debt. Rather grandly, and certainly foolishly, I assured him I had no need of money. Leaving Wyndham's, sad and worried, I started to wander back towards Westbourne Road and stopped on the way to gaze at the bills for a new play, called *Queer Cargo*, which was to open shortly at the Piccadilly Theatre. I decided that this might prove my last chance of a job and, on some strong impulse, instead of going to the stage door, took myself to the box-office, where I happened to encounter the stage-manager. Having talked to him for a few minutes he took me to a room, handed me a script and told me to read to him. The upshot was that I was given the understudying of nearly all the male parts (including Franklin Dyall) and told I would be walking on as a Chinese coolie, a French pirate and a British tar – all for the princely sum of £3 a week. I was given £1 as an advance payment and treated myself to a steak, chips and a glass of beer around the corner.

Several weeks later I went to a matinée at the Old Vic (of *Richard II*, with Maurice Evans) and, seated in the pit, glimpsed Gielgud in the front stalls. In an interval I followed him to the coffee bar, not with the intention of speaking to him but just to be in his presence. He suddenly spotted me and came over, saying, 'Where have you been? I've made enquiries for you all over London. I want you to play Osric in *Hamlet*. Rehearsals start on Monday week at the New Theatre.' Through the kind offices of the stage-manager at the Piccadilly I was released from my understudying and various disguises. My joy was almost out of control when I heard my salary in *Hamlet* would be £7 a week. But I hadn't foreseen the agony of rehearsals.

I revered Gielgud as an artist and was totally glamourised by his personality, but he was a strict disciplinarian, intolerant of any slovenliness of speech and exasperated by youthful tentativeness. He was a living monument of impatience. At that time he was thirty years old, at the height of his juvenile powers and, with *Richard of Bordeaux* behind him (I saw him in the part fifteen times), commanded a huge following throughout the country. He held his emperor-like head higher than high, rather thrown back, and carried himself, as he still does, with ramrod straightness. He walked, or possibly tripped, with slightly bent knees to counteract a childhood tendency to flat-footedness. His arm movements were inclined to be jerky and his large bony hands a little stiff. A suggestion of fluidity in his gestures was imparted by his nearly always carrying, when on stage, a big white silk handkerchief. His resemblance to his distinguished old father was remarkable and he combined an air of patrician Polish breeding with Terry charm and modest theatricality. There was nothing he lacked, as far as I could see, except tact. His tactless remarks, over the decades, have joined the ranks of the happiest theatre legends of our time and, apart from their sheer funniness, they have always been entirely forgivable because they spring spontaneously from the heart without a glimmer of malice.

It was after a week of rehearsing *Hamlet* that he spoke 'spontaneously' to me, with shattering effect. 'What's happened to you?' he cried. 'I thought you were rather good. You're terrible. Oh, go away! I don't want to see you again!'

I hung around at rehearsals until the end of the day and then approached him cautiously. 'Excuse me, Mr Gielgud, but am I fired?'

'No! Yes! No, of course not. But go away. Come back in a week. Get someone to teach you how to act. Try Martita Hunt.' So I went back to Westbourne Road, sat on my narrow, rickety bed and had a little weep. I didn't dare tell Martita, who had become a friend, what had happened as I felt she would be as upset as I was and might start telephoning John. I mooched around for a week, mostly walking in London parks, and then, heart in mouth, reported back for rehearsals in St Martin's Lane. He seemed pleased to see me, heaped praise on my Osric and laughed delightedly at the personality (very water-fly) which I had assumed. I could swear I wasn't doing anything differently from what I had done before but, suddenly and briefly, I was teacher's pet. 'Motleys! Motleys, you should give him a hat with a lot of feathers, like the Duchess of Devonshire!'

We opened in November; the production was a sell-out, running for about ten months, and John's Hamlet was his definitive performance in the part. I watched most of it from the wings every single night, as did two or three others of the younger actors. At Christmas he gave me a handsome edition of Ellen Terry's letters in which he wrote, 'To Alec, who grows apace', and then a quotation from Act V, which has remained my motto throughout life, 'The readiness is all.'

I worked for him in *The Seagull*, *Noah* and *Romeo and Juliet* over a period of two years; left him for a season at the Old Vic under Guthrie's direction, and returned to him for the four plays he did under his own management at the Queen's Theatre in 1937, *Richard II, The School for Scandal, The Three Sisters* and *The Merchant of Venice*. He directed the Shakespeares, Guthrie the Sheridan and Michel St Denis the Chekov. His companies were always happy and the only distress I remember experiencing that season was just before we opened *Richard II*, in which I played the tiny but pleasing part of the Groom. We had a quick canter through sections of the play on the morning of the first night and he said to me, 'You're not nearly as good in the part as Leslie French was when I did it before. Try coming on from the right instead of the left tonight and see if that makes a difference.'

There was no time to rehearse it and very cheekily I asked, 'Which right?'

'Oh, have it your own way,' he replied wearily. 'Do it as you've always done it. I can't be bothered.'

Later, when I was beginning to play leading roles, he stopped me one day in Piccadilly, saying, 'I can't think why you want to play big parts. Why don't you stick to the little people you do so well?' 'I wasn't awfully good as the Groom in *Richard II*,' I said. 'No. I suppose you weren't.' 'And I was even worse as Aumerle.' 'Possibly. Shall we go and see a flick?' I excused myself saying I had quite a lot to think about.

Touring with John was always delightful not only because the country flocked to see him, but he thought up such marvellous outings for the company on afternoons we were not working. He arranged a fleet of cars to take everyone to Fountains Abbey, for instance, or a vast lunch in an hotel in York because he wanted us all to fall in love with the Minster. It was at the lunch in York, I remember, that a waitress asked him to sign the tablecloth. 'I'm sure she doesn't know me from Adam,' he said. 'She'll be terribly disappointed if I put my own name.' So he signed 'Jack Buchanan', and the waitress was thrilled. Wherever we went he spent a lot of time in the art galleries and, if he wasn't entertaining us, his afternoons at the cinema. John must have seen more films than anyone I can think of; the quality of what he saw didn't concern him at all. In fact I had the impression that the trashier the films were the more he enjoyed them. He did very little filming until twenty-odd years ago. (*The Good Companions* and Hitchcock's *The Secret Agent* before the war were outstanding and he was charming in them.) But in recent years he has turned up, always giving impeccable, witty performances in almost every other British film; not that his presence has guaranteed the agreeability of all the pictures.

Three years ago, while being made up for a film I was doing in New York, the very jolly lady make-up artist said, 'Know any good limericks?' 'Very few,' I replied. 'When I used to make up Sir John Gielgud,' she went on, 'he used to tell me a dirty limerick every morning.' She fell about laughing at the recollection. What with the *Times* crossword and limericks he obviously begins each day with much mental activity, while most of us are still rubbing the sleep from our eyes.

In the theatre of our time there have been, and still are, some distinguished Johns and Jacks (to his family Gielgud was always Jack) but for over fifty years if you said to a fellow actor, 'I saw John the other day,' there was never any doubt about whom you were talking. When he walked on stage, in the thirties or forties, the theatre took fire; from his very first line you were aware of being in a very special glamorous presence. Even the vocal tricks – eventually abandoned – were pleasing and warming, like old and trusty friends. And, behind the theatricality, the tears and the staccato diction, could always be glimpsed the intelligence and feeling of a superb artist. His bright and wary eye hasn't dimmed with age. In my opinion Gielgud and Guthrie did more to liberate the English theatre than any others; and John in particular paved the way for what is best in London today. He introduced new directors and designers from home and abroad, encouraged unknown actors, and always cast around himself the finest established performers he could lay hands on. Not for him the follow-spot or seeking to show off his ability against third-rate talent, though he fostered the unknown. His humility, both as a man and an actor, is perhaps his most remarkable quality; and his enthusiasm for work leaves those of us who are ten years or more his junior flabbergasted and envious. But then he is a workaholic, even in his eighties.

CHAPTER SEVEN

Rising Above It

Tyrone Guthrie was the true *enfant terrible* of the British theatre of the thirties and forties, and quite the tallest *enfant terrible* to be found in the English-speaking world – standing six foot four in his socks. His height, his military hair-cut (*very* short back and sides), his clipped moustache and everything, except his sandals and old grey cardigan, suggested a gentlemanly sergeant-major who had slipped into something loose after a vigorous day of putting a bunch of rookies through some tough and complicated square-bashing. His clear, bright, aquamarine eyes transfixed you as if he was some greatly amused eagle, surmising if you were a rabbit fresh from the warren or possibly the fledgling of some other bird of prey. Whatever conclusions he came to on a first meeting I doubt if he ever changed them. Nothing much escaped his glance (or his comment) but, if it did, it was probably because he chose to ignore it. A shivering, scantily-clad Titania, trying to loll on the mossy bank of 'a wood near Athens', during a bitterly cold dress-rehearsal of *A Midsummer Night's Dream*, would be quickly spotted and a rubber hotwater-bottle surreptitiously eased across the stage towards her; and a demon of a star actor who had twisted his ankle would be sharply recommended to get a move on with his exit, as if the poor man could do more than hobble. New recruits were always treated with the utmost kindness and encouragement, the very old or incontinent with sympathy, but anyone in between, particularly if they were well-known personalities, was likely at some point to be verbally humiliated or reduced to anger or hysterics.

His rehearsals were always stimulating, usually great fun – often too much fun, perhaps – and always something to be looked forward to. They never became stodgy or finicky, and never, never, deteriorated into the dreary academic lectures with which so many modern young directors feel impelled to bore their companies. There was a spontaneity in all he did, a sort of whirlwind of activity and invention. I don't think I ever saw him consult a script or catch him with notes in his hand; all was straight off the top of his head, blessed as he was with a phenomenal memory, both visual and aural.

As an actor he was quite appalling; fortunately he only permitted himself to perform on very rare and special occasions, and yet he had a feeling for good acting and was highly appreciative of what was true in a performance. His personal taste was largely of an operatic theatricality and consequently often execrable – wild meaningless gestures (his arms, when demonstrating what he had in mind, seemed to bend backwards at the elbows like broken wings) and he encouraged speech of such rapidity that few could follow it. But, like a very keen games-mistress, he whipped a company up to great vitality and enthusiasm, and his rich, mocking humour was irresistible to anyone under the age of forty. He saw talent in unlikely places but sometimes refused to recognise it in the well-established. One day, cashing a cheque in a London bank, he spied a cherubic face behind the grille, a man quite unknown to him, to whom he said, 'What are you doing in a cage? Come out and be an actor.' It was like a call from the Sea of Galilee. The young man left his money-changing and took up a career in the theatre, not perhaps a tremendously successful one but at least it was a happy life.

Tony's interest in the theatre became increasingly decentralised. He rejected London or any other capital city, feeling their theatres were over-commercialised and in a rut, but more importantly that the provinces had been disgracefully neglected by the profession and were ripe with untapped audiences who were crying out for culture, and that there was a rich vein of talent to be unearthed in the Midlands and the North. In the long run he did more than anyone to revitalise the English theatre; and probably, through his pale imitators, did more lasting damage than any. The rash of drab concrete piles of car showrooms which now so uninvitingly pass for theatres can be laid at Tony Guthrie's door, though I am sure he would be horrified if asked to acknowledge them. He is not to be blamed, for too many followers in his giant footsteps mistook what he looked on as passing experiments as permanent establishments; they are shackling the theatre once more, binding the actor and deceiving the playwright. The theatre, when the performer cannot make a clean entrance or exit seen by the entire audience at the same time, and is obliged to make artificial moves purely for the sake of movement so that different parts of the audience, weary perhaps of a back, can get a glimpse of a face; where, when stillness is called for, the actor must rotate through 180 degrees to reach most spectators as well as other actors, is not so much a theatre as a circus. Exposed lighting, inevitable in these new arenas, is another form of distraction, catching the spectator's eye with every light change before he can see what is happening on stage. The passing of footlights has taken light from the eye and the excessive top-lighting (by which one is so often blinded in the stalls) turns all but the most rotund faces into cadavers. (Incidentally, Francis Bacon, writing as a contemporary of Shakespeare, greatly extolled the use of candles in theatrical presentations, and most likely he meant candles placed on the ground, similar to footlights.) Apart from the magic of over-complicated lighting, and the actual shape of things that have come, we have to do without a curtain, making it impossible to reveal or conceal; if a black-out is used between scenes it is nearly always accompanied by the sound of actors shuffling into position or stage-hands shifting furniture. Theatre must, of necessity, be artificial and use all the arts of make-believe. Only very occasionally, I believe, is a totally bare stage called for, and then only if it is to be occupied by supremely good and well-disciplined actors who are aware that almost every gesture will come over like a pistol shot. As a spectator I, for one, don't wish for a background of other people's flaccid faces (always highly illuminated) nor, as a performer, do I wish to become fascinated by a panoramic view of exposed chubby knees in the front row, nor distracted by embarrassed feet, interesting as it is to see what people do with their feet. I doubt if some or any of these objections occurred to Tony and if, with foresight, one had brought them to his notice he would have said, as so often, 'Rise above it.'

The idea of an open-stage theatre must have been in his mind, however vaguely, for years before I knew him, but the determination and enthusiasm to put such an idea into practice came to him, I am sure, during a night of terrible storm in June 1937, in Denmark. It was the first night of Olivier's *Hamlet* at Elsinore, with the Old Vic Company, before a cluster of crowned heads gathered from all over Scandinavia. The performance was supposed to have taken place at Elsinore Castle, on a set similar to what we had used in London placed at one end of the large courtyard, facing serried ranks of slatted chairs. Weather conditions were so appalling by four in the afternoon that messages were sent to the royal parties cancelling the show, but they were already making their sedate ways and could not be turned back. It was decided to present the play in the ballroom of the Marienlist Hotel where the company was staying. It was a large cream, ochre and gilded room with a pocket-sized stage standing high at one end, on which there was sufficient room for an upright piano, a potted palm and a three-piece band. Tony quickly marked out a circle in the middle of the room, which would be the acting area, surrounded it (with everyone's help) with little gilt chairs, leaving two or three avenues for entrances and exits and access to the little stage, which could be mounted by a few steps. The company was given the briefest instructions: 'Suggest you use the platform for Claudius and Gertrude in the play scene. Get rid of the piano. I love the palm. Could leave it. As you will. Larry will be in charge. Use any entrance you can find. Be polite to Kings and Queens if they get in your way. Alec, make your entrance as Osric through the French windows.' 'But, Tony, they give on to the beach. There's a roaring wind, heavy seas and lashing rain.' The telegraphese continued: 'Arrive wet. Very dramatic. Polonius, use the service door. When you are killed, wrap yourself up in those vulgar velvet curtains. Rather startling. No time for more. Larry will work out a few details. Enjoy yourselves. I'm going to explain to the old lady [Lilian Baylis] what we're up to. She's having a little lie-down. Must break it gently.' And he was gone, taking the gleam in his eye with him. Larry arranged things swiftly and to the point but much had to be left to improvisation.

It was the most exciting theatrical experience most of us had ever had. There was an energy, company-spirit and sense of achievement which were quite remarkable. My own small part in the evening was not very creditable. Knowing I was going to be hovering on the beach, soaked to the skin, my Danish dresser handed me a large schnapps. Skol! Then another schnapps. Skol! Tusen tak. Tak for tusen. Tit for tat. Tanks all the same. When I blew in through the French windows (which I shut *very* carefully) I was decidedly unsteady, more like a weary Greek Messenger than a Tudor fop. I managed the words with Larry all right, though I smiled too much, and the brief scene over I took up a comfortable position, resting my sword on the King of Sweden's lap and blocking the view of at least two crowned heads. Lilian Baylis, in cap and gown and twisted lip (the result of Bell's palsy), sat throughout looking wary and astonished, though God knows she had seen some sights in her time, including the genitalia of a previous Hamlet, when his tights had split in the death scene. Tony Guthrie was more than satisfied; his eyes were brighter than ever – quite a few schnapps had been thrown back there too, I suspect. His tall head nodded with approval and he saw before him, I know, his dream theatres of the future beckoning and glittering. Scandinavian royalty, homburged or heavily scarved, climbed back into their limousines and retreated to the safety of Copenhagen, leaving the Marienlist Hotel to our excited, undoubtedly drunken mercy. Many bedroom doors were locked, or slammed, or opened that night. In the morning the sight of the Kattegat, brilliant in the sun and as flat as plate-glass, was too much for puffy eyes.

The principal buildings that stemmed from that evening, over the next twenty years, are the Shakespeare Festival Theatre at Stratford, Ontario, and the Guthrie Theatre at Minneapolis, the Octagon at Perth in Australia, and the new Playhouse at Sheffield. Also the Chichester Festival Theatre, but Tony was rather critical of that, though many improvements have been made since he first saw it.

Tanya Moiseiwitsch, with Tony at her elbow, designed the theatre for Stratford, Ontario for its opening in 1953, as well as costumes for the two productions of the first season, *Richard III* and *All's Well*. We rehearsed on a mock-up of the stage placed in a vast tin barn. (The original theatre at Stratford was housed within a great marquee.) After we had been rehearsing about a week Tony and Tanya asked me if I found the stage comfortable; I replied that, apart from the necessity of some rather odd moves, it was comfortable enough but there were moments when I felt a great need for an extra twelve inches all round. (It is important to realise that if three actors are on the stage together and two of them have a dialogue which the audience can accept as the third not overhearing, then the space must be sufficiently wide to allow this, without, of course, depriving the audience's sense of intimacy. It is a matter of careful proportion.) Tony and Tanya agreed with my feeling and an extra foot – which they always referred to thereafter as 'Guinness's foot' – was added all round. When the Playhouse at Sheffield was built Tanya noticed that the architects had removed the extra width and complained to them, 'You have taken away Guinness's foot, and we need it.' Their reply was, apparently, 'What do actors know about theatre architecture?' The answer to that is, if I may say so, quite a lot; because theatres are their homes, while they occupy them, and the stages and auditoriums are their sounding boards. They are, on the whole, more theatre-conscious than directors, and a quick look and a few spoken words from stage to empty auditorium before a performance will tell them more in seconds than ever seems to penetrate architectural heads after months or years of planning. But I will say for the Playhouse, although I have never acted there, it is the most attractive new theatre I have entered; from a spectator's point of view.

I first met Tyrone Guthrie in the summer of 1936, when he engaged me, at £7 a week, for various smallish parts for the forthcoming season at the Old Vic. Money, though important, was of little consideration compared with the excitement of working for him, and at a theatre all actors loved. (No difficulty about being seen or heard there, until 'improvements' were made by Michel St Denis and later by Lord Olivier.) I had seen most of Guthrie's work in London from Bridie's *The Anatomist* onwards and always had found it brilliant and exciting. One came away from all his early productions with the knowledge that life had been enhanced and, as a young actor, a yearning to be part of them. *Measure for Measure*, with Charles Laughton, Flora Robson and James Mason was the finest evening of Shakespeare I had as yet experienced and only to be rivalled by Granville-Barker's *Lear*. It was ahead of its time by almost a decade, cold-shouldered by the critics and audiences alike.

My two years in the theatre, before going to Guthrie, had been spent almost entirely under John Gielgud's meticulous and somewhat impatient direction. I loved and admired him, and he could do no wrong, but rehearsals were a nightmare; a whole morning could be spent on a few minor details and in the afternoon everything would be entirely re-arranged, to be altered again on the day of a first night. The pages of my script were a filthy grey with the rubbing out of contradictory instructions in soft lead pencil and sometimes smudged with tears. With Tony Guthrie it was very different. He hated readings of a play before rehearsals began and did his best to avoid them. The first day I rehearsed with him he spotted me marking my script and immediately demanded to know what I was doing. 'Marking in the move you've just given me, Mr Guthrie.' 'Don't,' he said. 'Waste of time. If I've given you a good move you'll remember it; if bad, you'll forget it and we'll think up another.' I have never marked my script since and it has served me well; particularly when I have been able to say to an over-enthusiastic director, as I have often, 'I'm sorry, but I can't remember the move; perhaps it's not necessary anyway; what do *you* think?' In most cases they have improved their homework.

After working with Tony in *Love's Labours Lost* (with the Redgraves), *Twelfth Night* (Olivier and Jessica Tandy), *Henry V* and *Hamlet* (both Olivier), I returned to Gielgud for a season of four plays at the Queen's Theatre, a freer, less inhibited man and much more sure of myself. Guthrie was engaged to direct one of the plays, *The School for Scandal*; but I don't think he and John always saw eye to

eye and it was the least satisfactory production he ever did. Some of
the older actors wished everything to be 'lovely', fluttering lace
handkerchiefs and with a lot of fan-work; they resented Tony's
harsher attitudes to the period and the result was an uncomfortable
compromise. (Incidentally, I have seen only three actresses manipulate a fan with real wit – Athene Seyler, Irene Vanbrugh and Edith
Evans.) It was during the last play of that season, John's production
of *The Merchant of Venice*, that Tony came round to see me after a
matinée and asked me to call on him at the Vic the following
afternoon. When I got there he took me into a small dressing-room;
he sat on a rickety chair and I perched on a table. 'Liked you in *The
Merchant*,' he said. 'How about coming here next season and giving
us your Hamlet. Think you're about ready for it.' I nearly fainted.
'Think we should do it in modern dress. You could wear that nice
grey suit you've got on.' It wasn't at all a nice suit and a bit threadbare.
'Oh no,' I said, 'not this. Not at all right.' Which was the first of a
dozen violent disagreements which plagued us for the next twenty
years or so. I won on the grey suit issue, when the time came, and
invested in a tip-top navy blue piece of tailoring which cost about as
much as a suit could cost in those days. Some years ago, writing a
cheque to my very grand tailor, I sighed and said, 'It's a far cry, Mr
Whitley, from the first suit you made me, in 1938, for £15.' 'With
respect, you are wrong,' said Mr Whitley. 'I remember the suit well.
It was a navy blue hopsack with a Prince of Wales waistcoat and it
didn't cost £15. It cost twelve guineas.' Well, I remember most of
the parts I have played, so I suppose Mr Whitley is entitled to his
tailoring memories.

Merula and I had first met during Michel St Denis's production of
Obey's *Noah*, in which she was marvellous as the tiger and I was
limp as the wolf, in July 1935; we became engaged during a very
late-night dress-rehearsal of *The Merchant of Venice* at the Queen's
Theatre in the spring of 1938; and in June got married at Reigate
Register Office. As we left for the wedding the great French actor,
Bovario, shook hands with me across a rose bush and thorns pierced
both our hands. Not only did I set off to my wedding with a bloody
hand but I kept dropping my hat and having to retrieve it; also, when
we reached Reigate, I found I had no money on me and had to
borrow the cost of the licence from the taxi-driver. A nervous and
muddled beginning to a happy married life. We had decided, for our
honeymoon, to go to Dublin for a day or two and then set out on a
walking tour of Donegal. Tony and Judy Guthrie suggested we

might like to break our journey by spending a week with them at Anna-ma-kerrig, their house and ramshackle estate in County Monaghan, an invitation we were swift to pick up. It enabled me to discuss *Hamlet* with Tony at leisure and fully – we were to start rehearsals in August. After Anna-ma-kerrig we could ramble to our hearts' content for as long as our money lasted. Which wasn't going to be for long. After paying our air fares from London to Dublin and back and putting aside £10 for the Gresham Hotel, I found I was worth exactly £12, but Merula had a private allowance of £4 a week, which was going to prove most helpful for a few years to come.

The Guthries met us at the station, gave us a marvellous welcome, and drove us in their battered car the few miles to their house through greener country than I had ever seen, little rounded hills, an abundance of hawthorn and never a soul in sight. The house was a large Victorian pile with a red brick turret and no electricity, overlooking acres of rhododendrons and fir trees towards a long wind-swept lake. We occupied a large uncarpeted room with a high brass bedstead, a broken basin on a wobbly stand, and had the use of a lavatory with a ribbed glass door at the end of an echoing passageway. A few hours' notice was required if one needed a bath. The rooms were well-proportioned, the hall spacious and stone flagged, and a wide staircase, painted black, curved upwards to our quarters and, through a heavy black door, to regions we never penetrated. There was a Chekovian atmosphere of gaiety and decay about the whole place. At any moment one expected to encounter the Irish equivalents of Madame Ranevsky, Trofimov, Constantin, the Three Sisters or Uncle Vanya.

Anna-ma-kerrig was presided over by Mrs Guthrie, Tony's elderly and near blind mother, a lady of enormous charm, intelligence and gentle wit. If the estate conjured up Chekov, the inmates, we discovered, really had greater affinity to Dickens. There was a sprightly middle-aged lady who was companion to Mrs Guthrie, and who turned out to be a distant relative of Merula's family, and a visiting male cousin of advanced years who might have been a model for Mr Dick; in the kitchen quarters were delightful Irish equivalents of Peggotty and Mr Barkis. And yet, for all its Irishness, the house remained the home of a Scot. I never felt such awareness of Tony's Edinburgh forbears as I did there. Everyone in the household was always busy at something; from verifying in old horticultural books wild flowers gathered on walks, to rug-making and mending broken china, but mostly busy making lively conversation, which had us floored. The weather was perfect. After dinner on our first night there, Judy asked us if we would like to play bridge and when we said we would prefer to go for a walk on our own, and that anyway we didn't play, her relief was only thinly disguised; they had their regular four consisting of Mrs Guthrie, Tony, Judy and 'Mr Dick'.

Dusk had fallen by the time we got back to the house and from outside we witnessed a most extraordinary sight. Sitting by lamp-light in the downstairs room of the turret were the bridge-players, each clasping a hand of giant cards measuring about twenty-four by eighteen inches. These, it turned out, could just be seen by Mrs Guthrie and had been made especially for her. Each time a card was played it was lifted high in the air and wafted down on the table, making the oil lamp splutter and the ladies re-adjust their hair. Rubbers were collected in piles at the side of their chairs. They played silently, seriously and with enormous concentration. It could have been a scene from *Alice in Wonderland*. Shortly after our return they joined us in the drawing-room, offered us cocoa or whiskey, and then Tony sang a ballad and a hymn or two at the piano, in his pleasing baritone, before it was time for candles and bed. It was the same routine almost every night.

All assembled for breakfast, which was a porridgy affair eaten out of pretty chipped bowls (which Tony left me in his will). If Merula and I couldn't cope with the bridge we were equally put out by the breakfast conversation, which was a quick-fire quiz game on the lines of who said what and to whom ranging through the entire works of Dickens. Every now and then Tony or the lady companion would jump up to verify a reference in the set of Dickens kept in the dining-room.

There was a heavy, leaky old boat, with fishing tackle for coarse fish, in the lakeside boathouse, so some of our mornings were spent with me rowing and Merula sitting in the stern hearing my lines for Hamlet. They had told me at the house that there was a huge 'grandfather pike' in the lake, which had been known to snatch duckling and had become a sort of Moby Dick for Tony. I fixed a line to the stern and on our second morning out, pulling against a strong wind which was ruffling the water, Moby Dick struck. The boat was swivelled round and dragged backwards across the lake for a quarter of a mile. The beast shook itself free amongst a large clump of reeds. I never saw it, but when I reported the incident all the household nodded sagely, said the fish hadn't been spotted for about four years and was probably about sixty pounds by now. (Once, in

Canada, I hooked a muskalonge which I reckoned weighed about thirty pounds and gave me a hell of a fight for twenty minutes before getting away, so the Anna-ma-kerrig pike, if really sixty pounds, was a very formidable fellow.) Tony was exhilarated by the challenge of the fish and was always persuading me to have another try at it, but wouldn't come himself.

On one of our rowing mornings, calm and sunny, we saw smoke drifting from the side of the lake and sparks rising among the fir trees so we pulled across to see what was going on. We found Tony and Judy, both totally naked – Judy with her beautiful black hair, which she usually wore in a bun at the nape of her neck, hanging down her back, looking like an imperious squaw – making a bonfire. They waved and coo-eed casually and went on gathering sticks, not the least abashed. I had the impression it was some childhood fantasy they were playing at, for many of their youthful years had been spent together, which may also account for how similar in looks they often appeared to be, as well as being identical in manner. Their marriage suggested a marriage of twins.

Tony and I worked at *Hamlet* in an empty nursery at the back of the house. ('This is where we sometimes gave plays, as children,' he said.) He interfered with me hardly at all but seemed to be grasping at anything slightly original I had to offer, which wasn't much, and encouraging me to develop it. He knew I could never emulate the pyrotechnics of Olivier, or the classical formality of Gielgud, and that basically I was too inexperienced to carry a whole evening on my narrow shoulders. (It was to be a full-length version of the play, lasting over four hours; partly because he considered it was better entertainment when uncut, and possibly because he realised it would give the audience a half-hour breather without my presence.) Vocally I was light, but with good diction, and I was none too pleased when he told me my voice had much the same quality as Sir Robert Helpmann's. But he helped me to find the confidence to be, so to speak, the stillness in the eye of the storm.

When working with Larry, Tony had been under the influence of the Freudian psychoanalyst Professor Ernest Jones, whose essay on *Hamlet* was treated as holy writ, but there was no talk of such things where I was concerned. He often labelled a play in the Shakespeare canon with a single word, such as Spite (for *The Merchant of Venice*), Adolescence (*Romeo and Juliet*), Ambition (*Macbeth*), Spiritual Pride (for *Measure for Measure*), etc., to convey its essential element. He asked me to say in a word what *Hamlet* is about, and before I could give a floundering answer he said, with a frightening smile, 'Mummy!' Unfortunately, for all his loving care, he failed to wean me away from, or even mention, my pale, ersatz Gielgudry. I was over-familiar with Gielgud's manner and timing. (Dr Johnson says somewhere, 'Almost all absurdity of conduct arises from the imitation of those we cannot resemble.') If only Tony had said to me, 'Forget about John and any previous Hamlets you have seen,' I might have come up with something truer to myself and have been spared many theatrical blunders in later life. In this particular production I invented only two things; the first being Hamlet's attitude to Ophelia after the 'To be or not to be' soliloquy, when usually there is some accidental tip-off to Hamlet that he and Ophelia are being spied on by the King and Polonius. I rejected all the old business and any newer scheme, saying I must get the notion that Ophelia was a decoy from her attitude and false 'orisons', so that when she lies in answer to Hamlet's simple question the storm of abuse can break fully on her head and he can give full vent to his misogyny. That one we worked out in the Anna-ma-kerrig nursery. The second invention happened, almost without thought, during a rehearsal at the Old Vic. Tony had arranged for the players to leave on stage a whole pile of props when they are led away by Polonius, shortly before 'Oh, what a rogue and peasant slave', etc., and I squatted by an upturned drum to work out the lines which would 'catch the conscience of the King'. I found my hand beginning to tap out a rhythm on the drum. It made a splendid curtain to the first third of the play and we kept it in. Tony used it in a subsequent production, when it received critical acclaim. The startling effect of everyone carrying open umbrellas at Ophelia's graveside was, of course, pure Guthrie and totally memorable, creating a melancholy that overshadowed the remainder of the play. And it made ephemeral headlines in the press such as '*Hamlet* With Umbrellas'. The critics also talked of cigarettes and cocktails though no such things were used; in fact it was a very pure production, with no gimmicks beyond the umbrellas.

During the war I saw the Guthries quite a few times and managed to spend a week-end's leave, with Merula and Matthew, at their sooty rented house in Burnley, where the Old Vic Company had temporary headquarters. Judy spent much of her time writing a play (which was eventually performed by Sybil Thorndike and called *Queen Bee*) on little scraps of paper. When the wind whistled chillily through the sitting-room Judy would grab her scattered pieces of manuscript and stuff them in the window to stop the draught. She was going through a period of great enthusiasm for the works of Ivy Compton-Burnett and her eccentricities were on the increase, as well as a mild form of snobbery. One day, when they were to be out for a few hours, Merula decided that the house was so filthy she ought to do something about it and, finding a garden spade, she dug out the kitchen floor which had a marbled effect from well-trodden vegetables and refuse about four inches deep. When they returned in the evening Judy was furious to find she had a sparkling clean kitchen with apparently new flooring. 'Little interfering Miss Bourgeois Missy,' she hurled at Merula, and immediately downed a tumbler of scotch. Neither of the Guthries could tolerate anything which they took to be an implied criticism of their way of living. Dinner that night was almost silent and very glassy-eyed: a lot of concentrated work was done on the play.

Just at the end of the war they lent their flat in Lincoln's Inn to Anthony Quayle for two or three weeks while they were away somewhere and I spent a night or two there when up in London to do a screen test for David Lean's film of *Great Expectations*. Tony Quayle and I were aghast at the dirt in the sitting-room and decided that it would be charitable, as well as more comfortable for us, if we had a thorough clean-out. We started with the book-shelves. Removing a handful of books we discovered behind them, glued to the wall with old congealed fat, a green tin plate with a sausage stuck on it, a blue-grey sausage petrified with age. The bathroom – a cupboard-like room with a cracked and sagging ceiling – housed a chipped iron bath with three claw legs; support for the bath where the fourth leg was missing was provided by a huge sponge, a gift Merula and I had brought the Guthries from Malta in the Spring of 1939. Mice had made it into a sort of palace and were living in it very chirpily. And yet for all the squalor in which they so often chose to live, when not at Anna-ma-kerrig, Judy could present herself most elegantly when she wanted to, pouring herself into an evening gown in seconds to make an entrance like a tall, handsome, distinguished duchess. Tony had, for official occasions, what he referred to as 'my navy'. I think he had a tweed suit as well.

Disasters, theatrical or family, left them as unflappable as Harold Macmillan. There was a Sunday in County Monaghan, probably in 1950, when Tony received an urgent call to go to Glasgow immediately. There was no available transport so Tony arranged for a small private plane to collect him and Judy from a field near the house. It was a four-seater with a young pilot. They climbed aboard with their raincoats and string bags, and settled themselves comfortably. The plane bounced across the field towards a low stone wall. Tony turned to Judy and said, 'Don't think we're going to make it.' And indeed they didn't. The plane, not yet airborne, swerved and the wall carried away the port wing. It then lurched in the other direction and it was goodbye to the starboard wing. They sat for a few moments in the chrysalis in complete silence, except for the whirring of the propeller. Then Tony said, 'Think it would be wise to get out,' so gathering their junky belongings they stepped down. 'Not to worry,' Judy told the pilot, who had joined them, 'just a little accident.' The three of them strolled towards the house. They hadn't gone a hundred yards before the aircraft exploded. 'Horrid for you,' Judy said to the pilot, who was in great distress. Tony nodded sympathetically and said, 'Glasgow must learn to wait. Now, I think we all deserve a strong cup of tea.' When they told me the story they fell about laughing, and when I asked what had been so urgent in Glasgow, Tony said, 'Can't quite remember. Leading lady taken poorly at a matinée. Understudy *much* better in the rôle: leading lady not very pleased about that. Had the vapours. Silly woman. But we did enjoy our little adventure. And the pilot was a dear.'

A committee was formed at Stratford, Ontario, early in 1952, to explore the possibilities of starting a summer Festival of Shakespeare in the pleasant park which surrounds a lake in the middle of the town. The instigator of this scheme was Mr Tom Paterson, a starry-eyed enthusiast of touching qualities who felt that as Stratford boasted a rather pedestrian statue of Shakespeare it should also perform his works. He was detailed to contact someone in Britain who would advise the committee; accordingly he approached Guthrie, who accepted an invitation to visit Ontario and see the proposed site. Tony met the dozen or so people concerned – a well-heeled and fairly affluent cross-section of the Stratford community – liked them immensely, thought the idea was sound but was appalled by the suggested theatre, which was a tiny, pink concrete scallop shell, just large enough to house a small seaside pierrot show, prettily facing the lake and with space for an auditorium of a hundred deck-chairs. He soon swept that aside while at the same time sweeping the committee off their feet, deriding their parochial ideas with wit and charm, and firing them with the notion of a national effort which would require a vast amount of money. They would have to approach Ottawa, big business enterprises in Toronto, make an appeal throughout Canada and gain all the local support they could. Which is exactly what Tom Paterson set about doing, aided, I have no doubt, by the admirable committee dipping deeply into their own pockets. A sort of Greek amphitheatre with a canvas top and sides was what Tony proposed, to be made into a more solid structure after a year or two, when and if the venture proved a success. The design of the whole thing was put, at Tony's suggestion, into the hands of Tanya Moiseiwitsch, with whom he had worked so often. He also suggested that half a dozen actors from Britain, including Irene Worth, Michael Bates, Douglas Campbell (who lived in Canada anyway) and myself, should be approached to form an experienced nucleus to the company. It was his intention that after a season, or possibly two, all the British should withdraw and leave it an entirely Canadian enterprise. Paterson made his bid and we all accepted. The money wasn't much but we were promised free accommodation in various households and our food. Two plays were to be done in the first season and Tony and I spent hours in his dusty sitting-room in Lincoln's Inn thumbing through the entire works of Shakespeare, arguing the pros and cons of each play. We wanted plays that would give plenty of scope for the mostly unknown, to us, talents of the Canadian players, plays that weren't too hackneyed, and parts for me which I hadn't tackled before. Also Tony, who was always at his best with new material, wished at least one of the plays to be something with which he was unfamiliar. Eventually we settled for *Richard III* and *All's Well That Ends Well*, which we hoped would satisfy Irene and the others. The committee was hoping, I believe, for *Hamlet* and *A Midsummer-Night's Dream* or *As You Like It*. There was one stipulation which we both insisted on, and that was that we wouldn't be required to open before we had had three weeks' rehearsal in the completed theatre, and we had a clause to that effect written into our contracts. That clause proved useless; the theatre wasn't ready for our occupation until a few days before the first night, for which tickets had been sold well in advance.

When I arrived in Canada, two weeks ahead of the rehearsal schedule, the theatre was just a muddy hole in the ground about six feet deep and ten feet square. It didn't look promising. Tony and I gazed at it with foreboding; then he said, 'Rise above it.' Not a difficult feat, physically. 'Rise above it' was his catch-phrase for anything tiresome, undesirable or even disastrous, from undrinkable, tepid, canteen coffee, to toothache, or to the loss of all costumes and scenery on tour. Having arrived early in order to familiarise myself with my surroundings, and with time on my hands, I accepted an invitation from three delightful young Canadians to go on a canoeing and fishing expedition, for ten days, up the French River. When not engaged in back-breaking portage round waterfalls and rapids, batting off mosquitoes, avoiding poison ivy, heroically paddling a canoe or casting a line for muskalonge – a sort of large game pike – I tried to learn my lines, to the round-eyed astonishment of my companions, who were not used to muttering actors. It was one of the most spectacular and enjoyable holidays I've ever had and I returned to Stratford fit and fairly trim, only to find the theatre had barely progressed. However, Cecil Clark, who was our English manager, had done wonders of organisation and a mock-up replica of the stage we would be using had been housed in a barn-like disused warehouse with a tin roof, on which the rain thundered, drowning the loudest human voices. Also Tanya was busy in the wardrobe's workrooms and beautiful garments were beginning to appear on tailors' dummies. There was an air of bustle, and striding through it all, clicking his fingers, issuing orders, answering queries, was that tall military figure. And then the entire company took to bicycling and Tony's rehearsals.

It was fascinating to see the great Tyrone Guthrie manipulating a large company of whom he knew half a dozen, had met half a dozen more, and to whom the rest were strangers. He won their hearts and adoring confidence in an hour; made them laugh, made them jump with activity and held them all in the palm of his hand, including myself, who had been in eight previous productions of his and was familiar with his ways.

We were rather surprised that in Ontario we had to register at the local liquor store as alcoholics. On the car journey to the French River my companions had pulled in to a little roadside hut, saying, 'If you want whiskey this is the last place you can get it until the North Pole.' I think the ration was a bottle a month. The dear old man who ran the shack – a sort of sub-post office which also sold lumber jackets – took one look at me and said, 'Whiskey! I've seen your picture in the papers. You're Alisdair McSims.' Before I could put him right he had made out a form for me to sign and I hadn't the heart to disappoint him, except to say, 'Alistair – with a t – not Alisdair.' And I signed myself McSims, as an alcoholic, for the rest of my stay in Canada. The ghost of the delightful Alistair Sim has never haunted me.

Many of the sponsors of the Festival and people putting us up in their homes were teetotal, being strict Presbyterians, Christian

Edith Evans and A.G. in
Cousin Muriel, 1940

Tony and Judy Guthrie

Martita Hunt in *The Mad Woman of Chaillot*. Photo: Angus McBean

Vivien Leigh, 1937

, as Hamlet, 1938

Admiral of the Fleet Sir Roderick
McGrigor, 1953

. . . and a naval officer

Scientists or Baptists. (I was staying with the Anglican Archdeacon and his wife, so that was all right.) On one occasion Tony, Judy and I, driven out to Lake Huron for a bathe by a kindly Presbyterian couple, burst in to tears at their thoughtfulness when, opening the boot of their car, they revealed scotch, rye, vodka and gin. They had registered themselves as alcoholics to accommodate us. But then, it was like that all along. Although many of the townsfolk were unsympathetic to the idea of the Festival many more, who had been divided by their various sects and social standing, got on to speaking terms with each other and became friends and, at the service of dedication of the theatre, even the Roman Catholics joined the whole congregation in saying the Lord's Prayer. It was, of course, Tony Guthrie's influence which had broken down so many barriers, and perhaps the local conception of actors as a race of giddy whore-mongers with painted faces slowly gave way to the realisation that we were ordinary, fairly law-abiding citizens. The opposition to having a theatre in their midst had been similar to the antagonism felt at the first Edinburgh Festival. Christians of all denominations began to vie with each other in hospitality and providing plants to surround the entrance to the theatre. The only people who didn't pitch in with something were the Dukhobors, the extreme puritanical sect, of Russian extraction, who consider it vanity to wear buttons.

It was after the first dress rehearsal of *Richard III* that Tony and I, who had often had little tiffs, had our longest and most sulky flare-up – nerves on both sides, I am sure – and we barely spoke to each other until we exchanged cool 'good lucks' on the first night, which was two days later. I had asked that Hastings' head, which is presented to Richard after execution, should be in a plain canvas bag with nothing to suggest oozing blood or anything that might make an audience titter, and this was agreed. At the back of my mind I felt I could do something rather horrid by just feeling the contours of the head within the bag, which would be impossible if it was blood-stained. Then, at the dress rehearsal, I saw the bag on the prop-table just before it would be handed to me, and it was ghoulishly stained in the most realistic way. I was furious and at the end of the rehearsal voiced my anger loudly and petulantly. 'More important things to think about' was the only comment I got from Tony. On the day of the first night, during a technical run-through, he silently offered me a cherry from a soggy bag. 'Squashy!' I said, and moved away. During the performance that night I was presented with Hastings' head in a brand-new, spotless bag. I was so taken aback

that I dried up stone dead. After the show I said to Tony, 'Thank
you for the bloodless dorothy bag.' We gave each other a hug and
burst out laughing; anyway we knew the Festival had got off to an
emotional and blazing start (in spite of my poor Richard).

All's Well at Stratford, Ontario was one of Guthrie's finest productions, immensely inventive and the script thoroughly explored.
Irene Worth and Douglas Campbell, as Helena and Parolles, were
brilliant and Tony's direction of the war scenes hysterically funny,
bringing out the best in the young Canadian company. The fact that
he and I had put our heads together three weeks earlier and threatened
to return home (because of the incompletion of the theatre) was
entirely forgotten, though we never quite warmed to the man in
charge of all business affairs, including our contracts, who we felt
was more at home manufacturing the local orangeade, and advising,
we understood, the Canadian government on chemical warfare, than
dealing with actors. The season was undoubtedly a success, virtually
sold out and visitors came from Toronto, Ottawa, New York and
even further afield. Audiences seemed appreciative and attentive,
except for a hefty young man in the front row, at a performance of
Richard III, who rolled up his copy of *Playboy* or *Cute* quite early on
and whacked his mother across the head with it, shouting, 'Shite!
I've had enough of this fart arse stuff!' and waddled out of the theatre
muttering obscenities. Only his mother dutifully followed him.

I never had the opportunity of working for Tony again after
Canada, though we often discussed the possibility when we saw each
other. The last time I saw him was at Anna-ma-kerrig, not long after
he had had a mild heart attack and had been advised to take things
more quietly and decline invitations to lecture in New Zealand or to
the Ladies' Guild of Timbuctoo. (He was a great one for fitting in
odd assignments which meant criss-crossing the world.) I was staying
in Dublin for a short time and invited myself up to Anna-ma-kerrig
for the day. When I arrived I found him loading heavy logs on to a
barrow, having felled a tree after breakfast. He looked a little flushed
and weary. When I remonstrated with him for tackling such a job
his bright eyes gleamed sardonically. 'Nice of you to care,' he said,
'but what does it matter when I go? The jam factory is doing very
promisingly, thank you.' His passion in the last few years of his life
had been the setting up of a jam factory (the Monaghan soft fruits
are notoriously good) to ease the terrible burden of unemployment
in the district. Most of his savings went into this venture, which at
that time was not particularly successful – the first assignment of jam

to USA had been dumped in the Atlantic by the American authorities for not meeting the required standard of hygiene – and, as a result, when he died he was able to leave only something like £10,000 in his will.

That day at Anna-ma-kerrig was typical of so many others, with gossip, laughter, fruitpicking and a short walk. Old Mrs Guthrie had died years before and the house was somewhat rearranged. We lunched in a bay-window of the drawing-room and in my honour a bottle of suspiciously scarlet wine was produced. Judy took a sip and nodded approval. 'Not bad,' she said, 'for three shillings. Got it from Posty at the Post Office.' God knows what it was; it tasted of red ink. Back in Dublin I arranged for a case of decent Burgundy to be sent them; tactless perhaps, but I assumed they would appreciate it. Not at all. Not hearing from them for three weeks and knowing they had received the wine, I telephoned on some stray excuse. Tony picked up the receiver at the other end and when he heard my voice was decidedly cool.

'Oh, by the way,' I said, after I had chatted a little, 'did you ever receive some wine I sent?'

'Yes.'

I waited for further comment but none came.

'Oh, good!' I said. Still no comment. So I added, 'Well, I'd better ring off. Goodbye.'

'Goodbye.' And the receiver clicked down. Clearly my gift had given offence and was considered a criticism of Posty's vintage or their hospitality. I could hear them saying, with pinched lips, 'Film Star's got above himself. Fallen for the flesh-pots. Needs pulling down a peg.' It was the last conversation we had, though later on he sent me a postcard asking me, when next in New York, to go to the grocery department in Bloomingdale's and demand a jar of Irish Mist Plum Jam. But Bloomingdale's had never heard of it.

Tyrone Guthrie died on May 15, 1971, when probably the haw-thorn was in full flower. On June 16 a Memorial Service was held at St Paul's Church, Covent Garden, which was crowded to the doors. The day before there had been a violent storm in London and a large tree in front of the church had been uprooted by the wind and now lay partly across the entrance. It seemed almost symbolic – particularly as the Guthries' friend and factotum at Anna-ma-kerrig, who had discovered Tony dead in his study, sitting by a fire doing his morning mail, had announced his death to Judy with the words, 'A great tree has fallen.' Judy asked me to speak at the service and I

sought her permission to quote that but was nonplussed as to how
to refer to him: factotum, estate manager, employee or friend. 'Not
employee,' she whispered to me as the congregation was assembling.
'Too Ivy Compton-Burnett! Friend!' She was very calm and looking
beautiful. It was something of a Bunyan occasion, with choir and
congregation vigorously singing, in a way Tony would have loved,
'He who would valiant be', and Larry Olivier reading the passage
from *Pilgrim's Progress* which ends, 'So he passed over, and all the
trumpets sounded for him on the other side.'

The range of Tyrone Guthrie's achievement in opera and drama is
formidable; ninety-six productions, not including those he did for
the Scottish National Players and the Cambridge Festival Theatre
between 1926 and 1930, together with several works for radio and a
handful of plays and books he wrote, as well as founding three
theatres. His interests were wide and very human. He loved and had
a knowledge of wild flowers and trees, and retained to the end a
boyhood passion for steam railway engines. He was fond of singing
– charmingly, rather loudly, sonorously and with brilliant diction.
He was caught up with Freudian and Jungian psychology, admired
Victoriana and loved cats. Politically he was liberal-minded and in
religious matters fairly tolerant – his taste was more or less confined
to the English Hymnal and the Metrical Psalms – but he didn't care
for the brand of Roman Catholicism to be found in Ireland. Seeing
me set off for Mass one day he said, 'Going to nod to the statues?'
Another time, having listened to a Papal broadcast, he commented,
'The only words the Pope spake that I understood were "Short
sleeves".' And yet, in general terms, I would say he had a religious
sensibility.

He was an Honorary Doctor of Literature of St Andrew's, and
also, a distinction he greatly prized, Chancellor of The Queen's
University, Belfast. On the other side of the Atlantic he liked to be
known as Dr Guthrie, which on one occasion led to some confusion.
He and Judy were staying in a large hotel in Brooklyn; in the middle
of the night the telephone rang and the operator said, 'Dr Guthrie?
There's a gentleman in Room 204 having a heart attack. Would you
please go along there?' In slopping slippers and torn dressing-gown
Tony hurried to No. 204. When I asked him, some days later, what
he had done for the man, he said, 'Made him a nice strong cup of tea
and held his hand. *Much* better in the morning. Advised him to call
his own doctor.' Tony advised the hotel staff he was *not* a medical
doctor but it made no difference; at three the following morning the

telephone operator was on again, 'Dr Guthrie, the lady in Room 903 thinks she's got Spanish 'flu.' Tony let fly a stream of expletives and slammed down the receiver. 'Feel a little guilty about that,' he said to me. 'Probably not the same party, but I *did* see yesterday a STIFF being wheeled in to the service elevator.'

For all his occasional schoolmasterliness, his capacity to snub and his relish in putting down people he considered self-important, such as Lord Mayors and other dignitaries, he was loved by all who knew him. There was an innate humility about him and he always hoped to find a shadow of it in others. But perhaps his greatness lay not merely in his enthusiasm for taking total risk but in his truth to himself; unlike St Paul he was never all things to all men but always, and steadily, the same man to all men. He never referred to his knighthood, which came very late in life.

Judy declined rapidly after his death, occupying the old dining-room at Anna-ma-kerrig as a bedroom, sometimes sitting at the window, wrapped in a shawl, so that she could watch the birds and look towards the lake. Eventually the squabbling of the birds upset her too much so that she preferred to just lie on her bed. The last time I visited her I was warned I could only see her for ten minutes at a time and that I was to tread quietly in the house in case she was asleep. We talked quietly about old times; of evening picnics on a punt on the Avon, swigging whisky mixed with river water from old tomato soup tins; of mishaps and the war and old friends, and of Tony's work and death. 'A very tiresome man. He could be very tiresome,' she said. And laughed. Then she would be seized with her dreadful hacking cough.

In the middle of my last afternoon in the house I crept in to the drawing-room to get a book. To my amazement Judy was standing, a little unsteadily, at the grand piano, which had its lid open. She was in a dressing-gown, her hair flowing over her shoulders, and was gulping brandy from the neck of a bottle. She looked magnificent. She squeaked the cork back in the bottle and put the bottle in the piano. 'My little store,' she said, looking at me gravely. And then added, with all her charm and a radiant smile, 'Strong waters! Time for bye-byes.' She walked slowly and very carefully across the room and went out through the door, which she closed quietly behind her, only to open it again immediately. She stood in the doorway for a second or two, said 'Sh!' in a whisper, and left. I never saw her again.

CHAPTER EIGHT

Cockerell of Kew

Armed Sudanese guards, black-faced and red-tarbooshed, lolled outside the wide gateway to Mr and Mrs Chester Beatty's palace in the desert, a longish stone's throw from the Pyramids. They rolled their eyes over the modest car in which we were being driven, looking as if they might prefer to use the butts of their rifles on us rather than waste bullets. Inside the gates there was a well-irrigated, sandy garden of palm trees, eucalyptus, exotic shrubs and giant oval beds of purple pansies; the afternoon air of a hot Sunday in March 1939 was heavy with the unmistakeable dusty, peppery and aromatic smell of Egypt and the Near East which can make even drab places seem glamorous, but here it was about as far from drabness as you could get, and everything glistered when not actually gold. The whole atmosphere went straight to my young head.

Merula and I had lunched with a kindly English couple, almost strangers, who had told us that they would be taking us to tea with the Chester Beattys. 'She is great fun,' they said, 'and you must see the house and gardens. The only tiresome thing is that they have a cantankerous old man called Cockerell staying with them and he's a frightful bore. Perhaps we can avoid him.' We were made welcome, shown around the place and were served an elegant tea under a tree which provided shade and dappled sunlight. Burnished silver pots and bowls flashed at us; hot water simmered over a methylated spirits burner; silver covers were removed by butler and frilly-capped maid to reveal muffins and cucumber sandwiches; fine cambric napkins were provided to wipe away the crumbs and stains from our greedy mouths of cake and chocolate éclairs; and tea itself came in varieties of Chinese and Indian. Into this oasis of luxury and pleasure trotted the dreaded Sir Sydney Carlyle Cockerell, a seventy-one-year-old greybeard in panama hat, linen jacket and very crumpled grey flannel trousers. 'Qui vive!' whispered my lunchtime hostess. Behind his gold-rimmed spectacles I was sure I detected tolerant and amused eyes. I liked him instantly.

When I first met Sydney Cockerell, he had retired from his curatorship of the Fitzwilliam Museum in Cambridge two years previously and had settled, with his invalid wife, in a small house in Kew, where they were ministered to by a fleet of devoted, self-deprecating ladies in jumpers and brocades; ladies who were usually talented artists or writers and, invariably, good bakers of cakes. At the Egyptian tea-party Sydney took over the conversation as soon as introductions had been made; informing, putting right, gently snubbing, wincing ever so slightly at abysmal ignorance – 'The name is pronounced Kooch! Quiller Kooch. Not a couch, such as you lie on. And the poet, a good friend of mine, incidentally, is Walter de la Mare, DELLa-mare, not de la MARE!' Everyone expected to be corrected and my hostess from lunch kept pressing my knee as I slid slowly to the bottom of the class. But he hadn't taken against me, I feel, for he said, 'We came to see you play Hamlet in Cairo a few days ago. Very good for such a young man. Mrs Chester Beatty has been approached by the committee which intends to build a National Theatre in London – opposite the Victoria and Albert – and although she is happy to contribute she doesn't wish to use her own name. I have suggested she should make a donation in your name. One day, when you are famous, there will be a seat in this beautiful theatre bearing your name on a brass plate. Does the idea appeal to you?' I nodded, blushed and spluttered some cake at Mrs Chester Beatty. The money was given, undoubtedly; the site of the proposed theatre was shifted from the museum area, and shifted yet again, but no brass plate that I know of has commemorated Mrs Chester Beatty's contribution. Sir Denys Lasdun's theatrical fortress faces the Thames with concrete severity, making no acknowledgement that I have seen to the original donors who made its existence possible.

When tea was over Cockerell, who had told us that he was returning to England the next day, suggested I should accompany him to his suite as in his trunk there was something he would like to give me. My thoughts leapt immediately to treasures fit only for museums – a rare Codex, a First Folio Shakespeare, Keats's walking-stick, T. E. Lawrence's dagger – anything, in fact, which had passed glamorously through his teatime talk. I followed him with alacrity. In the middle of a blue-tiled ante-room stood a vast Saratoga trunk which would take about four hefty fellaheen to shift. Great leather straps were unbuckled, the heavy curved lid creaked open, and Sydney rummaged inside. 'You won't find anything like *this* in Cairo,' he said. 'It's a real bargain.' He produced with a flourish, and presented to

me, a Penguin paperback of *Twelfth Night*, which sold in those days
for about sixpence. I thanked him profusely, of course, and slipped
it in my pocket. It was a lesson in values, salutary and probably
necessary in those golden surroundings, and I only wish that particular copy of *Twelfth Night* had survived the war, so that it could take
a central position among my books.

Presumably Sydney had taken to us, because as we said good-bye
that afternoon he told us to get in touch when we returned to London
as he would like to arrange a lunch for us to meet Mr and Mrs
Bernard Shaw.

Shaw completed writing *In Good King Charles's Golden Days* on
the morning of the day he had invited Sydney, a niece of Mrs Shaw's,
Merula and me to lunch at Whitehall Court. It must have been at
the very beginning of May, shortly after the Old Vic company had
returned from its tour of the Continent and Egypt; I remember it as
being bright and warm, and the threat of war seemed to recede. Mrs
Shaw received us in a kindly, reassuring way; pointed out with pride
the quite hideous pictures and bronze statuettes in the drawing-room;
explained that G.B.S. would join us as soon as he had finished a piece
of work in his study, and kept up a general chicken-like clucking
which meant we hardly had to utter a word. As the clock struck one
a big mahogany door was thrown open by a flunkey in braided
uniform and white gloves who announced, as if at an embassy
reception, 'Mr Shaw.' I was standing nearest to the door and nearly
caught the old gentleman as he hurtled into the room in his purple
woollen suit and green knitted tie. He was unexpectedly tall and
rather beautiful; his fluffy blanco-white beard and pale baby-smooth
skin were particularly striking. He entered smiling and full of greeting, with a hand extended to be shaken, but I hadn't been told how
poor his sight was: I put out my hand to take his and he missed me
by a yard, scampering past but calling out joyously, 'I have just put
the finishing touches to the play.' 'Oh, well *done!*' cried Mrs Shaw,
clapping her hands. Sydney gave me a nodding, smiling, satisfied
look, as if to say, 'Young man, you are witnessing history in the
making.' The footman announced luncheon and we trooped out of
the drawing-room to the rather dingy dining-room, furnished with
a long table and high-backed Windsor chairs which were pulled out
and pushed in by two further flunkeys as Shavian bottoms were
settled. Before our arrival Merula and I had speculated, depressingly,
on the likelihood of dewberry soup and nut cutlets, but we were
totally wrong. For Cockerell, the niece and ourselves it was roast

chicken and white wine; the Shaws pushed little bits of greenery around their plates and sipped water. There wasn't much conversation to speak of as G.B.S. talked continuously, mostly recounting the jokes to be found in *In Good King Charles*, etc. and falling about with laughter in his slatted wooden chair. Sydney attempted to get him on to heavier things, such as the likelihood of war, but he dismissed everything as 'bally-hoo' except what he had given Newton or the King to say in his comedy.

Back in the drawing-room Mrs Shaw gathered her niece, Merula and me at a bronze bust of Shaw, standing on a pedestal, while we had our coffee. 'This side,' she said, 'shows Shaw the philosopher. Now come round here!' We shifted a few paces and were joined by the great man, who stood listening, smiling and approving. 'From this angle,' Mrs Shaw explained, 'you see Bernard the humourist. You will notice the mouth turns up at the corner; while from this side' – we all shuffled back to our first position – 'the corner of the mouth turns down. The Philosopher!' We inclined our heads gravely; Shaw looked serious so we took our leave and Sydney shepherded us away. I knew I had met an undoubted man of genius but what had impressed me most, in spite of the overriding garrulousness and the evident self-satisfaction, was the exquisite, almost eighteenth-century courtesy. Shaw's manners were a delightful mixture of formality, ease and charm, of a sort rarely encountered nowadays, except in the very old and very distinguished. Sir Osbert Sitwell had the same cultivated gift, as did the U.S. Ambassador to Britain, Mr Douglas, the film director Anthony Asquith and, still in our midst, Lord Stockton and King Hussein of Jordan – men who manage to make civilization appear attainable.

As a result of that lunch in Whitehall Court Shaw, unknown to me though possibly not to Sydney, sent a postcard to Gabriel Pascal in Hollywood suggesting me for a part in a film. Nothing came of it; but Pascal managed to exchange the card at Dunhill's in Beverly Hills for a box of cigars. Many years later the manager at Dunhill's kindly gave me a photostat of the card, but nothing would induce him to let me have the original.

Fairly early in the war I appeared in a short-lived play at the Globe Theatre, supporting Edith Evans and Peggy Ashcroft. Partly from frustration, and also in pale emulation of the lunchtime concerts which had been inaugurated at the National Gallery, the three of us decided to give weekly poetry readings in aid of various war-time charities; no entrance fee was charged but a silver collection taken at the end of each performance. The programme changed each week, although Edith was very keen to include at every reading, 'Say not the Struggle Naught Availeth', in which she saw, prophetically – America not having yet entered the war – President Roosevelt's Lease-Lend or the Marshall Plan. On one afternoon, when I had been allotted 'La Belle Dame Sans Merci', Sydney Cockerell turned up, accompanied by Sir Edward Marsh, who at one time had been Churchill's secretary. After the performance I took a slow walk with the old gentlemen under the barrage balloons and among the trenches and sandbags of Hyde Park. 'Ah, beauty! Beauty!' piped Eddie Marsh, whose voice was quite astonishingly high. His head was thrown back, his heavy black eyebrows knitted with pain, his amber-topped malacca cane was waved sadly in the air, and I couldn't make out whether he was referring to my reading or merely commenting on the silver Blimps floating above us or having ancient memories of his protégé, Rupert Brooke.

Whatever may have caused Eddie Marsh's emotional enthusiasm Sydney cut across it with, '*Quite* good. Not perfect. It wasn't what Keats meant, you know. He did *not* mean "And there she lulléd me asleep", with that hard éd at the end of the word. I know it is printed like that in all the anthologies, but it shouldn't be so. William Morris told me – and he got it from Joseph Severn, the painter, who, as you must know, was with Keats when he died. Keats meant a triple "l" – lullld – but the printer mistook the third "l" for an accent.' Difficult to say aloud but I guess Severn, Morris and Cockerell were right. Sydney was a gold-mine of rare pieces of information, collected from friends like Ruskin, Morris, Burne-Jones, Hardy and Tolstoy, and meticulously noted down the days they were gleaned in diaries covering fifty years or more. Born as he was in 1867, many of his elderly friends in, say, 1890, had memories of Queen Victoria coming to the throne, of Disraeli, Gladstone, the young Dickens, Thackeray and Trollope and the Catholic Emancipation Bill. Sometimes there was a lot of pedantry in what he chose to pass on to me, but now and then the vividness of what he remembered makes me feel that, in more dramatic circumstances, he could have been an English equivalent of Alexander Herzen.

In 1903, when Tolstoy was living at Yasyana Polyana, Sydney had an opportunity of visiting him there, and two things in the account he gave gripped my visual memory as if I had seen them myself. When he arrived at the Tolstoy home he was shown down to the apple orchard, where the entire family – with the exception of

Tolstoy, who was resting – was taking tea. He said they were all sitting or lying in long grass under the trees, drinking tumblers of black tea and eating cucumbers spread with honey. The samovar was crooked, the conversation nil, the only sounds were of hissing steam, bees and the crunching of cucumbers. Later, up in the house, Tolstoy said he would like Sydney to see the billiard-room. The door was pushed open and they stepped into a large room, but there was no sign of a billiard table although it was there all right. The table was entirely surrounded and covered, nearly to the height of the ceiling, by tens of thousands of unopened letters which Tolstoy had thrown there. Stamps from all over the world, a philatelist's dream, could be glimpsed and Sydney turned to his host with a look of astonished enquiry. Tolstoy shrugged, muttered something about vanity and propelled him out of the room.

During the war I used to receive short letters from Sydney, written in his beautiful italic hand which, with the years, deteriorated into something so small and cramped that each letter looked like the Lord's Prayer written on a postage stamp and sometimes required a magnifying glass. I took to writing to him occasionally in my swift, ugly scrawl and he used two or three of my letters in his collection, *The Best of Friends*; he also begged me to improve my 'unformed hand', as he called it, and sent me Patrick Barry's Handwriting Sheets, for which he had written the introduction, to encourage me. As a result I suppose my hand has improved, but more often than not it is neither fish nor fowl and with advancing age I notice it getting smaller and smaller, not unlike Sydney's towards the end, but without his distinction.

Undecided, in 1939, as to what I should do, and not wishing to join up until Merula's child was born, I thought I might go round hospitals reading short stories at the bedsides of the sick. I told Sydney of this intention and he promptly sent £10 (I think it was that) towards my expenses. I only read once, at a cottage hospital near Dorking, where I was a nuisance rather than a help. I had chosen a Chesterton 'Father Brown' story and for twenty minutes mumbled away at a young man who looked tired and indifferent, and when I left I asked the sister in charge what was the matter with him. 'It hardly matters, does it?' she said. 'He won't live through the night.' I felt that she should have told me that before I embarked on reading; I wouldn't have disturbed, then, his peace or distant thoughts. I abandoned the idea of hospital readings and Merula returned the money to Sydney after I had joined the Navy.

In about 1951 Sydney had a bad fall and from then until the end
of his life was bedridden. I called on him at Kew quite a few times.
He lay propped up in bed in the downstairs front room of his house,
a blue velvet skull-cap on his head, gold-rimmed spectacles perched
on the end of his nose, a writing pad on his lap and surrounded by
letters, books, pens and paper. 'You've just missed the Archbishop
of Canterbury,' he would say, or, 'If you had come half an hour
earlier I would have introduced you to Archie Wavell.' Later on I did
meet Major Wavell at 21 Kew Gardens Road, saw something of him,
and felt we would have become good friends if only his life had
not been cut short so tragically when he was butchered by the Mau
Mau.

When I came to play T. E. Lawrence in Rattigan's *Ross*, in
1960, I took myself to Kew before rehearsals started to pick at
Sydney's memories. 'He was a terrible fibber, you know!' he said.
' "Why do you bother to lie?" I asked him once. "Because my lies
are more interesting than the truth," he replied.' Miss Dorothy
Hawksley, Sydney's faithful and almost daily companion, whose
portrait drawings were of exquisite delicacy, was in the room when
Sydney recounted this and said, in her shy way, 'I came in here one
day and saw a small man, dressed as an airman, looking out of the
window. His back was turned to me. I wondered why Sydney should
be talking to such a very undistinguished little man. Then, just as if
he could read my thoughts, the little man turned round and stared
hard at me. I was stupefied; I don't think I have ever encountered
such a strong personality. I didn't know who he was, of course, until
introduced. He rather gave me the creeps. But Sydney was fond of
him. Weren't you, Sydney?'

'Fond of whom?'

'Lawrence of Arabia.'

'M-m-n. Perhaps. But he was such a terrible fibber.'

Sydney gave me a coarse, striped robe which he had bought from
a Bedouin when he and Wilfrid Scawen Blunt had been wrecked off
the coast of Sinai in 1900. He used it as a dressing-gown later in life,
lent it to Lawrence who in turn handed it on to G.B.S. Eventually
it found its way back to Sydney, and shortly after it came in to my
possession I handed it over to Clouds Hill, T.E.'s hideaway cottage
in Dorset, as a memento. Of all the people who were T.E.'s friends
whom I questioned about his personality, only Sydney and Sir
Basil Liddell Hart seemed to me to have a straight, appreciative but
unemotional view of him. Many, including Siegfried Sassoon, Robert

Graves and David Garnett were, I guessed, jealous of Lawrence's friendship, each thinking himself the one, true and intimate friend. They seemed like schoolboys who had a slight crush on the captain of the cricket team. The most useful picture of him I formed came from the custodian of Clouds Hill who, looking from the window of his own cottage one evening, said, 'I can see him right now as he was thirty years ago, walking like a duck, toes turned out, his arms stiff at his side, straight down the middle of the road in the dusk of a summer night. I always used to watch him. Of course I was just a kid. But he was my hero.' When I mentioned this to Sydney he smiled rather sourly and said, 'I expect he knew he was being watched; and hero-worshipped.'

Opposite his bed, propped up against books, were three or four large framed photographs, one of which was of Dame Laurentia McLachlan, Abbess of Stanbrook, and another of Dame Felicitas Corrigan, also of Stanbrook. 'Great women,' Sydney would muse, peering at them over his spectacles. He had been largely responsible for Bernard Shaw visiting the Abbess in 1924, from which stemmed the correspondence of playwright and nun which includes one of Shaw's finest letters. When Dame Laurentia died, her biography was written by Dame Felicitas and a continual and substantial exchange of letters took place between her and Sydney – a genial non-meeting of minds so far as Christianity was concerned but for all his antipathy to the Church he cherished a high regard for intellectual nuns. When I told him I had become a Catholic he was genuinely puzzled, saying, 'But *how* can you believe in a creative, all-good, all-wise God, knowing that you have an appendix, which is a totally useless organ and can prove dangerous?' Nothing would convince him that to be a Christian did not necessitate rejecting evolution or explosive theories and embracing Biblical fundamentalism. He enjoyed the derisions of his period, class, attainments and scholarship; blinkering himself, as so many of us do – but his generation particularly – with the worship of art and science and the hope of social change. As a young man Sydney had worked for a few years among the poor of south London. His nature was totally without frivolity.

He had charm but could be cantankerous; he was kind but often snubbing; generous but with the instincts of a bullying magpie; a good friend who could take umbrage. His taste was for the medieval or Victorian – I cannot remember him ever mentioning anything of the seventeenth or eighteenth centuries – and the already-vanishing world of post-World War One left him politely indifferent. When I mentioned him one day to Edith Sitwell she said, 'I could kick Cockerell!' and, dismissing him without further thought, continued knitting a sea-boot stocking.

CHAPTER NINE

Damage to the Allied Cause

The Colonel stood with his back to the sitting-room fire, warming his shoulders and his behind. He was very small. He wore a hairy tweed suit and, although he was trying to be helpful, he only managed to look rather cross. He was a revered 'uncle', but no relation, of my dear friend Peggy Ashcroft, who had kindly arranged for me to be interviewed by him. This was in 1940.

'Drive a car?' asked the Colonel.

'I'm afraid not,' I said. The Colonel looked crosser, so I added, 'Sir,' which mollified him slightly.

'Motor bicycle?'

'No, I'm afraid I don't do anything like that.'

'Sport? Rugger? Cricket?'

'Absolutely no. Sir.'

'My niece says you act.'

'Yes.'

'Well, that's that. I suggest you offer your services to the Royal Navy. Good afternoon.'

So I left. It was the Navy I wished to enlist in anyway, but I had no idea of the preliminary steps to take. A few days later, somewhere off Piccadilly, I ran in to Dennis Price, who was a casual friend from the time we had been together in one of Gielgud's productions. 'You should join us at Sevenoaks,' Dennis said encouragingly. 'It's an anti-aircraft battery and there is simply nothing to do. Major Cazalet is a dear, and there are lots of chums. Johnnie and Jack and Hughie and Sebastian among others. [I won't recall, now, who all those Christian names represented.] You can swing as much leave as you want; all you have to do is say you have a dinner engagement at the Savoy which you simply can't get out of. I think we should sit out the war very comfortably. Do join us. I'll have a word with Cazzers.'

Dennis looked very smart in his khaki; a sharp crease to his trousers, shiny boots and a rakish tilt to his cap.

So, a week later, I took the train to Sevenoaks and walked from the station, very nervous and undecided, but in my best suit and head held high. I arrived at a large suburban house which didn't have the air of being occupied by the military; in fact it appeared to be totally deserted. The hall through which I strolled was empty of furniture or any sign of human life. Very gingerly I pushed open a door. There, in a small room, each lolling over his typewriter, sat two sergeants, knitting. They looked up with some surprise but busily continued their two plain one purl.

'Yes?' said one of them, affably enough. 'And what can we do for you?'

'I am hoping to see Major Cazalet.'

'Are you expected?'

'I think so,' I said.

These were not what I had expected sergeants to be like and I wondered, briefly, what Peggy's uncle would have made of them.

'Well, hold on a tick,' said the one nearest the door, 'I'll go and have a peep. What name did you say?'

I gave my name, and the sergeant wearily put down his knitting and left the room. The other eyed me roguishly.

'Going to join us?'

'I don't know yet.'

'What, may I be so bold to ask, do you do in civvy street?'

'I'm an actor,' I said.

'Oh, my Gawd! Not another! My dear, the place is swarming with them. It's a positive snake-pit. You know we've got Dennis and Hugh?'

'So I heard.'

The door opened and Sergeant No 1 reappeared.

'She'll see you now, toute suite.' He flipped a wrist in the direction I was to take. As I made my exit I heard No 2 say to his colleague, but for my benefit I am sure, 'Not exactly a dish, but quite sweet.' I took a deep breath and knocked on the Major's door.

Major Cazalet was a smallish, benign-looking man. He rose from his desk and motioned me to a chair opposite him. The room, which was in a Victorian turret, was uncarpeted and almost bare.

'Do sit down,' he said. 'It's lucky you've caught us on a slack day. Most of the fellows are out learning about the Bofors gun. Dennis has spoken to me about you. You found your way all right?'

'With no difficulty, sir.'

'Oh, good.' There was a silence, as if he was searching for something to say. Then he went on, 'We are rather over-manned at present.' Another silence. 'What do you think? Would you like to join us? Of course, I do realise you've seen nothing. Take your time.'

I shuffled and fumbled before finally saying, 'Might I have a day or two to think it over, sir?'

'By all means. Good heavens, I'd hate to rush anyone. Let's see; it's Tuesday. Could you possibly let me know by Thursday?'

'Yes,' I said, knowing perfectly well I could let him know there and then, if I had the courage.

When I left the building both sergeants were peering after me out of a window. One of them waved. As I wandered back to the station I fussed as how to make suitable apologies to Dennis.

Not long after this there were questions in the House of Commons about the Sevenoaks battery; the whole thing was broken up; and Jack and Johnnie and Dennis and Hugh and Co. were dispersed to different and less pleasant duties. A year or so afterwards I heard Victor Cazalet lecture a group of Naval personnel at Inveraray; and excellent he was. Tragically, in July 1943, he was one of the seventeen victims, along with Sikorski, to be killed in the abortive take-off from Gibraltar; and it was about this tragedy that Hochhuth wrote his scandalous play, *The Soldiers*, much championed by Kenneth Tynan, which more or less accused Churchill of collusion in Sikorski's death. But that play wasn't for another twenty years. The immediate future for me was the Navy.

My next port of call, after Sevenoaks, was a large, disused school in North London being used by the Navy for enlistment. Very courteously they referred to all of us who turned up there as volunteers. I was sat down at a small desk opposite a hatchet-faced Chief Petty Officer. He made it clear that he didn't think I was a very suitable candidate and did his best to dissuade me. (I am reminded of him by lines in a poem by Charles Causley: 'He surveys with a prehistoric eye the hostilities-only ratings' and 'Waiting for tot-time, His narrow forehead ruffled by the Jutland wind'.) When I answered his various questions he made little despairing shakes of the head, which were almost like a nervous tic. But I persisted. Eventually, with a gloomy sigh, as if he had caught me out, he said, 'Well, can you swim?' I answered, triumphantly, 'Yes!' He stamped a piece of paper and said, 'If the doctor passes you, you'll get your call-up, my lad. One day.' Then it was the shuffle, totally stripped, along with a few dozen other young men of various shapes, sizes and physiques, to dentists who cursorily looked in our mouths, to eye-specialists who wanted to make sure we weren't colour-blind, and then to a genial, burly, elderly doctor. He ran a tape-measure round my chest;

told me to breathe out and then breathe in. He looked puzzled, as if
he had miscalculated, and repeated his measurement.

'Chest expansion over four inches. How do you account for
that?'

'I'm an actor. It's part of the job to use your lungs.'

'I see,' he said, rather impressed. He grabbed me, somewhat
intimately.

'Cough! Now bend over.'

While I did so he suddenly asked, 'Know Ivor Novello?'

I told him I didn't.

'Like his music?'

'Yes,' I said.

'Straighten up. I'm passing you A1.'

He scribbled on my piece of paper. I got dressed and walked out
into the grey light of day, not quite sure what I had done for myself,
rather alarmed at what fate might have in store, but somehow relieved
and happy. It was about ten weeks before I was drafted for training
as an Ordinary Seaman to HMS *Raleigh*, a shore establishment a few
miles west of Plymouth.

At this time Merula and I were living, with our baby son, who
had been born in June 1940, in a tiny bungalow at the edge of a
wood. It belonged to Mr and Mrs Deuchar of Standon Farm (not far
from Ockley in Surrey) who were kindly people and rented the place
to us for seven shillings a week. It was a life of oil-lamps, candles,
solid fuel and water-pumps; it suited us admirably, although we
thought the bungalow haunted, in a not too unpleasant way. Small
birds, mice, owls, rabbits and other wild creatures abounded, and
seemed to take our presence quite casually, as if we had as much right
to nest there as themselves. They were almost welcoming. The nights
were always full of tiny sounds, of rustling feathers, snapping twigs
or gentle tappings. I had recently embraced, very briefly, not to say
flittingly, Anglo-Catholicism; I was inclined to interpret everything,
from sight or smell or sound, as an insight, as I thought, into some
other world. It was all, I suppose, a psychological bulwark against
the uncertainties of war and fear of the future and it stood me in good
stead, while it lasted. Evenings were mostly given up to reading by
lamplight: the works of St Teresa of Avila, St Francis de Sales,
William Law, William Temple or Bishop Gore, a high-flown diet
which was sometimes brought down to earth with some Dickens or
Beachcomber. It was also brought down to earth, one day, when I
was machine-gunned by a hedge-hopping Luftwaffe fighter while

innocently bicycling to Ockley Station. I fell in a ditch with shock. I got up, unscathed, but outraged and ready for anything.

When my call-up finally arrived I was seized by my dreadful sense of over-punctuality and left Ockley for Plymouth a day early. Perhaps I felt that if I waited to the last moment I wouldn't go at all and they would have to come and fetch me. I have rarely felt so lonely and lost as I did walking down the gravel road from our bungalow that dismal afternoon. My face, I know, was stained with tears as I thought of the sad bleakness Merula was going to undergo; but at least she had the baby to occupy her. My thoughts simply wouldn't budge from either of them or look to the immediate, practical future. I stayed the night in a Plymouth hotel and went to an early-morning Anglican Communion service; there were no other communicants. The young priest was over-dressed and had a flouncy, arrogant manner and I wanted, meanly, to knock his biretta sideways. It was the first faint tolling of the knell to my High Anglicanism.

HMS *Raleigh* was a vast parade ground, with concrete quarter-deck and rows of long wooden huts housing two-tier bunks, offices, gym, dining hall and bomb shelters. My world was peopled with Lofties and Nobbies, Geordies and Taffies, Chiefs and the Master-at-Arms. Noise and barking voices filled the air; there was no quiet corner, except the Mission hut chapel, in which to read or ruminate. Swabbing floors, pushing wheelbarrows of kitchen gash, polishing boots, simple squad drill and attending lectures on discipline seemed to be the order of each tedious day, interspersed with PT and sessions in the gym. My fellow sailors, if that could be the right word for us as yet, I found agreeable and simple-hearted, with only two or three exceptions. We came from every sort of background, numbering among us butchers' assistants, a housepainter, a maker of pianos, a couple of schoolmasters (whom I thought rather intolerable, with their condescending airs), an aggressive, foul-mouthed Post Office clerk from Manchester, who could have served Hitler well, a Scottish Laird of great distinction and a dozen or so drifters from all over. Most of them were great swillers of beer. When in small, intimate groups, they chatted quietly of their mothers and sisters; once they were gathered in larger numbers, however, the conversation, loud and hyphenated with four-letter words, was of football and the crudest sex. Nearly all wished to be taken for old salts within days of joining up: they spent hours bleaching the midnight blue of their stiff sailor collars so that they would appear to be paled by sea and sun. Tall stories were already fermenting in their minds, to lure the

'birds' in Plymouth pubs, but transport to Plymouth was thin on the
ground. Mostly, if we went 'ashore', we had to content ourselves
with weak tea and buns, served in a local hall by kind, hard-working,
elderly Methodist ladies, who treated each of us as an image of Christ
and were reluctant to take our tuppences.

After I had been at HMS *Raleigh* a week I discovered that Peter
Bull, who was to become one of my closest friends, was in the
infirmary, suffering from some leg complaint. I had only met him
once, some four years previously, when he had offered me a job at
his Perranporth summer theatre, but which, for financial reasons, I
had declined. (Another job turned down at the same time was to
play, at two days' notice, Captain Fluellen in an all-female production
of *Henry V* which was touring schools. It hadn't been the lack of
rehearsals or money which had deterred me from that one.) Peter
was soon up and, when we weren't stamping around the parade
ground, we gravitated towards each other. I think our friendship
started when I was able to whisper to him, while we were both
standing rigidly to attention at some ceremony, that Madame Katina
Paxinou, the great Greek actress, had been torpedoed. Peter was a
great giggler.

One disturbing day the officer in charge of entertainments, hearing
that Peter and I were actors, approached us about doing a play in the
garrison theatre. He and some of the WRNS were rather keen to be
seen in Patrick Hamilton's thriller *Rope* and he wanted to know if
we would like to help with the production and also act in it. We
couldn't make up our minds whether our acceptance might further
our naval ambitions (to obtain commissions in the RNVR), or hinder
our very necessary training. Unless we gave full time to what we
were already doing we felt we would never master how to make a
Bowline on the Bight, a Double Matthew Walker, or what the hell
you did, if anything, with Bullivant's Fixed Nipper. The offer, of
course, had its temptations; excusing us, perhaps, from various
unpleasant fatigues. We said we would give it a try and a reading of
the play was called in the vast, rectangular, red barn of a theatre.
Peter, who had done *Rope* at Perranporth, was going to give the part
of Brandon and I, who had seen Ernest Milton play it at the old
Shilling Theatre at Fulham, was to be the decadent Rupert Cadell;
we were to direct jointly. The reading was quite excruciatingly
dreadful and we knew on the spot that we couldn't go through with
it: our problem was how to back-pedal without giving offence. So
we decided to blame the size of the theatre and its acoustics. We had

found out that no other play had been done there, only concerts. I stood at the back of the auditorium and shouted at Peter that he couldn't be heard; then he would do the same for me. Then we announced, as our professional opinion, that the theatre was unsuitable to act in. In spite of the obvious disappointment of the cast, the shrugging and sour smile of the officer in charge of entertainments, the whole thing was successfully called off. A couple of years later I ran into this same officer.

'You remember,' he said, 'that you and Bull expressed the opinion that the garrison theatre at *Raleigh* had rotten acoustics and was useless?'

'Vaguely,' I said.

'Well, it's a funny thing, but shortly after you two had left Michael Redgrave joined us. He put on a simply A1 show and had no difficulty with the acoustics at all.'

'He's a fine actor,' I said, smiling myself away from any further explanation.

Although Peter Bull and I went through the same process of being transformed into officers and gentlemen, each of us serving our time on the lower deck for about a year and then three months' training at Lancing College and HMS *King Alfred*, at Brighton, our paths diverged. We didn't meet again until May 1943, when I bumped into him, almost literally, in Djidjelli harbour, on the Algerian coast. By that time he was in command of an anti-aircraft ship, with seventy marines on board, and I was in dubious command of LCI(L) 124 with a crew of twenty and, most fortunately, an efficient and charming First Lieutenant, John Bostock. We were all very young and inexperienced; my own lack of know-how and swift rash judgments hampered the Allied Cause like small but irritating gnat-bites.

LCI(L) stood for Landing Craft Infantry (Large); the ships had a displacement of 250 tons, were 153 feet long and 22 feet in the beam. They were powered by diesel-electric engines, had variable pitch propellers and were capable of sixteen knots. Their function was to carry 200 troops and put them ashore, dry-shod if possible, on various invasion beaches. Lord Mountbatten told me, many years later, that he had roughed out the design for them on the back of an old envelope. The only armament they carried was four Oerlikon anti-aircraft guns. The ships were admirable in many ways, not desperately uncomfortable, but their landing ramps for the troops were far from satisfactory. As they had a draft of (on average) only 4 feet at the bow and 6 feet at the stern they appeared to be alarmingly shallow for crossing the Atlantic.

About a year before I contacted Peter Bull in Algeria I went for my commission. Roger Furse, bearded as always but now sporting two gold rings on the sleeves of his uniform, acted as a sort of secretary to the Admiralty Board in Portsmouth in front of whom I found myself standing, rigidly at attention, to be questioned about my suitability. Roger was one of the finest scenic artists we have had; among dozens of notable productions he designed were the Olivier Shakespeare films, Guthrie's modern-dress *Hamlet* and Gielgud's *Duchess of Malfi*. Along with Oliver Messel, the Motleys, Tanya Moiseiwitsch and Cecil Beaton, he helped rid the theatre of much that was fustian. He was always relaxed, charming and helpful, and he managed to display all three qualities on this particular occasion. Before announcing me to the eight or ten aged Admirals, sitting at their long, green-baize-covered table, he whispered, 'Nothing to worry about. Just *act* the part.' It was simple but splendid advice which I often conjured up for the rest of the war. When, nowadays, I am asked what I consider the best performance I have given, I reply, 'That of a very inefficient, undistinguished, junior officer in the Royal Navy Volunteer Reserve. It also proved to be the longest-running show I have ever been in.'

Each of the Admirals had paper and pencil before him. They looked as if they were about to take part in a quiz and I had hardly completed my hat-off salute before their pencils started to scribble. One or two just stared at me with wind-watered eyes. The Admiral in charge of the proceedings appeared to be a shrewd, friendly-disposed frog. He glanced at the papers Roger Furse handed him.

'Navigation not too good,' he rumbled. 'Mathematics very poor, I see. Gunnery marks are appalling. You don't like guns?'

I levelled my eyes at him.

'I wouldn't say that, sir. It's just that I'm not very sympathetic towards them.' I had a suspicion I might have scored a near miss.

'It says here you were an actor. Do you by any chance know Sub-Lieutenant Gantwhistle?'

'I know of him, sir, but I can't say I really know him. I met him once – I think.'

Gantwhistle wasn't his real name, but as he is no longer alive it is only fair to let him rest in peace. He was a Sub-Lieutenant with a green stripe alongside the gold, which meant, in his case, that he was considered unfit to go to sea, being flat-footed, white and portly and, so far as I could then judge, of limited talents. He was also rather pompous.

'You've seen him act?' the Admiral persisted.

'Yes,' I said, with a tiny hesitation.

'He's a very clever actor, wouldn't you say?'

I perjured myself immediately with an enthusiastic, 'Yes, sir.'

'Mind you, I'm no judge of these things, but I would say Gantwhistle should rise to the top of his profession. Become a regular star. Do you agree with me?'

'Undoubtedly, sir.'

Pencils all round the table were doodling or being chewed.

'He gave us a very enjoyable show here,' the Admiral added. Then he said, rather dreamily, 'I can already see his name in lights. Gantwhistle in . . . in . . . give me the title of some play.'

I took a deep breath and said, '*Bunty Pulls the Strings.*'

'Ah, yes. Well, back to business. Drill, good; Smartness, yes.'

I thought, with pride, of the exquisite trouble I had taken with my black silk ribbon, collar, boots and tiddly suit. I was dismissed curtly, but I had the impression that the dear frog face watched my exit keenly. Roger collected the papers with their pencilled comments and afterwards told me that scrawled across my paper by the senior Admiral were the words, 'Probably more to him than meets the eye.'

So I was commissioned. As quick as lightning I got measured by Messrs Gieves for my midnight-blue Sub-Lieutenant uniform, with its thin, squiggly, gold-braid stripe. It was goodbye to Devonport, Portsmouth, and the abysmal horrors of Chatham Barracks. Chatham had been the nadir of my lower-deck experiences, where thousands of men slept, snored or vomited – their hammocks slung three-deep in a cavernous tunnel which served as dormitory, bomb-shelter and lavatory; Chatham, where to get a meal you had to fight your way to the food – which was something I refused to do. If it hadn't been for kind, tough messmates who took pity on me, I think I might have starved but somehow, in the general struggle, they managed to salvage meals for me as well as themselves. Eventually, embarrassed by being waited on, so to speak, I abandoned all messing and spent my pittance on chocolate and biscuits at the local store. However, it was not goodbye to oily decks, feeling a misfit, or being the victim of nautical martinets or the witness of authoritarian absurdity. It was goodbye to my wife and small son (not to be seen again until he was four years old) and hello to two and a half years of service overseas; the same life that tens of thousands of others were

undergoing but clearly not as horrible as the trench warfare of
1914–18.

Of course the war, with its threats and reverses, small triumphs
and anxieties, was always with us; but somehow at a remove. Blood
chilled at Lord Haw-Haw's rasping propaganda on German radio –
'This is Germany calling' – there was fury at bombing of towns (I
don't think we realised that we had been bombing Germany, fairly
indiscriminately, for about five months before Hitler retaliated) and
tears were shed by many, including myself, at the loss of great
battleships such as HMS *Hood*. And yet it still wasn't quite a reality.
It was a bad dream from which, one day, we would wake up to
resume our former ways of life. Privations and a common fear held
us together – defeat was unthinkable – but there were far too many
people around who met simple requests with a snarling, 'Don't you
know there's a war on?' and the black-marketeers, for whom I must
admit we were, occasionally, guiltily grateful, looked as if they might
grab the future once victory was achieved, and possibly grab it even
more fiercely in defeat. Many of us in the Services moved around
like zombies, fretting about our families and hearing our own hearts
thump whenever a buff envelope arrived containing orders to report
to some remote, usually unheard-of, desolate place.

One of the early and silly amusements to be found, after com-
missioning, was collecting salutes, as if they were car numbers, from
poor aircraftsmen doing duty outside the Queen's Hotel in Brighton.
I gave this up promptly after an overdressed lady, mistaking me for
a commissionaire, handed me her ticket in the foyer of the Theatre
Royal. I tore off the stub and misdirected her; but it made me realise
that my present status wasn't as grand as I had imagined. I have
found, in subsequent years, that a day or two after receiving an
Oscar, or a doctorate, or even an accolade, there has had to be a
similar readjustment.

In the early summer of 1942 I was appointed to be First Lieutenant
of a grubby Tank Landing Craft TLC 24 (not to be confused with
LCI(L) 124) on Loch Fyne, up and down which we did ragged naval
exercises. The weather was cold, the ship rusty and greasy. I never
knew exactly what my job was and I hardly got to know the crew,
but the CO was friendly and casual and, as he liked to spend most
of his evenings ashore in a convivial way, I had nothing better to do
after the day's work but read or write, crouched in a duffel coat over
a little coke stove, very long letters to those I loved and even to
people who were only acquaintances, in a desperate attempt to keep

in touch, somehow, with a familiar world which seemed to be vanishing. Bollards and sisal rope, marlin spikes and diesel fuel had replaced spotlights, proscenium arches, wings and make-up in my daily round but not in my imagination. When I did go ashore it was usually to the Manse, to have high-tea with the Rev. Penn Collett and his sisters Gwen and Olive. They were kind, hospitable Anglo-Catholics, very anti-Roman – living in a rather mouse-like present but gloriously in the past. For Gwen the past was 'artistic'; for Olive memories of being a governess in Russia; and for Penn what Bishop Gore might have said to Archbishop Temple. They had billeted on them Julian Trevelyan, then a lieutenant in the army, but I rarely glimpsed him. 'You should look in his room,' Gwen said to me one day. 'He paints!' Her eyes revolved with agony. 'You've never seen such stuff. *Very* modern. We simply don't understand it. I do hope he's happy.' Trevelyan, needless to say, is a fine painter. Gwen, who was a semi-invalid, always wore a hat indoors and on one occasion, when she was in bed with a migraine, I found it in the lavatory with bits of grey hair safety-pinned to the brim. They were a dear, good, eccentric trio and we kept in touch for quite a few years after the war, when they had left Inveraray and settled in the West Country.

Among the crew of TLC 24 was a young burly Scot of great innocence and charm. He looked on me as quite remarkably well-educated because he had seen me reading *Bleak House*. One night he knocked on the cabin door and asked me to settle a dispute on the lower-deck; it was true, wasn't it, that there were giant birds with bat's wings, that flew round and round the moon? He had read about them in a comic. No, I was pretty sure it wasn't true. Another evening he came asking, very solemnly, if it was true that when a man died his soul could be seen leaving the top of his head like a puff of smoke. The Coxswain had said he didn't believe it. The Scot was insatiable for knowledge and philosophical truth. My gloom deepened. Everything seemed out of proportion and drab. Then I remembered that tucked away in my suitcase was a diminishing glass, which Martita Hunt had given me recently. It was a small, gold-rimmed, elegant eighteenth-century glass which, when held a few inches in front of the eye, produced a brilliant miniature picture. The grimmest sights could be made to appear delectable; the mountains of Argyllshire dwarfed to colourful hills; the grey water of the Loch achieved a dizzy sparkle and, above all, people could be reduced, when required, to exquisite manikins. I searched out this pretty object and, from then on, nearly always had it in a pocket. It proved a great

comfort. I quizzed Admirals through it (furtively and at a distance)
gunnery officers or anyone who enquired if I knew there was
war on. Martita's glass, which I am sure she gave me only as an
afterthought, feeling the need to give something but having nothing
suitable to hand, such as a bottle of champagne, stood me in good
stead, alongside Roger Furse's advice, throughout the remainder of
the war.

One bleak dawn, on Loch Fyne, I stood in the bows of the TLC
impeccably dressed (to compensate for the CO, who was looking, I
knew, scruffy and unshaven) with a white silk scarf round my neck.
We were on some exercise and finally landed on a small beach
crowded with senior naval and army officers. The most senior of
them all, an RN Captain, bawled at me, 'Why are you incorrectly
dressed?'

'By your leave, sir, I am correctly dressed.'

'You are not wearing a collar and tie!'

'I am wearing a scarf, sir.'

'Go and put on a collar and tie immediately.'

'Aye, aye, Sir,' I said. I saluted; about-turned; threw off my scarf
(I was wearing collar and tie, of course); about-turned again; saluted
again and said, 'Sir.' The old horror didn't even apologise but
stumped away over the muddy shingle. I watched the departure
through my quizzer until he was as small as a mosquito. I rehearsed
to myself Hamlet's lines to Polonius, regarding the actors; 'Let them
be well used; for they are the abstract and brief chronicles of the time.
After your death, you were better have a bad epitaph, than their ill
report while you lived.' Many years later, when making a sequence
in the film *Kind Hearts and Coronets*, in which I had to play a senior
officer going down on the bridge of his ship, my mind jumped back
to that cold morning near Inveraray. I am ashamed to say it now,
but I had my little revenge and it tasted sweet.

Job promotion in the services in 1939–45 was, of necessity, swift:
after three months or less, as First Lieutenant of TLC 24, I found
myself crossing the Atlantic, in comparative luxury, aboard the
Queen Mary, to take command, in the USA, of an LCI(L).

The *Queen Mary* sailed from the Firth of Clyde, shrouded in mist
and great secrecy. Her course was an elaborate zig-zag, to avoid
possible submarine packs, so we had days of near-Arctic conditions,
followed by days with flying-fish in sub-tropical seas, and then back
to the North again. The only near-disaster was on the morning I was
detailed as an extra look-out on the bridge. As I went on watch the

officer of the watch said to me, 'We're missing a Sunderland, out of Iceland. She should have rendezvoused with us five minutes ago. As soon as you spot her, give a shout.' I sauntered out on to the splendid wings of the bridge, which were so shaped that you felt no wind in spite of our great speed, and there, circling above us, was a Sunderland. 'Well, he can't have meant that one,' I thought, 'as obviously that's been there for ages.' So I didn't report it. Which was my mistake. Because that was the one they were all hooked up about. When I was questioned, a little later, about not reporting it, anyone listening might have thought I was suspected of being a German spy. If they could have foreseen the damage I was going to inflict on the USA in the next few short months, doubtless they would have felt their suspicions justified. The Sunderland was an albatross, tied round my neck until we docked in New York. It was my first visit to the USA and the New York skyline, hazy in the hot afternoon sun, was a sight which thrilled me then and has done so ever since. And then there was the excitement of seeing city lights again: we had all forgotten that for nearly four years, back home, the world had been blacked out, on land and sea; we sailed from a dark world into one that was hopping with brilliance.

It was a steaming hot September. There were probably about fifty RNVR Sub-Lieutenants who had disembarked from the *Queen Mary* and we were put up at the Barbizon Plaza Hotel. The first thing I did was to scan the theatre columns to see if there was anyone I knew playing on Broadway. I was in luck. That evening I managed to worm my way into Gladys Cooper's apartment (I barely knew her) and from that there stemmed much generous hospitality. Gladys abandoned her other guests in order to cook me bacon and eggs, being under the impression that I was battle-scarred and exhausted after some terrible Atlantic crossing. The same evening I ran in to Peggy Webster, whom I knew a little. The following morning I found at the hotel an envelope containing fifty dollars, with a note from Peggy which just read, 'I know what your pay is. It isn't enough for here. The enclosed will help for a day or two. Telephone me and I'll take you to a slap-up lunch.' Which she did. But the gloriousness of New York was short-lived on this occasion; within four days I was posted to Asbury Park, a small seaside town in New Jersey, where my job was to assist in the conversion of the Berkeley–Carteret Hotel to something resembling a British naval barracks. My LCI(L) was still being built in a shipyard on Quincy Bay, near Boston, and I was told I would probably be in New Jersey for about three weeks.

There were only two other officers and about a dozen ratings so living was easy-going, with little to do except arrange for the shifting of beds, to make dormitories, and to decline tremendously over-hospitable invitations from local ladies. They would telephone, and say something like, 'We thought we would give a party for you Britishers on Saturday night. There'll be lots of simply gorgeous girls, so send along about twenty of your handsome sailors.' It was useless pointing out that we were only a handful and that the sailors couldn't be commanded to go to a party. Down the telephone would pour further inducements, besides the implied sex. 'Each British sailor who comes will be given a red rose – you know, a Red Rose for England. And there'll be lots and lots of ice-cream.' I asked a very serious-minded stoker, who had accepted one of these kind invitations, what it had been like. 'The grub was smashing,' he said, 'but it was a bit embarrassing. There was this old bag who kept shoving a rose at me. I think she thought I was a Nancy Boy. Or maybe she was pissed.' Kind, kind ladies, who hadn't a clue about the mores of Southend, Huddersfield or Liverpool.

I had been in Asbury Park barely a fortnight when I received a frantic call from, of all people, Terence Rattigan. He was in New York, on leave from RAF bomber duties, and his play *Flare Path* was about to go into rehearsal for Gilbert Miller's production company. Peggy Webster was to direct it. There was no one available, he said, to play the juvenile; I *must* do it. When I pointed out that it would be impossible, because of naval duties, etc., Terry said that everything had been fixed already; Gilbert had approached the British Ambassador, who had contacted the Admiralty, informing them of the propaganda value of the play: the upshot was that I was to be given eight weeks' leave to do *Flare Path*, if I was willing. Well, I was willing. It would be, in any case, just as useful a war effort as shifting beds while waiting for a ship to be built. Gilbert Miller summoned me to his New York office. 'How much do you want?' he asked. I had heard, in the past, that with Gilbert you should always fly high. Tony Quayle had once lost a job because he had only asked for twenty pounds a week and Gilbert had squealed, 'I never use actors who want less than sixty.' So, as casually as I could, I said I should consider something like five hundred dollars a week as appropriate. The highest salary I had received to date had been thirty pounds. I think even Gilbert was taken aback, but he didn't quibble and generously threw in all taxes and Equity dues.

It was only a short respite: We rehearsed *Flare Path* for three weeks and then played New Haven for a week, prior to its New York opening. (The New York run lasted all of three weeks.) At the dress rehearsal in New Haven we were disturbed by seagull cries and scrabbling noises which filled the theatre and seemed to come from a ventilator shaft in the auditorium. Gilbert Miller was telephoned in New York. He turned up the next morning wearing an Alpine hat, expensive shooting-jacket with leather patches, plus-fours, woollen stockings and thick brogues. Under his arm he carried a double-barrelled shotgun. Gilbert was very stout and in this outfit looked like a rich gamekeeper. 'Where's this goddam bird?' he squeaked. When told, he inserted his gun in a small trap in the ventilator and fired. There was not only a very loud, reverberating bang, but also a great shattering crash. The glass chandelier parted from its mooring in the ceiling of the auditorium, splashing itself into a thousand pieces in the stalls. There followed a deep silence. Gilbert was well satisfied, saying, 'That's the end of that lousy bird.' The stage management spent hours picking up the bits. But Gilbert was wrong. When the curtain rose for that evening's performance, before the actors had a chance even to open their mouths, the wild gleeful squawks started all over again. The only other sound was the mother of the leading lady (Nancy Kelly) remarking loudly on my personal appearance as I came on stage, 'My, he's got big ears.'

Peggy Webster, with her gruff voice and dangling cigarette, her rich and ready laugh, together with her huge commonsense, was a joy to be with. My fellow actors, including Arthur Margetson and Nancy Kelly, were all pleasant but it was little Pixie Hardwicke, Cedric's ex-wife, to whom I most warmed. Almost nightly she and I hunted out, in the Madison Avenue area, the dottier fortune-tellers. Never a word of truth was revealed to us, or anything like a reasonable prognostication of the future, except by a Romanian woman in the Village, who used Tarot cards. She gave me what turned out to be a fairly accurate picture of the life Merula was experiencing in Sussex. The Tarot, which I had never seen before, made a disturbing impression on me, which was to revive after the war; and if, as I have already noted, I hadn't had the good impulse, in about 1950, to chuck cards, books and all to do with the Tarot, into the fire, I might well be under their baneful influence today.

New York, which can be as lonely, of course, as any great city, hands out, even more so than Paris, a generous welcome to all artists, of whatever breed. In a delightful little book by E. B. White, called *Here is New York*, the author says, 'The residents of Manhattan are to a large extent strangers who have pulled up stakes somewhere and come to town, seeking sanctuary or fulfilment or some greater or lesser grail.' I found in 1942 that, although I was disguised as a British officer, the fact that in reality I was an actor gave me entrance to a wider circle – of painters, writers, musicians, poets and sculptors – than I had ever enjoyed at home. I was particularly lucky in having been given by John Gielgud letters of introduction to Rosamund Gilder (then the editor of *Theatre Arts*) and to Ned Sheldon, the author of *Romance*. Sheldon had been struck blind and totally paralysed some years before I knew him. He was a rich man, fortunately, and sometimes held magnificent court in his penthouse overlooking Manhattan. Stretched on a hospital-like bed, his body covered by a sheet, his eyes bandaged in black velvet, he looked like a model for a Roman sarcophagus. He had been a tall man, finely-built, but now his limbs were wasting away to chalk. He had many friends in the theatre and consequently Broadway plays were often performed on his terrace, as affectionate tributes. He laughed a lot, with a deep throaty chuckle, and his hearing was alarmingly acute. To have a meal at a table near his bedside could be a little unnerving; he would suddenly ask, for instance, if you required salt, as he hadn't heard you put salt on your plate. His room was stacked high with books and gramophone records. Usually, when I visited him, he would ask me to read something from the daily papers (and while I did so he invariably fell asleep) or to put on a particular gramophone record, probably something by Schubert. He would tell me that he thought it must be, say, the fourth from the top in the third pile on the floor, right of the door. When the record had been played I suggested replacing it where I had found it, but he would say, 'No, just put it anywhere convenient, but tell me where. It's the way I exercise my memory.' He was, I think, one of the bravest men I have ever met. Privileged, talented, handsome, successful; something of a womaniser, I imagine; rather spoiled; a man who, in younger days, must have seen the world as his oyster and now found that world a place of utter darkness, robbed of all sensation. He never complained or showed any sign of bitterness, or even disappointment, but retained a vigorous interest in everyone he knew or had heard of.

The short life of *Flare Path* led me to report back for duty and I was dispatched to Boston, there to pick up my completed LCI(L) – No. 124. She was sitting neatly on the slipway in Quincy, ready to be commissioned, when a crew could be assembled, and little aware how she was going to get knocked about and finally lost, if being turned into a concrete jetty at Termoli, on the Adriatic coast of Italy, can be called final loss. While waiting for crew and First Lieutenant I was sent, as a third officer, on a trial run from Boston to Brooklyn in another LCI(L). It was a bitter winter, with snow-drifts up to sixteen feet deep and the sea, off Massachusetts, frozen in places for as far as five miles out. Cape Cod Canal was impassable for two days. We bumped into the thick, soft ice, opening up gaps a few yards long, withdrawing and then bumping again; a weary, fretful process which gradually enabled us to nose our way south. 'And Southward aye we fled.' Not that it got any warmer. When we came alongside a Brooklyn pier the ropes, like coils of crystal, were impossible to handle. A friend of mine, standing huddled on the pier, just about recognising my unshaven, puckered, yellow and purple face, shouted out, 'God save thee, Ancient Mariner, From the fiends that plague thee thus!'

It wasn't a popular greeting; particularly as I had to return to Boston straightaway, to be in command of a similar trip. No. 124 was commissioned, slid safely into the water and started her mild adventures. The first of these was to take on fresh water and diesel oil, and by some miracle we managed to get them in the right tanks. But not before I had snapped off most of the starboard stanchions and severely cracked a wooden jetty. The crew, very young and friendly, stood about, their mouths wide open with amazement, until bawled at to *do* something. But quite what anyone could do none of us knew. The only thing which occurred to me was to carry out some earlier instruction, go out into the middle of the bay and 'swing compass'. I wasn't at all sure how this was done and the results were far from satisfactory. The Americans shrugged off all our mishaps with muttered 'Bloody Limeys!' but it was only the reactions of my own crew I cared about. You didn't have to be hypersensitive to be aware of their apprehension. Crews of otherwise friendly ships, seeing us approach, would put out all their fenders and then flee in mock terror. The resounding impact, the sight of metal folding like blotting-paper, the feeble attempts to look indifferent or modest, as if it was all part of a skilful manoeuvre which had gone only slightly wrong, are still with me, after more than forty years, on nights of indigestion or when the wind is blowing great guns.

It was the swing bridge, at Newark, New York, I think, which was put out of action for twenty-four hours by the intrepid action of an LCI and then given a very tiny *coup de grâce* by me as soon as it started functioning again. By then I was growing in confidence. My first trip from Boston to New York under my own steam was not, I am happy to say, spectacular, though it reached a curious climax. Having furrowed an unpredictable course down Long Island Sound, we had just entered the East River when dense fog descended. There was no chance of mooring. Fierce notices, illuminated with flares, forbade dropping anchor in any circumstances. With the tide flowing swiftly, the fog worsening, the only possibility of avoiding a major catastrophe and also of getting a necessary night's sleep was to sidle gently in alongside a rather posh embankment, and make fast to a convenient lamp-post and park bench. This proved a great success. (A little further up-river that same night another British naval vessel successfully rammed an ammunition barge, which sank with hardly a gurgle, leaving only its name, *John D. Jefferson Jr*, just above the water.) It was a pity, I must admit, that I had miscalculated the rise and fall of the tide, which can be quite considerable in those parts. I did, of course, warn the Quartermaster to take in slack and pay out rope as necessary. No doubt he was as sleepy as the rest of us. He was certainly wide-awake, and indeed wide-eyed, when I appeared on deck at dawn. The fog had lifted; we were in the same position as before. But we had managed to dislodge the park seat, dragging it over the embankment as an anchor, and the lamp-post was bent in two, like a hairpin. Main engines were started immediately, and we slipped quietly away to our proper berth. I didn't report the incident. No doubt the rich folk, when they descended from their great apartments to walk their dogs, grumbled of vandals and racial unrest, but no word of it reached me.

The remaining days in New York were spent preparing ourselves for an Atlantic crossing. Our final loading was to be done in Norfolk, Virginia; from there we would hop over to Bermuda and then make for North Africa. So far as I was concerned, after the welcome arrival of John Bostock as First Lieutenant, all my free time in New York was taken up with constantly having goodbye parties thrown by old friends and new, such as Rosamund Gilder, Val Stavredi, Betty Parsons, Guthrie McClintic and Peggy Webster (who gave me an enormous silver flask to protect me against shrapnel and cold weather). I stocked my tiny wardroom with a few carboys of New York State wine and as many Modern Library books as could be crammed into very limited space. The Modern Library was a godsend, similar to our Everyman editions, and the prices ranged from about sixty cents to a dollar. I spent money on a few volumes of

Dickens and Jane Austen, all available Tolstoy, Dostoevsky, Proust, and Boswell; also some William James, Meredith and two or three anthologies of verse (Shakespeare and Milton I had with me anyway) and whatever I could find of Evelyn Waugh and Graham Greene. As a 'Desert Island Disc Castaway' I was well off; and yet, when I was wrecked, on New Year's Day 1944, it wasn't one of the books I had bought that I pushed into a duffel-coat pocket, but a sleazy-looking paperback thriller which I saw lying around. Loaded with wine and books, typewriters, pineapple juice and low in the water with stacks of goods for Algeria, we sailed from New York and straight into trouble. In Chesapeake Bay, across the entrance to the estuary of the James River, there was a great defence boom. Night had fallen, weather conditions were appalling, there were no navigational aids (I could spread out the excuses) and I managed to get one third of my ship straddled across the boom designed, so they thought, to stop penetration by the enemy.

We struggled off our spider's web in an hour or so, thanks to the patience of the engine-room staff and our excellent unflappable Geordie coxswain. Visibility was nil, so, having backed away from the boom, I dropped anchor. The first light of day was an alarming revelation; together with half a dozen other LCIs we had anchored in the middle of a minefield. The tide had gone down and the mines could be seen a foot below the surface, slowly swaying like sinister black balloons. I experienced something similar a year later, in the Gulf of Taranto, where our predicament was complicated by whirling waterspouts. On that occasion I was making a confident exit; on this, an extremely cautious entrance.

In Norfolk we were encouraged to camouflage our ships with paint in any style we fancied. I devised a pattern of pale blue and white rectangles, rather like a Braque. My fellow officers complained that I had made mine look like a hospital-ship and far too conspicuous; but when we were out on the ocean they equally complained that they couldn't see me. If they really couldn't see me some mornings it was largely the fault of the steering-gear, which was electrical and had a nasty habit of seizing up. For hours, on two nights running, shortly after leaving Bermuda, I found myself doing small circles in the middle of the Atlantic. In command of the squadron for our crossing to North Africa was a delightful RN Lieutenant-Commander. He had a gentle, dry wit and was a dab hand at Biblical signals. On the morning after one of my individual night manoeuvres, when I was recognised on the horizon as a pale blue spot, he flashed on his Aldis Lamp, in Morse code, 'Hebrews Chapter thirteen verse eight.' A watchkeeper was sent to the wardroom immediately for a Bible. It was a lovely sunny morning and the breeze tugged at the india paper pages, which kept sticking together. I found the place and certainly got the signal, 'Jesus Christ the same yesterday, today and forever.'

The little town of Djidjelli lies on the North African coast about a hundred and twenty miles west of Algiers. What it is like today I have no idea, but in 1943 it had a certain charm. The French, who had been in Algeria for so long, had placed a small wrought-iron bandstand in the scruffy central square; vegetables in the market always looked fresh (the meat less so) and there were a couple of excellent pâtisseries. Stately Arabs moved slowly through the heat of its dusty streets. Old gentlemen in turbans sat at rickety tables, sipping coffee, smoking hookahs, praising Allah and totally ignoring the Allied presence. Most of the British personnel around the place seemed to have found themselves 'up-homers' – little families where they took their laundry, drank mint tea, hoped for some sex, or just passed a few quiet, off-duty hours. Those of us who were less privileged, or on whom such fraternisation would be frowned, contented ourselves, when not bustling with pre-invasion activity, with bathing from the superb sandy beaches. It was an almost idyllic life, after our wearing Atlantic crossing of sixteen days. That late spring and early summer were taken up, for the most part, with exercises at sea and practice landings; and each day, when dusk fell, we scattered to various inlets or coves in the hope of avoiding detection by the occasional enemy spotter plane. A few casual bombs were dropped near us, in a half-hearted way, but there was never a concerted attack and only once was damage done. We were thought of, probably, as inexplicable or of no consequence, particularly as we never retaliated as we lay silently at our anchorages. The future might be full of apprehension but the immediate present, for me at any rate, sharing the harbour and much of my spare time with Peter Bull, was extremely pleasant. The colour of the Mediterranean, looking north with the noonday sun behind us, was a miraculous surprise every day. It was hard to remember that, so far as we were concerned, the war was to the north, with France and Greece overrun and Italy an enemy country. We had no idea of where and when the invasion would take place, but obviously it would be one of those countries, unless it happened to be Yugoslavia or Albania, which seemed unlikely. Naturally there was a lot of speculation and, as it turned out, security, which was supposed to be absolute, was not entirely inpenetrable – as Peter and I discovered almost accidentally.

How Vivien Leigh and Beatrice Lillie found out where we were (our personal whereabouts not being a matter of vital importance) I do not know, but one blustery morning the officer commanding the Djidjelli outfit received a signal which read, 'Miss Vivien Leigh and Miss B. Lillie request the presence of Lieutenants Bull and Guinness at the Garrison Theatre, Bougie, at 1400 hours this afternoon.' Bougie is halfway to Algiers. There was no available transport and the CO affected to be unimpressed by our invitation. He certainly wasn't pleased but reluctantly gave his permission, on condition that we returned before nightfall in order to take our ships out of Djidjelli harbour. We promised to do so. Dressed in our smartest white uniforms we thumbed a lift to Bougie on the back of an army lorry, arriving at the theatre at about three in the afternoon, caked in red dust. At the theatre, where the performance was almost half over, we were told we couldn't possibly be admitted without passes from the Town Major. Pleading that we were guests of the Misses Leigh and Lillie was of no avail. We were directed to the Town Major's office, about half a mile away. We found it without difficulty, but no one there. The street door was wide open, as were the doors to all other rooms. There was a droning silence, flies buzzed and papers on the notice-boards curled in the heat. Then we heard a voice down some distant passage, clearly speaking on a telephone. I recognised the voice, with its gentle emphasis, immediately. It was saying, 'You can tell Basil Dean that, if that's his attitude, we are not going to play Cairo. Repeat *not.*' There was the click of the receiver and we followed the sound. There, occupying for the afternoon the Town Major's swivel chair, was Binkie Beaumont, in navy-blue silk shirt and white cotton slacks.

Binkie, as head of the firm of H. M. Tennent, had been for many years the most influential theatre manager in Britain and was to remain so until his untimely death in 1973. It was astonishing as well as delightful to find him in a small Algerian town, conducting business on his usual lines. He accepted our sudden presence as perfectly normal, as if he had been expecting us, and very possibly he had been responsible for the signal we received from Vivien and Bea. There was nothing he could do about getting us into the theatre so late in the afternoon, but he took us backstage as soon as the curtain had fallen. (I encountered many visiting theatre friends during my stint in the Mediterranean, all of whom asked for Merula's address, saying they would write to tell her they had seen me, that I looked fit and so on, but somehow they never managed to get pen to paper. The only two who never asked, but took pains to find out where she was and *did* write, were Binkie and Emlyn Williams, neither of whom I knew very well.) Backstage, Peter and I had a happy twenty minutes with our two hostesses and Michael Wilding, who was appearing with them, until gloom set in and we began to fuss about our return journey. Vivien said she would fix it for us and went straight into bold action. She buttonholed, with all her wheedling charm, a starry-eyed Admiral. Caressing the lapels of his uniform, admiring his campaign ribbons, she suddenly asked him what he was doing for the next few hours. His eyes danced with excitement as he blushingly replied, 'Nothing!'

'Then,' Vivien went on, 'you won't be needing your car.'

'It's at your disposal, fair lady.'

'You are *too* sweet,' she said. 'You see, I have two darling friends here, and they've simply *got* to be driven back to a little place, just round the corner, called Djee-Djee. So you are going to be the dear thing you are and send them home in your car.'

The Admiral's face fell: he bowed acceptance and defeat.

'To show you how grateful I am,' Vivien went on, 'I'm going to give you a little kiss and then, perhaps, a nice big drink.'

So, to our immense relief, it was fixed and we were driven away smartly by an astounded Lieutenant-Commander. We arrived back just in time to see our ships passing the harbour wall, making for the open sea. We managed to scrounge a motor boat to ferry us out to them. I apologised profusely to my No. 1, who, as always, had taken my absence very philosophically. There was no comment from higher authority.

It must have been about a week later, on a Sunday morning, that all LCI commanding officers were summoned to a top-secret exhibition of photographs, taken from a submarine, which showed us the beaches on which we were going to land, when the time came. The security precautions were elaborate; and there was, of course, no indication of which country was to be invaded. The photographs were presented in a vastly long strip, about three inches deep, pinned on hessian screens. They had been taken through a periscope, from about a mile off-shore, and, understandably, were grainy and in places obscure. Certain areas were marked with red lettering. I was instructed to study carefully a section marked A–B, and Peter studied it with me: his ship, being anti-aircraft, was not going to land but offer protection from the sea, so his concern was not so immediate as mine. The view we gazed at was a long stretch of rather flat land with very few memorable features; however, on the stretch marked A–B, there could be seen a small, white, pretty lighthouse. Under the lighthouse, on the edge of the photograph, there was a white scribble, which looked like the number 58, or something similar. Looking at this, with total incomprehension, I whispered to Peter, 'What do you think that number represents? Something to do with the length of film exposed?' Peter suddenly looked rather pale under his rich tan.

'Let's go back on No. 124,' he said.

And we left. We didn't speak all the way back to my ship, but once we were in the cabin Peter suggested we might thumb through the two volumes of *The Mediterranean Pilot*, a vade-mecum for peace-time mariners but not always useful in our blacked-out world. In the section on the height of lighthouses we found the only one listed as being 58 feet high, with a nice little drawing of it as well. It was the lighthouse at Cape Passero, on the extreme south-eastern tip of Sicily. On that Sunday morning Peter and I knew where the invasion was to take place; information which was supposed to be known to a mere handful of Top Brass. We were shattered, I think, by the realisation that this, at last, was reality and not a dream. We never breathed a word about our discovery but when I opened my strictly sealed sailing orders, an hour after leaving Malta on the night of July 9, 1943, as instructed, I was unable to go through the antics of surprise.

About two weeks before the invasion of Sicily, a Captain RN was sent to Djidjelli to take charge of us. He stood on a wooden crate in the shade to address us; we, the officers, were lined up in the sun under the harbour wall. (Mountbatten would have been far cleverer, psychologically, and reversed the position.) I had the impression we were about to be shot. He was a tall, fine-looking man, peremptory in his manner and quite incapable of grasping the 'hostilities-only' attitude. He tried out his own brand of humour. 'I shan't bother to get to know your names,' he said, 'for in two or three weeks' time there will be a lot fewer of you to remember.' It went down very poorly indeed. Fortunately another senior officer, the late Commander Villiers, was present; I think it must have been he who reported this demoralising speech in Algiers, for the following day we were all lined up again, this time to be addressed by Vice-Admiral Sir Rhoderick McGrigor, 'Wee Mac', who was really our boss and

whom we hadn't seen before. He was tiny and charming; he soon
became very much our hero and father-figure. He made no reference
to the previous day's harangue but he did say, 'I have been watching
your exercises at sea and, in my opinion, experienced Royal Naval
officers could not have kept better station or behaved more promisingly. I have only one request to make: when the day comes and we
all go in, would you please, please, *not* eat your lunches on the
bridge.' It was exactly what was required; we were happy and
confident again and, although we expected no picnic, the impending
invasion didn't seem quite such a stomach-turning enterprise.

Nerves, I suppose, took their toll, in spite of the outward calm.
There had been a lot of talk about Italian mini-submarines and I was
prepared to see them everywhere. Sailing quietly along the coast
towards Tunisia, one of the crew reported a dark shape following
us. Could it be a sub? It was probably a porpoise but I was taking
no chances and, in panic, I ordered a depth charge to be dropped.
John Bostock asked what depth to set it at for explosion and without
hesitation, knowing nothing about it, I said, 'A hundred feet.' For
me depth charges were just oil-drums, inconveniently cluttering up
the quarter-deck, and I was quite happy to be rid of one. I rather
looked forward to what I expected would be a spectacular sight.
After much puzzlement over technicalities, and racing ahead at full
speed, it was eventually jettisoned. Nothing happened; it just went
on sinking. The porpoise, if it was a porpoise, lost interest in us. We
possessed three more charges but I decided it would be best to forget
the whole incident. When I reported the matter, I was asked by an
amused Commander what depth I had set the wretched thing at and
I told him. 'And what speed were you making?'

'Sixteen knots,' I said.

'You're lucky, aren't you? Because if it had gone off it would have
blown your arse off.'

We sailed for Sousse, carrying two hundred soldiers from the 5th
Battalion of the Black Watch, running through a plague of locusts
and little yellow flies which got into everything, including our eyes,
temporarily blinding us; and a magnificent salmon leapt across our
bows, dripping blood from a wound in its side, and followed, in the
same arc, by a swordfish. I wondered if the plagues of Egypt were
upon us and that the Angel of Destruction might be lurking round
the next headland. In a way, it nearly was. In Sousse harbour I
climbed on the binnacle in order to see better, slipped and cracked a
rib. I didn't dare go to see the doctor; too many men were suffering

from odd complaints, mostly psychosomatic. Breathing was still painful when, a few days later, we left Sousse, together with a portion of the invasion fleet, and made our way to Malta.

It was late in the afternoon of a grey, sultry day when we arrived in Malta. I hadn't seen the Grand Harbour, Valletta, since the Old Vic tour to the island in the spring of 1939. Then all had been sparkling, with great battleships and cruisers, very spick-and-span, at their huge moorings, brass-funnelled Admirals' barges speedily chuffing their way to the Customs House steps hooting shrilly, Liberty Boats full of raucous sailors, dghaisas – gaily painted red, green and white – plying for trade, bugle calls echoing from Fort St Angelo and flags flying everywhere. Now all looked dilapidated and sulky. The Navy was there in force, but grim and unlit. Valletta had suffered terribly from bombing, its honey-coloured houses sliced in half like pieces of cheese, the streets choked with rubble and the inhabitants, many living a troglodyte existence in caves, seemed scarce and very war-weary. I was to find, when I got ashore, that the splendid Opera House, where the Vic Company had played, no longer existed. The sadness and horribleness of war were self-evident. My immediate task, however, was to berth where instructed; which proved an impossibility. I was required to squeeze my craft between two others, bow on to the quay, which meant slewing my stern within about four feet of my favourite ship, the crack minelayer, HMS *Manxman*. She was beautiful, swift, and with a first-class hand-picked crew, most of whom lined their gunwale to watch, with concern, my cautious and useless endeavours. There was a rather unpleasant snapping sound: I had managed to crack the *Manxman*'s gangway. I promptly sent a signal of apology to the Captain, who replied immediately, 'Whoever told you to berth in that position is a fool. Stop. You did very well considering. Stop. Good luck. Stop. End of message.' A further signal reached me from shore telling me to berth at the far end of some muddy creek half a mile away. Darkness was falling. We reached the sloppy, garbage-strewn spot all right – it reeked of oil and refuse – but I could see no means of mooring except to an old wooden stump. There was certainly no way of getting ashore. Near the stump, standing on the muddy shore, I could see three men. It was too dark to make out how they were dressed. The crew repeatedly failed, understandably in the conditions, to secure a line ashore so I seized a loud-hailer and bawled at the three figures, 'Don't just stand there. One of you take that rope and put it round the post.' There was no movement so I

shouted again, 'Frightened to muddy your boots?' After some hesitation one of the men stepped forward and did what was required.
'Thank you,' I called out, in a very sarcastic tone. As he turned away
to join his companions I caught a glimpse of red tabs and a glitter of
gold. It was Lord Gort, then Governor of Malta; one of the others
was, I believe, Admiral Sir Andrew Cunningham, C-in-C Mediterranean. Who the third was I never found out. They vanished into
the darkness and I lay in my muddy creek to await events.

What we did with our brief days in Malta I cannot remember, but
I have the impression that the men were cooped up on board with
no permission to go ashore. On the afternoon of July 9, I received
and signed for a sealed envelope, which had to be put immediately
in the ship's safe, together with our sailing orders for that night. The
envelope was not to be opened until we were at sea, some ten miles
from the island. Such tremendous security precautions; but I knew
the essential contents of the envelope (other than the actual hour of
invasion) and all that could possibly be known about Cape Passero
without having visited it. The wind was rising, the barometer falling.
In spite of the hot weather everything suddenly felt damp and chilly.

It was a beastly night at sea. When we cleared Valletta harbour all
had been quiet except for the ominous whine of the rising wind;
now, an hour from Malta, the wind increased and the sea, which had
been just choppy, became unpleasantly rough, the crests of the waves
breaking into white water. Troopships, destroyers, cruisers and an
aircraft-carrier were converging from places as far apart as Alexandria
and Algiers on a position a few miles west of the southern part of
Sicily, where we were to rendezvous, and where each of the LCIs
was to embark two hundred soldiers. Getting alongside a troopship
in that wind, with the sense of urgency making for rash judgments,
was far from easy. Waves lifted and dropped us a good six feet every
time they struck. The ramps on either side of the bow – the smooth
working of which was essential in order to get the soldiers swiftly
ashore when we landed – were dislodged by the high seas and couldn't
be replaced in position. There was nothing to be done but embark
the military as best we could and, instead of being able to walk on
board, each soldier had to wait for a wave to lift us sufficiently high
and then, with gun and equipment, jump for it. It was a slow process,
one at a time and at long intervals. The whole operation took about
three quarters of an hour longer than planned. In the confusion I
never received the signal postponing the actual time of invasion by
an hour. Once we had our full complement aboard, many of whom

were already sick, and were free of the troopship, I carried out my instructions by making straight for the beach just left of Cape Passero lighthouse.

It was a trip of about eight miles, buffeting against a turbulent sea, but we made good time and I was confident of carrying out my orders to the letter. A mile offshore we encountered half a dozen other LCIs which appeared to be lost, or at least in a quandary. Knowing exactly where I was – thanks to Peter Bull, *The Mediterranean Pilot* and the time I'd had to study the coastline – I hailed one of them, in a cavalier way, and suggested it should follow me. So in we went. My ship hit Sicily very hard. We were on a narrow sandy beach, waves pounding our stern and water about four feet deep swirling round the bow. A kedge-anchor had been dropped well astern to enable us to winch ourselves off when necessary, but another ship, coming too close, managed to sever it. In no time my stern, pushed by the waves, had swung round to an unenviable angle. The soldiers crouched on deck ready to spring ashore but the ramps proved immovable. There was nothing for it but to use ropes to lower them into the surf. Wet, miserable and silent they scrambled up the beach to take up their first positions. They had a very raw deal. There was no firing or sign of opposition. It was 'first light'. Suddenly, from out at sea, there came a spectacular barrage of rockets, which landed in devastating salvoes about half a mile inland. According to my reckoning this should have happened an hour earlier; and I was puzzled. The soldiers disappeared into scrub and olive trees; our companion ships withdrew without offering to give us assistance; the ship's engines failed to shift the stern; so we just lay there at 45 degrees to the shoreline, thinking that later in the morning someone would surely come to our aid. The wind died down at dawn, the sea regained its friendly blueness and the sun appeared, blazingly. I got ashore to stroll on the sand, stretching and yawning, delighted to be alive, even on enemy territory.

There was a cry from the olive trees and then three soldiers appeared, frog-marching a little Italian corporal. The soldiers grinned but the Italian was in a great state of terror and in hysterical tears.

'A prisoner, sir,' they said.

'I don't want him,' I replied.

The little Italian broke into a stream of resentment and kept touching, very fearfully, a shoulder. He said he had been shot after having surrendered.

'Not a word of truth in it, sir,' said one of his captors. 'No one

has touched him. No one has even fired a shot. There was a bunch
of them in a shelter. They thought it was an RAF raid. We flushed
them out. They were ever so surprised. They came quietly.'

The Italian continued to insist he had been shot in the back so I
told him to take off his shirt. No wound. But there, on his shirt
sleeve, was a sleepy bee, and on his shoulder the small mark of a
sting. He was so overjoyed when this was pointed out to him that,
brushing away his tears, he attempted to embrace us all. He was
marched off, chatting happily, in a lingo the soldiers hadn't yet
mastered. All I heard them say to him, by way of conversation, was
'Listen, Iti! You-a come-a this way-a, OK?'

Later in the morning an irate Commander RN appeared, angrily
asking why I was so late in landing. I considered he was out of touch.
I pointed out that, far from being late, I considered I had been the
first to arrive. He clearly didn't believe me and muttered something
disparaging about RNVR officers.

'What did you do in civvy street, Sub?'

'I was an actor, Sir.'

The familiar question and the equally familiar twisted smile at the
answer. My temper has always been short-fused, particularly in those
days, and I suddenly saw red and gave way to a cold rage.

'An actor I was, Sir, and an RNVR officer I am. My ship was the
first to arrive here, leading others – which was not part of my orders
– and I beached at exactly the right spot at exactly the time I was told
to. And you will allow me to point out, Sir, as an actor, that in the
West End of London, if the curtain is advertised as going up at 8 pm,
it goes up at 8 pm and not an hour later; something which the Royal
Navy might learn from.'

'You'll have to get your ship out of here,' he said, rather peevishly.

'Impossible,' I said, 'without assistance. Perhaps you would be
good enough to arrange for a destroyer or tug to tow us off.' I
knew I was being impertinent, possibly risking a court martial or
reprimand, but I didn't much care. We had to wait ten days for the
destroyer, other craft having failed to shift us.

Apart from anxiety about the likely shortage of fresh water, we
had a relaxing stay at Cape Passero. There was nothing to do except
bathe and organise games on the beach. The local peasants began to
appear, very timidly, offering us, with shy smiles, a few eggs or
melons which we gratefully received. Children began to come down
to the beach and were soon persuaded to play with the crew. The
only tiresomeness was the day one of the sailors developed acute

toothache and I decided he must be got to the nearest army camp; and I didn't know where that might be. The two of us set off in what we knew must be the right direction, plodding over rough ground and very carefully, so as not to damage it, through an enormous field of beans. We spotted smoke, as if from a cook-house, and found the camp and a doctor. He dealt successfully with the tooth and then said, casually, 'How did you get here?'

'Through a bean-field,' I said.

'My God! It's a *mine*-field. We by-passed it. Practically every bean is a booby-trap. You'd better go back along the shore.'

Our walk to the camp had been about four miles; our return journey, over rocks and gulleys, was three miles longer, in the heat of the afternoon. But the sea, when we reached the ship, was clean and cool, the crew were splashing about stark naked and spirits were high. I refused to contemplate the ridiculous position in which No. 124 was lying. That evening John Bostock and I sat down to play gin-rummy. They could come and collect us when they wanted, but not too soon I hoped.

The Sicilian campaign was swift. Mussolini was overthrown on July 25 (he was shot by partisans in April 1945) and in September 1943 the Italians signed an armistice. The invasion of mainland Italy, commenced at Salerno, was quickly successful in the south but slowed down as it encountered stiff German opposition further north. Somehow I missed the landings at Salerno and Reggio; I think I must have been, by then, plying between Syracuse, Augusta and Catania on endless ferrying jobs. A similar assignment, on the east coast of Calabria, was to occupy me for much of the remainder of the year and the constant crossing of the Adriatic with supplies to the Yugoslav partisans. The Germans were still very much a force in the Balkans, although we understood they mostly appeared only by day, the nights being under partisan control.

By this time Tony Quayle, now a Major, had been dropped by parachute, carrying bags of gold to fierce Albanians in the mountains; Peter Bull, with his marines and anti-aircraft guns, was sailing up and down the Tyrrhenian Sea; Evelyn Waugh was sharpening his pen and being excessively, not to say foolhardily, brave in the Balkans; an eccentric Colonel, whom I ferried with his merry men, was busily polishing his bows and arrows ('The Hun doesn't like it, you know. I hide behind a tree, and – whizz – Jerry bites the dust, not knowing what has hit him') and General Montgomery, standing in a jeep, was distributing cigarettes to hundreds of clutching hands,

playing to the gallery with his sharp order, 'These are not for the
officers – only for the men.' Back at home rehearsals were well under
way for the ENSA concerts which were to be sent out to entertain
us.

Entertainment was not entirely lacking. A fellow-officer who was
to become a good friend, Malcolm Harvey, discovered that the
Brindisi Amateur Operatic Society, having swiftly recovered from
the shock of defeat, was to give a performance of *Madam Butterfly*
and persuaded me to accompany him. Malcolm was musically appreciative, flamingly red-bearded and full of zest for life. Apart from
his beard we were alarmingly conspicuous as the only two present
wearing British uniforms in the tiny, gilded, dusty and crowded
theatre. The orchestra was a local brass band, the Pinkerton enormously fat and squat – he came out splendidly with the word 'whisky'
– and all the Japanese wore their wigs back to front. We enjoyed it
hugely. To begin with I had been slightly apprehensive that we might
be stabbed in the back or lynched; later I had the impression the
audience was rather flattered by our presence, happy to show the
barbarians from the North some Italian culture. Malcolm and I
staggered back to our ships, after too much grappa, humming – or,
in his case, singing – a variety of Puccini arias. Not up to Tito Gobbi
standards but rewarding to ourselves and astonishing to the natives.

A rather more sophisticated show which came our way, though I
cannot remember exactly where, was a production of *The Barretts of
Wimpole Street* by Guthrie McClintic, starring his wife, Katherine
Cornell. It was quite dreadful. With the exception of Kit Cornell,
who made a very statuesque Elizabeth Barrett Browning, all the
actors played down to the troops (mostly American) with the result
that the villain was hissed, the hero cheered, the heroine cat-called,
and all the other characters treated, encouragingly, as jokes. It was
good to see the McClintics again, but although we admired their
effort and courage it was vaguely dispiriting. I found I could not be
as effusive as was expected.

*

The nearest I came to death, though not through enemy action, was
on January 1, 1944, when I lost my ship. For over thirty years I kept
a copy of the report I wrote to my Squadron Commander but that
is now missing; All I have are a few scribbled notes I made after the
war. Not that many of the details have escaped my memory; and I
truly believe that time has not exaggerated them.

On December 31, 1943, I was ordered, together with LCI(L) 127, captained by Lieutenant Nick John, who was senior to me, to sail from Barletta tc the Yugoslav island of Vis, where, between us, we were to evacuate four hundred women and children. The Germans were expected to invade the island at any moment. (They never did.) We were supposed to reach Vis under cover of darkness and return to the western shore of the Adriatic before daylight. The day we set off was one of perfection; sunny, warm, windless, and the sea like a pale sheet of mother-of-pearl. I should have guessed they were ominous signs. We were to sail for the Manfredonia headland and, when dusk fell, alter course for Vis, which lay about seventy miles to the north of us. Knowing I would be up all night, I left John Bostock on watch for a couple of hours in the late afternoon while I had a nap. It was a heavy dreamless sleep I fell into until just before 1800 hours, when I woke with a start, the sweat pouring off me, and frightened as I had never been since childhood. I was wide awake when, as it seemed to me, a very unpleasant voice spoke close to my ear; just one word – 'Tomorrow'. It was penetrating, gloating and undoubtedly evil. It implied that by the same time tomorrow I would be dead. Churning it over in my mind, as I have done countless times since, I am unable to dismiss it as something purely subjective. There was a clarity and intention which I couldn't mistake; and, whatever may have troubled me in my sleep, I know I was fully conscious when I had the experience. I hurried to the bridge and found Johnny Bostock as pale, under his tan, as I was. He is a very reticient man and said nothing. We altered course; Bostock went below, leaving me to gloomy thoughts and a sudden change in the atmosphere. A slight wind got up and the surface of the sea became ruffled. Within an hour it was rough and blowing hard. By the time we were within a mile of Vis a full hurricane had hit us. It would have been impossible to reach the little harbour and Lieutenant John flashed a signal to return to Manfredonia. The odd thing was that the signal came from about twenty feet above me; then I made out the dark shape of his ship, going in the opposite direction to mine, riding the crest of a giant wave. That was the last I saw of him for a few weeks. I managed to turn, with waves now about thirty feet high toppling around us and lashed by a wind which was later estimated to have reached a hundred and twenty miles an hour. I was faced in the stinging darkness by a world which seemed to have turned to scudding white. The Adriatic is shallow and when hit by a storm the sea throws itself up in confused pinnacles of water, each seemingly with a life of its own. The hurricane was from the south-east, roaring across the open sea from Egypt and Libya. I tried to keep it close on my port bow, attempting to make some headway south, but the ship was thrown about like a cork and any progress or direction proved very haphazard.

The phenomenon of St Elmo's Light, something none of us had seen before, seized the ship. This is an electrical discharge, occasionally caused by storms, which appears as ribbons of blue fluorescent light about the thickness of a thumb, and crackles its way along the edges of things, dividing itself but never diminishing in intensity or substance and giving off a powerful smell of ozone. With us, St Elmo started at the bow and progressed along every guard-rail and wire until the whole ship was lit up like some dizzying fairground side-show. It was beautiful and strangely comforting, like Aurora Borealis. One of the crew, a small Glaswegian, made himself heard over the wind as we clung grimly to the rail on the bridge, bawling in my ear, 'Is it spirits?' I think we all felt the end must be on us at any moment. A stoker's head appeared for a flash, took one look, said 'Oh, Christ!' and rapidly withdrew below.

With first light the full horror of the sea met our eyes and in my despair I almost felt resigned. Nothing original raced through my head; just wife and small son followed by son and wife – how would they manage in the future? – was it disgraceful to capsize in these circumstances? – would anyone ever know? – would we be classified as 'lost presumed drowned'? – why on earth was I wearing a collar and tie? – was the crew cursing me as an incompetent fool? – was it worth pouring out more oil? – should we sing 'Eternal Father, strong to save'? – would Merula be saddled with looking after my mother? – No, there wouldn't be anything like enough money for that; only her widow's pension. The grey, white and yellow towers of water continued to swish down on us, the spray reducing visibility to about a hundred yards or so. The island of Pianosa must have been passed on our port side but none of us had a glimpse of it. Then suddenly, immediately ahead of us, there was a tumult of white water; great waves virtually passing over the little group of low islands called Tremeti. By rights I should have turned hard to starboard and run with the sea but in my panic, and unsure how far we might be into the middle of the islands, I gave the order to put the helm hard to port and, with engines full out, we battled head on into the storm. It must have taken us an hour to work our way past that immediate danger. Once that was cleared, with tiredness and relief I decided to abandon all idea of trying to reach Manfredonia, and to run, with sea and wind almost dead astern, for the small port of Termoli further up the Italian coast. I didn't give a thought to where the Allied front line might be, and even if I had, I doubt if I would have cared. In fact it turned out that the Germans were just ten miles north of Termoli, and retreating.

At three in the afternoon I signalled Termoli for permission to enter harbour; purely a formality as far as I was concerned. Back came a message saying, 'Anchor off until further notice.' There was no question of anchoring off – the sea had carried away the anchor, and in any case no anchor short of a battleship's could have held us. I came to a swift conclusion that everyone on shore was insane, that their absurd signal was to be ignored and it was up to me to save my ship. We wallowed through the harbour entrance, followed by a monstrous wave which deposited us firmly on rocks astern of an abandoned tank landing craft. We lay there, at an absurd angle, buffeted by waves within the harbour. The ship was clearly a wreck but no one had been hurt. Orders were given for the crew to scramble ashore. It was all very orderly and quiet. They were a good lot. Private possessions, little gifts from home, picked up in North Africa, Malta or Sicily, were carried off as if moving house. I stood in the cabin, exhausted and wet, thinking it would be sensible to take a book with me. There were plenty to choose from. No, not Dickens, or Tolstoy, or the Bible. On the deck lay a paperback thriller. I pocketed that and said goodbye to LCI(L) 124.

The storm took three days to blow out. Aircraft on the mainland had been overturned, twelve fishing boats were reported missing and a storm-battered destroyer limped back to Malta for repairs. Bostock and I parted company, the crew was dispersed and, after a few days, I was flown back to Malta. It was decided there would be no court of enquiry. I was given two weeks' leave, some of which I spent with my old friends Kay and Ella Warren at their little house set in the walls of beautiful Mdina, in the centre of the island, before taking up an office job until another command could be found for me. Nick John and I rented a tiny, dilapidated house in Sliema for ten shillings a week, where we entertained, when we could, offering omelettes made from eggs which cost half-a-crown each, and our ration of gin. We lived there, escaping the noise and turmoil of the officers' mess, for over a month.

Finding a handful of actors, some of whom I knew, visiting Malta with a domestic comedy, we entertained them too. Eggs and gin disappeared quickly. One actor said he couldn't possibly stay in his slovenly hotel and asked us to accommodate him. He took one look at the house and decided he would be better off in his hotel after all. I began to go off actors. Strangely enough I didn't even envy them or their cosseting.

Before I was given command of LCI(L) 272 I was sent by the Squadron Commander, the admirable and very likeable Commander Sargent, RNR, to Algiers, to investigate, in absolute secrecy, what was suspected of being a case of account-fiddling and the selling, on the black market, of ships' stores. It was expected I would be there for only a few days; if anyone enquired what I was up to I was to say I was on leave. I am no George Smiley; my grasp of paperwork is minimal and I could make nothing of the documents shown me in the Naval accounts department. Unable to spot anything at which I could point an accusing finger, I prepared to return to Malta. It was unfortunate that, as I was leaving the building, a rather fussed Admiral waylaid me, wanting to know who I was, what I was doing and where I was going. I told him I was just finishing a spell of leave and was on my way back to Malta to rejoin my Squadron. 'Oh, no you're not,' he said. 'I need an officer. Some damn fool RNVR fellow has cracked up and poured a bottle of Lysol over himself. You will take over his command. It's an LCT There's no First Lieutenant and it's in a filthy condition. See to it.' I protested vigorously but he walked away. I sent a signal to Commander Sargent telling him I had been abducted and all but raped, and then went in search of the filthy ship. And it *was* filthy; with a demoralised, scruffy crew. After a few wretched, stifling hot days, orders came for me to take the beastly thing to Messina, in north-east Sicily. We chugged along like a floating refuse skip, angry and miserable, though I was cheered by the sight of a school of happy whales and hundreds of turtles. We sailed under the enchanting Lipari Islands, and on arrival at Messina rescue was at hand – a welcome signal to return to Malta forthwith to take over LCI(L) 272.

I never managed to feel quite the same affection for my new ship as I had for 124. She was spick and span, had a charming, very tall Canadian as First Lieutenant (John Keys) but we had not seen each other through the same teething troubles. Until my arrival she had been under the command of a dapper Canadian who was greatly given to smart dark glasses and expensive cameras. He was withdrawn, I think, for reasons of health. No one could explain the bullet marks round the bridge or why the White Ensign was in ribbons, the crew denying knowledge of any enemy action. Keys would only shrug and smile. All was clean and comfortable and I settled down to a life which was to consist, for the most part, in ferrying stores to the Yugoslav partisans and bringing back to Italy their wounded or battle-weary.

Dubrovnik, beautiful and quiet, was delightful to visit and in the early days we always received a friendly welcome, although the Yugoslavs couldn't resist shooting at us whenever we approached the harbour. The shooting, happily, was wildly inaccurate. Each time I protested to the very youthful Commissar and explained the look of our flag, but nothing much penetrated his skull. On one occasion some of the crew were invited to a dance, which had been arranged by British soldiers garrisoned there. They returned on board in the early hours of the morning, only partially satisfied. 'How was the local talent?' I asked the coxswain and received a graphic reply.

'Well,' he said, 'it was like this. There was this smashing girl, real nice-looking, but dressed as a Tommy, see. We got on all right, and I thought she had interesting boobs, so I put my hand on them. She didn't like that. Besides, they weren't boobs at all – they were Mills bombs. I might easily have pulled a pin out and then – whoosh!' I don't think he cast an eye ashore after that. Our visits became obviously less welcome. On Christmas Day we arrived, the ship dressed over-all with flying bunting (and still shot at), to find coils of barbed-wire cutting off the exit from the quay. We unloaded crates of butter, cheese, blankets and boots; all marked as gifts from the UK or USA. Partisan youths arrived immediately with pots of red paint and proceeded to substitute for our markings, 'From USSR', before loading the stuff on to lorries and driving it through the town to organised cheers.

Another time I put 272 alongside a small Russian merchantman in the harbour. The Russian ship turned out to be manned entirely by bulky women with incipient moustaches. The Russian ladies made signs at us, with a lot of mimed puffing and blowing, that they wanted cigarettes. Some of our crew were impressed by our Allies sending women to sea and expressed the wish to hand over their next month's supply, and although I was reluctant to comply I was touched by their generosity and weakly gave in. A few cartons were handed over the side. The cigarettes were in cardboard packets, which seemed to puzzle the Russians. At first the ladies pushed and pulled at the packets, not very intelligently, and then tore them in half, destroying the cigarettes. In their frustration and rage they pelted our

chaps with the remains or threw them contemptuously over the side.
If they had had cutlasses I believe they might have boarded us. Main
engines were started and we quickly slipped astern, seeking refuge
at another berth, safely out of reach of such alarming bedfellows.

The fall of Naples, Anzio (which we visited only once, fleetingly),
the fall of Rome – followed two days later by the Normandy landings
– were all taken into our awareness, almost casually. 272 was sent to
Naples for her engines to be overhauled and we arrived in the bay
just after Vesuvius had erupted violently. For a mile or so out the sea
was covered, several inches deep, with light, floating pumice dust,
as if giant tins of Johnson's Baby Powder had been emptied on land
and sea. The air was chokingly difficult to breathe and, the ship's
intakes and exhausts became partially clogged. Instead of being laid
up for a few days we were put in dock for three weeks, so half the
crew were sent on local leave. I remained on board with nothing to
do but suffer dockyard noises – welding, hammering, scraping – and
swelter in the heat.

A fellow CO whose ship was a short way up the coast, at Pozzuoli,
took pity on me and suggested I should spend a weekend with him
in pleasanter surroundings; an invitation I happily accepted. (Sophia
Loren told me, many years later, that she was one of the small kids
on the waterfront at Pozzuoli who were always clustering round our
sailors, cadging chocolate.) My weekend turned out differently from
what was intended. 'We've got to go over to Corsica,' my host said.
'Only for a night. Back in a day or two. Come with us.' I hesitated
and, thinking no harm could come of it, finally agreed to go. We
sailed to the east coast of Corsica and anchored in a lovely small bay
surrounded by dwarf pine-trees growing from pure white sand almost
to the water's edge, where the swimming was superb. It all seemed
idyllic until we realised we were part of the intended invasion of
Elba. Our ignorance of this was about the only well-kept secret in
connection with Elba. I had with me a toothbrush, razor, a clean
shirt, swimming trunks and nothing else; not even a helmet (obliga-
tory) which I was to regret.

The invasion of Elba was undertaken, as a joint effort, by a force
of Americans, Free French and British in about twenty LCI(L)s. By
the time we reached them the first assault had been driven off from
its objective and there was much milling around, confusion and many
contradictory signals being flashed. The Admiral in charge, we heard,
had given a 'pep talk' a few days earlier in which he had said that the
only formidable opposition might come from a German gunboat,

lurking in a bay on the south of the island, and that this would have to be put out of action before any landing could take place. He had called for volunteers, who would be armed with knuckledusters, to slip alongside the gunboat at night, climb aboard and knock out the crew. He had referred to it as 'The Nelson Touch' and had been vociferously cheered by the Americans. Volunteers had been found, and as they clambered aboard the Germans picked them off one by one and from then on were well alerted. Phosphorus shells were used against the first ships to enter the bay, which was the cause of their withdrawal. By the time the ship I was on went in, an hour later, things were quieter and more under control, although there was still uncomfortable mortar fire from the shelter of the wooded hills. A friendly acquaintance of mine, who had been hit by phosphorus, jumped overboard and was last seen, swimming deep down, lit up like a torch.

Having no duties to perform I wondered how best to make myself useful, in an inconspicuous way. I sought, and received permission, to man one of the Oerlikon guns, which I found rather enjoyable until it jammed and I couldn't remember how to clear it. Gunnery was never my strong suit. Not liking to go below, which might look un-officer-like, I stood around like a fool, fiddling with the incomprehensible mechanism of the gun, feeling very vulnerable without a helmet. By that time I was regretting the whole operation. A weekend with Noël Coward's Mrs Louseborough Goodby would have been far preferable. By happy chance a signal reached us, before I blew myself up, instructing us to return to base.

Before leaving the bay we picked up a totally naked American Negro and a young Frenchman. The American was unscathed but in a state of shock. As I helped him over the side he accused me of stealing his wallet and started to chase me round the deck. He had to be sedated and locked in a cabin. There was no sign of a wound on the French lad either but he had been blinded, possibly for life. He was twenty-two years old, good-looking, and said that before the war he had worked on a farm near Bordeaux. My assurances, in halting schoolboy French, that he was only temporarily blinded sounded hollow to me and probably to him, but he remained calm and brave. We got both men to a hospital ship. On our return journey two ratings, being towed in a small boat by another LCI at too great a speed (a speed which was twice queried by the CO but overridden by higher authority), were drowned when their craft capsized, trapped inside it. There was no enquiry. The invasion of Elba was recorded as a success; some of us felt, however, that much had been bungled and we would have been quite happy to see a head or two roll at a court martial – an unlikely event. The heads which should have fallen were wreathed with golden oak-leaves.

Luckily, no one knew of my absence on the Elba escapade and I returned, unobtrusively, to LCI(L) 272 at Naples to take up again my old routine in the Adriatic. The Gulf of Taranto surprised me, one lowering day, with the sight of dozens of water-spouts, looking like twisting grey funnels joining sea and sky – an everyday tale of sailor-folk, no doubt, but a new experience for us, who had to sail between them while at the same time dodging uncleared Italian mines. In Taranto I stumbled across Ben Levy, the playwright, who was later to become a distinguished Socialist MP but at that time was a Lieutenant in the RNVR Earlier in the war he had served gallantly on the lower deck, during the Murmansk runs, when he could so easily have had an Admiralty job in London. Ben was an old friend of Merula's family, always chuckling and delightful, with a habit of calling everyone 'ducky'. 'Anything I can do for you, ducky?' he said as soon as we spotted each other. I quickly talked him into letting me read him an adaptation I had recently made of *The Brothers Karamazov*. He suffered it admirably. We sat in a grubby little colour-washed office, with the shutters half closed against the heat, flies buzzing, children screeching outside, while I droned on interminably. Ben was patience personified, sitting perfectly still on an upright chair, absolutely concentrated. He made a few encouraging remarks, some useful suggestions, and then asked, 'Would you like to do something rather brave, ducky?' 'Not too brave,' I replied. He was in charge, locally, of various cloak-and-dagger operations, so I was suspicious. He said I would receive some interesting orders before long. We said goodbye and on my way back to my ship I couldn't help wondering if it wasn't all a ploy, to make sure he wouldn't have to undergo another such afternoon.

A week later 272 was temporarily detached from her flotilla. Ben's sailing orders were perfectly correct, in naval parlance, but in their cryptic phrasing managed to make me laugh. By his use of words such as 'prompt', 'timing', 'cue', and, finally, 'too long', I knew he was referring not only to my forthcoming trip to the Greek mainland but also to *Karamazov*. LCI(L) 272 was to sail from Brindisi, through the Strait of Otranto, and at a point well to the south-west of Corfu (which was still occupied by German troops) turn east to pass between the small islands of Paxos and Antipaxos, then on another fifteen miles or so to a little cove, where we would be met by British soldiers and Greek Partisans, to whom we would hand over ammunition and other stores. A moonless night had been chosen; when we were close to the cove a rubber dinghy would put out, flash once with a blue light, and on our acknowledgement lead us in. Total quiet was enjoined; the crew and few soldiers we had on board were forbidden to speak, except in whispers, from the time we neared Paxos and no cigarettes were allowed on deck. There was a German gunboat south of Corfu, continually sweeping with powerful searchlights. The searchlights swung our way as we slid out from the shelter of Paxos but, by the grace of God, missed the top of our mast by a few feet. An hour later we spotted the blue flash and eased our way in to the cove. For a moment or two the darkness was complete and the silence almost unbearable. Quite suddenly the whole cove sprang into a brilliant, unexpected light, with bonfires blazing on the tiny beach and the hillsides. A handful of British soldiers stood on shore, waving, and a large group of Partisans who, grinning and boisterous, fired rifles at random into the air. They all made as much noise as possible. When I asked a languid English officer if, after all the secrecy and quiet, this was advisable he replied, 'Oh, yes. Jerry doesn't like coming out at night in these parts. Thinks he might get his throat slit. Which he would. The fires and noise will make him think there are more of us than there are.' Stores were unloaded and carried away, some on donkeys, into the darkness behind the cove: we exchanged Pongos we had on board for those on the beach. It was all a gorgeous sight; the fires reflected in the water, which was so clear that by their flames we could see the sea-bed; the smiling faces and the smell of burning pinewood was almost intoxicating. Once we were safely away we voted it the jolliest night we had spent in the Mediterranean.

Apart from a few night landings on Yugoslav islands (I was never very sure which was which and once stranded the ship, briefly, on a sandbank between Brac and Kvar) the remainder of the year was reasonably uneventful, except for one night, when, thinking I had surprised enemy soldiery, I switched a searchlight on an old woman with a nasty cough taking her wheezing goat for a walk. Back in Barletta, on a grey morning, I found a signal informing me that a relief was being sent, and when he arrived I was to take myself to Naples for shipment back to the UK. I counted the days. After two and a half years away from home, I was on my way.

I felt very impatient with Naples, which I had never cared for, and

was obliged to wait ten days for a troopship. Ugly little scenes took
place in the streets: a drunken British soldier overturning an old man's
barrow of fruit, ruining his stock; gangs of touts and pickpockets at
work; heavily made-up youths offering themselves or their sisters
for sale. The aftermath of defeat looked very sordid. *Faust* and *Tosca*
were on at the Opera, in tired productions. I found social comfort in
Tony Quayle and Peter Bull, both of whom I discovered to be
around. Tony was acting as ADC to an American Admiral (late of a
New York department store) who appeared to be very deferential to
anyone who had actually been to sea. Most of my afternoons I spent
at the Admiral's headquarters, Count Ciano's villa – more recently
occupied by Goering – a short distance to the north of the city. In
the villa's minuscule harbour there was a dinghy, which Tony and I
frequently took out into the bay for a swim. One afternoon Tony
told me we had to be back from our swim before four o'clock and
that I would have to disappear, as someone important was arriving
from England, sent by Churchill. We mistimed our return to the
villa; we were standing in the driveway in wet bathing shorts when
a large, black limousine drove up. A tall man got out, was saluted
by a couple of US Marines and ushered indoors. Tony was a bit
fussed by our lateness. He said he had heard that the man was tipped
as our next Prime Minister. We scampered up to a bathroom to
shower and change. While drying myself I leant out of a Gothic
window, gazing across the Bay of Naples, ruminating. Over my
shoulder I called to Tony, 'If that's a future Prime Minister of England
he must do something immediately about that droopy moustache.'
As I looked back towards Vesuvius my eye caught a face, peering
out of the next window, smiling at me from under the moustache.
It was, of course, Mr Macmillan (now Lord Stockton). I hastily
withdrew and made my exit from the villa.

It was Macmillan's Private Secretary who wrote, in the autumn of
1958, that 'the Prime Minister has it in mind to propose to Her
Majesty' that I should receive a knighthood – 'if acceptable.' That
was to be in the New Year's Honours List of 1959. Mr Macmillan
cannot possibly have recalled the pink face from the next-door
bathroom window, but the moustache had been trimmed a little.

While we were in Naples I happened to mention to Tony Quayle
that Peter Bull was in the city. He barely knew Peter but generously
suggested that I should invite him to dinner with the American
Admiral at the Ciano/Goering villa. There were no other guests, the
Admiral was quiet, shy and courteous, but I am afraid that cannot

be said for Peter, or indeed myself, after we had had a drink or two
or three. I could tell at once that Tony had not greatly taken to Peter
and his dislike intensified as the evening progressed. The dining table
was immensely long and the Admiral sat at one end, Tony at the
other, while Peter and I faced each other in the middle, both in a
state of near giggles. Conversation was far from easy. Very soon
Peter discovered our chairs were on large swift castors and when the
Admiral made a remark which he didn't quite catch he gave his chair
a push and arrived, as if on skates, at the astonished Admiral's side.
I slid my way rapidly up to Tony; then we reversed positions. Tony
was furious – we were letting down the side, being vulgarly British,
etc., etc. – but he said nothing and held his fire.

It was a lovely balmy night and when dinner was over (much to
the relief of our hosts) Tony suggested Peter and I might like a stroll
in the garden, adding, 'I don't think you've ever seen the chapel.'
We followed him out rather drunkenly – the Admiral excused himself,
saying he had paper-work to do – and we staggered around gravel
paths under olive trees and cypresses until we reached the chapel,
which I had never previously noticed. It was a small Gothic construc-
tion with a flight of about five wooden steps leading up to a large,
closed, oaken door with iron hinges and lock. 'Half a minute,' Tony
said, 'I've forgotten the key. Oh, Peter, just try the door, will you?
Give it a push.' Peter mounted the steps and the third one gave way
under him, working a mechanism which violently threw open the
door and caused a giant, red-haired monk to loom out. Peter screamed
and nearly fainted and I sobered up on the spot. Apparently the chapel
was a folly which had been constructed by Goering to scare Fräulein
guests, who would automatically collapse on his ample bosom. By
the time we got back to the villa, steady, pale and sober, the Admiral
had retired to bed. Tony, obviously chuffed with the success of his
revenge on our bad manners, said good-night cheerily enough and
dispatched us back to Naples in a jeep.

*

Liverpool was my English port of arrival and, at the Adelphi Hotel,
Judy and Tony Guthrie were waiting to greet me. After a warm
welcome they quickly became rather cool and censorious, in the way
they could. Judy said, 'You have become very grand and veddy
Briddish. I suppose it is your officer's uniform.' They couldn't
disguise their disapproval of an actor they had once known as a 'bit'
player putting on what they considered 'airs'. They didn't realise I

had grown up a little. We spent an uncomfortable hour or two together before I caught the train to London, to meet Merula.

We met at Martita Hunt's flat in Upper Wimpole Street where, in the past, we had so often talked late into the night, planned The Actors' Company, had delicious meals and drunk fine wines. Merula was wearing her new, cherry-coloured woollen suit – a pleasing extravagance that had used up all her clothing coupons – and I think we were both somewhat astonished at each other. For all our joy in meeting, there was a nervous sense of strain. It took several days to get adjusted. I had over-glamourised England while away, was shocked by the drabness that had overtaken London, and had failed to imagine the privations people were still suffering. We spent a night in a gloomy hotel before making our way to the country. Air-raid sirens, which I hadn't heard for a very long time, seemed more alarming than anything experienced at Sicily or Elba.

Merula and Matthew had been living, with her sister-in-law, for a year in a farm cottage not far from Horsham, and that is where we went. Lovely country smells, bird-song and green fields abounded; but, although the collapse of Germany was imminent, the atom bombs were not to fall on Hiroshima and Nagasaki for over another three months. After four weeks' leave I took up desultory duties at Southampton, from where I made a couple of trips across the Channel in a borrowed LCT but did no damage. The theatre seemed remote and I hardly dared think if I would ever get work again. Then, a month before I was demobilised, a telegram reached me asking my availability to play Herbert Pocket in a film to be made of *Great Expectations*. My CO at Southampton, the genial and sympathetic Tom Sharpe, said, 'Of course you must do it. I'll cover for you until you are demobbed.' So, after a film test for David Lean, I embarked on a new career, in an unfamiliar world, but still wearing His Majesty's uniform.

CHAPTER TEN

Tall as a Crane

She was immensely tall, although slightly stooped, and in her early fifties when I first met her properly at the beginning of the war. The long, oval face was chalk-white, the mouth small, thin and straight, the arched eyebrows like faint pencil lines querying the tiny eyes. She was nothing if not striking to look at, but from top to toe the portrait was bizarre; on her head was a high black and gold turban and, in spite of it being a warm summer day, she wore a black Astrakhan coat which came to her knees, and floating under that a blue something in embroidered silk, which gave way to a black skirt which reached the ground, and from under that peeped two long sharply-pointed patent-leather shoes. The whole façade was clamped together by what appeared to be a large, bluey-green, gilded enamel saucer but was in fact a great tangle of gold and jade. The thin long hands were weighed down with splendid aquamarines. She rose, with great courtesy, from an upright chair in the front parlour of the Sesame and Imperial Pioneer Ladies Club in Grosvenor Street and gave me two or three fingers to feel. She also offered me a glass of sherry, which I declined, before asking, 'Who is your favourite poet?' The voice seemed to come from the back of her throat but was light, rather high-pitched, as individual as her clothes, and pleasing.

'I don't think,' I said warily and pompously, 'that any of the tremendously great could ever be my *favourite*; I need to live on rather cosier terms than the really great permit. Off the top of my head, and just for today, I'd say my favourite poet is Herrick.'

Her lips pursed with a prim smile; she inclined her head with what I took to be qualified approval and said, 'Let us go in to luncheon. Then we shall discuss your beloved Herrick.'

Had she expected me to say Edith Sitwell was my favourite poet? I wondered; and, oh God, I simply couldn't remember a line of Herrick, except –

> A careless shoe-string, in whose tie
> I see a wild civility.

Turban, Astrakhan and glinting aquamarines led me in stately
fashion to the dining-room, where Edith was greeted as if she were
a mediaeval royal personage stepping out of a Book of Hours. Elderly
Pioneer ladies were sitting at small individual tables, for the most
part, but a few were entertaining gentlemen friends with quiet
conviviality.

'Miss Sitwell,' I whispered, 'there is a lady bowing to you.' She
glanced round at a little lady who had half risen from her seat. 'Pay
no attention,' she warned me. 'She wrote "A Little Grey Home in
the West". Oh, how they plague me!'

We were ushered to a round table in a window embrasure flooded
with sunlight. As we sat down it struck me she was being very careful
not to get off balance; the saucer of jade must have weighed like a
small tombstone on her breast. She screwed up her eyes against the
brightness of everything and clapped her hands imperiously; an old
waitress appeared immediately.

'Miss Sitwell?'

'Gladys, there is too much sunlight. Please pull down the blinds.'
Gladys, only too delighted to obey the commands of someone who
so charmed her, rushed to draw down all the blinds in the room.
They were navy-blue and the room was plunged into semi-darkness;
the other guests, astonished, bent their heads closer to their plates to
find their food, but none complained.

'Herrick!' said Edith, and a troubled thought struck her; there was
a slight but angry bumping noise coming from behind our blind. 'Is
that a bluebottle I hear?'

'I think it is. Behind the blind.'

'They *know* I can't bear bluebottles.' And she clapped her hands
again.

'Miss Sitwell?'

'Gladys, there is a bluebottle. *Please* get rid of it – it is a tremendous
bore.'

Gladys got under the blind and manfully fought the fly; Edith
collapsed backwards, from the weight of her jade, and appeared to
be in a dead faint; I rose and thought that perhaps I ought to flick
cold water at her but hovered indecisively, and 'A Little Grey Home
in the West' put down her napkin with the air of someone on the
way to help, which I knew would be disastrous if Edith ever opened
her eyes. I waved a water-jug towards 'Home in the West' and shook
my head violently, which she took as a threatening gesture and
subsided, biting with anxiety on her napkin. All eating and conver-

sation in the dining-room ceased; forks were poised with dangling 'spam' halfway to open mouths. Gladys to the rescue. Emerging from behind the blind she shouted in Edith's ear, 'The bluebottle has gone, Miss Sitwell.' Edith's eyes opened, and with a great effort she swung herself into an upright position. She made no reference to the incident except to incline her head graciously towards Gladys; she looked enormously surprised to see me standing, holding a water-jug in a menacing way. 'Help yourself to wine,' she said. 'Now, Herrick!'

The invitation to lunch had come, to my excitement and alarm, after a very brief exchange when I had written to thank her for a book she had sent me. The only time I had met her, very briefly, was when she and her brother Osbert had come backstage to see me during a performance of *Great Expectations* during the winter of 1939–40. This was the first of a few lunches and teas (and one terrifying supper) to which I was bidden at the Sesame Club, and I think it was the only time I was invited on my own. She was hard pressed financially but the generosity of her entertaining was lavish; good food and fine wine were always carefully thought out, and sometimes we sat down as many as eight or ten to table. Usually the guests were, to my mind, glamorous: Kenneth Clark and his wife, Arthur Waley, Beryl de Zoete, Stephen and Natasha Spender, Dylan and Caitlin Thomas, William Plomer, Evelyn Waugh, Fr Philip Caraman and, on one occasion, the dreaded Somerset Maugham.

'There are only three people in the world who terrify me,' Edith once confided, 'and I am very fond of them. Aldous Huxley, Evelyn Waugh and Willie Maugham.' Huxley, whom I met twice in California and once in London, I found easy and delightful, Waugh (whom I got to know a little and lunched or dined with two or three times) was always kindness itself to me, and very dear and funny anyway, but Maugham, I must admit, slightly turned my stomach the only time I encountered him.

At most of her lunches Edith behaved with a grave courtesy, like a Plantagenet Queen, keeping a concerned eye on the welfare of her villeins below the salt. Conversation was inclined to be *sotto voce* and rarefied, sometimes quietly bitchy, with suppressed smiles and knowing looks, and occasionally came to a stop when great Papal pronouncements fell from Edith's lips like acid honey. ('Virginia Woolf's writing is no more than glamorous knitting; I believe she must have a pattern-book' or 'Beethoven is the world's greatest bore' or, in more generous mood, to engage my interest as an actor, 'Donald Wolfit's Macbeth, you will agree, is *transcendental*.') What-

ever statements Edith made, even outrageous ones, they were received with total acquiescence, and it took me no time to realise that,
being socially out of my depth, *lèse-majesté* was easily committed
and that safety lay in silence. It struck me that all her guests, including
myself took her at her own value – the Great Poet and heiress to
Plantagenet blood. Flattery was sometimes delivered, like a Shakespearean messenger, on the knee; on one occasion, when the ladies
had retired to powder their noses after lunch, Merula witnessed just
that – a grand lady kneeling to an enthroned Edith (on a chair, of
course) and kissing the aquamarines. Others followed suit, but not,
I am glad to say, my wife. In any case Merula, claiming descent, on
her mother's side of the family, from Hereward the Wake was treated
by Edith as a sort of cousin, at a vast number of removes, so Danegeld
was not exacted in her case.

I first heard of the Sitwells when still a schoolboy and must have
looked at *Gold Coast Customs* in someone's house. Its frightening
imagery was very different from Scott's *Marmion*, and when I discovered *Façade* I said goodbye for ever to Longfellow, Newbolt and
Swinburne. Until T. S. Eliot was to come my way *Façade*, with its
brilliance, wit and absurdity revealed a world I longed to inhabit.
For a whole term my catch-phrases were:

> A word stung him like a mosquito,
> For what they hear they repeat

and:

> When Sir Beelzebub called for his syllabub
> In the hotel in hell

and:

> – out went the candle,
> From dark Coramandel rolling on

and, when in mock rage:

> In a room of the palace
> Black Mrs Behemoth
> Gave way to wroth
> And the wildest malice.

As far as I know there was no gramophone record of the *Façade* poems then, so I was groping in the dark and missing much, but the rhythms were so insistent and varied that I caught, I believe, some of the intention. My lugubrious recitation of 'The Dream of Eugene Aram' – recited by Henry Irving in a way which made strong men pass out but which in my hands only reduced audiences to giggles – gave way to finger-snapping jazz when I attempted to do 'When Don Pasquito', etc., something I was to learn which could only be executed perfectly by Constant Lambert. Edith herself failed dismally as an executant. Much of her later work, particularly during the war years, I found moving and stimulating; then, after her death in 1964, it all seemed rather forlorn or even tiresome. From that time until quite recently I have neglected to re-read anything she wrote; but looking through her *Collected Poems* some months ago I was gripped anew by her brilliance and a profundity I hadn't recognised previously. 'Still Falls the Rain' and 'How Many Heavens' strike me as being very fine indeed.

In the summer of 1940 Edith invited me to Weston Hall, in Northamptonshire, where I would be the guest of Sacheverell Sitwell, whom I hadn't met, and his wife Georgia. It was beautiful weather and the only clouds on the horizon were angry letters, usually addressed to the *New Statesman and Nation*, and left by Edith for posting on the hall table. Mrs Sitwell (as she then was) would glance anxiously at the addresses. 'Perhaps we could ask Mr Guinness to post these in London,' she would say, adding later for my ear alone, 'There is no hurry about those letters, you understand: it wouldn't matter if they *never* reach their destination.' And she gave me a compelling conspiratorial smile.

Curiously enough I remember little of my brief stay, but I do remember Edith losing herself on the gravel driveway in front of the house. After lunch on the Sunday my hosts asked me which I would prefer to do – prune roses or pick raspberries. Raspberry-picking sounded safer so into the canes we went, Edith saying she would follow later. Half an hour went by and there was no sign of her. 'Oh, do go and look for Edith,' said Mrs Sitwell, 'she's inclined to wander off so.' I didn't have to look far. Moving in small circles on the space before the house was Edith in a vast, conical, straw hat which covered her entire face except for mouth and chin. She couldn't possibly see where she was, her vision being restricted to a small segment which included her feet and a yard or two of gravel.

'I am lost,' came a solemn but uncomplaining voice from under the hat. I led her to the raspberry canes; she could see no raspberries. After a few minutes the pointed top of her hat got caught in the netting and another rescue operation began. I took her and her empty basket back to the house, where she announced she was exhausted and retired to her room, to draft, no doubt, yet another vitriolic letter to the editor of some magazine.

That evening, when dinner ended, Sacheverell Sitwell passed me a handsome silver bowl heaped high with what looked like purplish-black cloves. 'George IV's snuff,' he said. 'Do try it.' I sniffed up a grain which lodged near my adenoids for several hours. We sat in a darkening study under the shadow of the vast painted trumpet of a wind-up gramophone. Something by Berlioz was put on the machine and while the others listened with intense concentration I tried to snort discreetly in an effort to dislodge King George IV.

Later in the year Edith persuaded Osbert to invite Merula and me to Renishaw Hall for a weekend. I was on tour with Robert Ardrey's *Thunder Rock* and we were at Leeds, which was not too far away. We had Matthew with us, still a baby in a carry-cot, and strict instructions were given us that Osbert must not be told of his presence in the house as babies made him feel ill. Matthew was smuggled into Renishaw and carried upstairs like a basket of dirty linen. By day, if the weather was fine, he was to be deposited in the walled garden, far from earshot of Osbert's study windows, and on paths Osbert was unlikely to take if he strolled out to gaze, past the statuary, to the slag heaps and dark Satanic mills in the near distance. David Horner, Osbert's other guest, was let in to the awful secret of what was in the basket. I began to think we were shifting a changeling around, but all worked well until dinner time.

There was no electricity at Renishaw so life at night was spent in the leaping shadows made by candle flames or under the hiss of great standard oil lamps. The house seemed vast and very dark; and at dinner there was much talk of a ghost who appeared periodically on the staircase disguised as a piece of black lace. By the time we reached cheese and fruit (delicious strawberry-vine grapes from the hot house) Merula and I were already jittery. Robins, the elderly butler-cum-factotum of the household, entered the dining-room and whispered to Merula, 'Young Master Guinness is in distress: he is screaming.' Osbert looked mildly surprised, but Edith's next remark was not reassuring. 'Nothing to worry about, my dear. I expect the baboon has been looking at him.' Without waiting to excuse herself Merula threw down her napkin and sped from the room and, crashing through the darkness of the hall, brushing aside any spectral black lace that might have been floating around, flew up the stairs. Edith explained, 'She is an old maid, quite harmless and full of curiosity.' In that household, I thought, it was just possible that baboons might be employed as maids and I was not entirely reassured when Merula returned to the room. 'She does *look* like a baboon, doesn't she?' Edith asked. Merula's 'Yes' was very firm. Osbert took Matthew's presence well and appeared not to resent the deception. 'I assure you I do not mind in the least,' he said with charm, 'so long as you will excuse me from looking at him.' The conversation turned to more frivolous things as we withdrew to the drawing-room, where Edith picked up her knitting, plying a collection of enormously long needles as she worked her way round the heel of a sea-boot stocking.

The Sitwell establishments were, I think, the only places we stayed in during the war where we were not expected to surrender our ration cards for little squares to be cut out, representing an ounce of butter, sugar, jam or meat.

During my time in uniform Edith wrote to me regularly; letters of two or three pages of affectionate scrawl which often contained a copy of a new poem and always included a diatribe about 'bores' who were plaguing her or monsters who dared to visit her with sniffling colds. Unfortunately, due to sea-going operations and the frequent changes of address ashore, most of these have been lost. And stupidly I never kept a long telegram from her, received at the end of July 1955, telling me she was to be reconciled to the Roman Catholic Church on August 4 and bidding me to the ceremony, with lunch afterwards at the Sesame Club.

August 4 turned out to be a hot, sunny day and when dressing to go to London I was perplexed as to what to wear. Eventually I decided that my navy-blue hopsack was suitably formal for the occasion but looked too severe with a black or grey tie; so I sported a bright blue tie, which I considered more in keeping for what I assumed was a joyous event, even though I didn't share Edith's faith. As things turned out I believe I struck the right note. With the exception of Evelyn Waugh, who was to be Edith's godfather, all the other men were dressed as for a funeral. Evelyn wore a loud black and white dog-tooth tweed suit, a red tie, and a boater from which streamed red and blue ribbons.

Farm Street Church was empty when I arrived but I was soon joined by Evelyn Waugh, whom I hadn't met before, and shortly afterwards by an elderly foreign lady, whose name I never caught

even when she barked it at us, who walked unsteadily with the aid
of two sticks. Her bare arms were encased in metal bangles which
gave the impression that she was some ancient Persian warrior.
Getting herself on to a rather complicated seat, half prie-dieu and half
collapsible deckchair, she entangled herself in the mechanism; the
sticks slid from under her, the chair heaped itself on the floor and all
the bangles rolled down her arms and sticks and propelled themselves
in every direction around the church. 'My jewels!' she cried aloud.
'Please to bring back my jewels!' Waugh and I put her to rights as
best we could and then, on all fours, wriggled our way under pews
and past candle sconces retrieving everything round and glittering.
'How many "jewels" were you wearing?' he asked. 'Seventy,' she
said. 'What nationality?' he whispered to me. 'Russian, at a guess,' I
said, sliding on my stomach under a pew and dirtying my smart suit.
'Or Rumanian,' he said. 'She crossed herself backwards. She *may* be
a Maronite Christian, in which case beware.' We both got barely
controllable hysterics. The bangles having been collected I counted
them into her hands; she looked suspiciously at us as if we might
have pocketed a few. 'Is that all?' she asked. 'Sixty-eight,' I said, and
Evelyn added, 'You are still wearing two.' At that moment the organ
struck a deep note and the other witnesses arrived, self-conscious and
gloomy in their mourning attire. Then up the aisle, swathed in black
silk, Edith made her stately entrance. About three years later *Time
Magazine* attributed to me, wrongly, a description of the ceremony
in which I was alleged to have described Edith being carried through
the church dressed in white lace and lying on a satin cushion. Of the
outcome of that – later.

Edith was received into the Church by Fr Philip Caraman, SJ, who
had instructed her, and in time was to become a loving friend of
mine. Lunch was a splendid affair at a long table in the dining-room
of the Sesame Club, Edith presiding like a bride in black and Fr
Caraman frequently casting his eyes heavenwards as if in ecstacy.
The lady in bangles demanded hard liquor, but was persuaded by
Evelyn to stick to the freely-flowing white wine. 'We couldn't face
another disaster from that quarter,' he said afterwards. A Portuguese
poet, whom I was to meet again briefly, on the publication of
Time Magazine's article, looked a little peevishly atheistic; the rest of
us were all somewhat bemused. Would we have to drink the Pope's
health? If Edith died on the spot would she go straight to heaven?
And should that be a case for ecclesiastical rejoicing or worldly
and artistic distress? The wine continued to be poured well on

Noël Coward with
Alec and Merula
Guinness

Ernest Hemingway

Ernie Kovacs in *Our Man in Havana*

Ralph Richardson

John Gielgud

Laurence Olivier

Pope Pius XII with Alec and
Merula Guinness, 1958

A.G. with the Abbot at Subiaco

es by Clive Francis

Anthony Quayle

William Hardy-Smith

Peter Glenville

Peter Bull

into the afternoon. I cannot recollect any of us leaving the table.

One of the unexpected sides to Edith was her compassion. The very poor and downtrodden gripped her imagination and caused her genuine distress. She was, for a while, obsessed with the work of Léon Bloy, that rather excessive Sufferer for Humanity, and sent me, as a birthday present, Albert Béguin's book on him, which is sub-titled 'A Study in Impatience'. Suffering, in all its shapes and sizes, became a particular topic in her conversation and letters. But for all that she was swift to consign mild offenders, such as I unfortunately turned out to be, to the dog-house. For at least two years, before her acceptance of the Roman claims, I was cast into outer darkness. As she said to Max Adrian, who repeated it to me with glee, 'Alec Guinness is *not* a Plantagenet.' Her long telegram inviting me to Farm Street Church and lunch was her form of absolving me from crass *lèse-majesté*.

The Apollo Society had arranged an evening of music and poetry at a London theatre one Sunday evening. The readers were Cathleen Nesbitt, Dylan Thomas and myself, and the pianist, who was to play some Beethoven, was Franz Osborn. Part of the programme consisted of poems by all three Sitwells and Edith arranged a small supper party after the performance at her club. At the table Dylan was placed on her right and I sat at her left. There were also present Stephen Spender and his wife Natasha Litvin, Caitlin Thomas and, I seem to remember, David Horner and two others. All went swingingly well until, towards the end of the meal, Edith expressed her disapproval of the piano-playing and of Beethoven in particular. 'Beethoven was a great *bore*!' she announced. 'Not a first-rate artist. I'm sure everyone here will agree that Beethoven is *deadly*.' There was a murmur of agreement from most people at the table; I was shocked. Then, unfortunately, she decided to elicit condemnation of Beethoven from all present. 'Dylan, you agree he is terribly boring?' 'Yes, Edith.' 'And Stephen?' 'Of course, Edith.' Pray God she doesn't come to me, I thought. She went round the table, from right to left, receiving nods of agreement. Probably everyone there knew she had suddenly fallen into an aggressive mood and that it would be wise, for the sake of calm, to agree with whatever she said but, bumptiously, I couldn't see it that way. At the moment when I thought I had escaped, as an uncultured nonentity, she turned to me with, 'And you, Alec, you agree Beethoven is a bore.' 'I got pleasure from the playing this evening,' I said, somewhat evasively. 'But you *do* agree about Beethoven?' she persisted. My face flushed and a sudden temper

surged through me. 'Not at all,' I replied. 'I imagine Beethoven will
be played and loved long after everyone at this table has been entirely
forgotten.'

It was an unpardonable remark, of course. There was a gasp from
the other guests. A deprecating look or two came from the Spenders,
as if to say, 'Oh, dear, you should have known better!' Conversation
flagged almost to a standstill, of the 'More coffee? Not for me at this
time of night' variety. Edith never spoke to me again or communi-
cated in any way until she took the Pope as her guide when, as she
expected to be forgiven any sins she may have committed, doubtless
she decided to forgive her supposed 'enemies' and I fear I must have
figured among them.

The largeness of her capacity to forgive, when truly and deeply
hurt, was apparent when *Time Magazine* printed an article about me
which contained the untruthful but not unfunny reference to her.
Luckily *Time* courteously sent me an advance copy, which I received
in the morning's post on the day of publication. Horrified at what I
read, and alarmed at its possible repercussions, I telephoned Edith
immediately asking if I might call on her at the Sesame Club as soon
as possible. She invited me to lunch with her that day but I declined,
saying she would not wish me for lunch after I had seen her – so she
was well alerted before my arrival. I found her sitting, alone and
forlorn, on a dingy sofa in an ante-room. As I handed her the
magazine I assured her that I had never said to anyone that at her
reception into the Church she wore white lace and had been carried
up the aisle lying on a cushion. She read the article in silence and
flushed deeply when she came to the offending passage; then she put
it down at her side and said, 'Stay to lunch.' I again refused. 'It
doesn't matter about this,' she said, tapping the magazine. 'I am
fortified against the press.' I could only apologise for the fact that
my name was coupled with hers in such a ridiculous way; she inclined
her head graciously and forgivingly. 'Do stay,' she said, 'as I am
expecting a very fine Portuguese poet, whom you may have met
before.' The words were hardly out of her mouth when a dark
haired young man arrived, waving *Time Magazine*. I recognised him
immediately as a fellow guest at Edith's reception but he failed to
recognise me. 'Edith, my dear,' – and he kissed her hand – 'have you
seen *this*?' He thrust *Time* at her. 'Isn't it disgraceful of that actor?' 'I
have just read it,' she replied. 'Alec brought me a copy. I don't need
to read it again.' The poet went pale and we bowed. He tried to stuff
Time into a pocket but it wouldn't go; then he concealed it in his

jacket, close to his heart. He fell silent. As I kissed her goodbye she whispered, 'Light a candle for me in Farm Street one day.'

Once or twice I have remembered to do so, but I have often remembered her in my haphazard prayers. When I pass the chapel where she was baptised I can still conjure up her tall figure, swathed in black, looking like some strange, eccentric bird and Fr Caraman pouring water over her forehead in the ancient rite. She seemed like an ageing princess come home from exile.

CHAPTER ELEVEN

A Broadside from a Taxi

It was an early evening in 1946 when I gave Edith Evans a lift in a taxi, for a reason I can no longer remember, to the theatre at which she was playing in an adaptation of Dostoyevsky's *Crime and Punishment*. Perhaps I had been to tea at her flat in Albany. Perhaps it was the day I told her I couldn't undertake to sell, on her behalf, a very tatty edition of the complete works of Dickens which had been collected by her late husband with Ardath cigarette coupons. Perhaps she had just wanted a drive round Green Park in the drizzle. Whatever had gone before, she was by now in a rather grumpy mood and I should have known, after a friendship of some twelve years, to tread, or at any rate speak, more warily. We chugged morosely up Lower Regent Street towards Piccadilly Circus. I had the impression she was neither happy with the play nor her part in it. (She was always uneasy when acting women who were ill as it caused a conflict with her Christian Science attitudes.) In the play with her was a young actress whom I knew slightly, of great porcelain prettiness – an area to avoid with Edith – and fair talent. Stupidly, to break a silence, I said, 'How's Audrey?' 'Audrey?' she echoed, as if Audrey was a handbag. Her great drooping eyes slowly swivelled in my direction, like sixteen-inch naval guns. 'Audrey?' she asked, in a deceptively tiny, high voice, mimicking Audrey uncannily. Then she fired; her aim being at the base of the Eros statue we were just rounding. 'She's no GOOD!' she said. It wasn't a moral judgment; a purely artistic one. She had used her great armament to blow a rowing-skiff out of the water. The eyes withdrew and levelled back at Shaftesbury Avenue. The effect had been of an ear-splitting 'Boom', but it dawned on me later that the voice had been, in fact, light, clear and quiet. The 'Boom' had been in her intention. People imitating Edith frequently make the understandable mistake of gravelling her voice with some sombre quality. 'A handbag!' has come down, in theatrical tradition, as a rumble of outrage. It wasn't. It was a series of spread-out high-pitched vowels which swooped round the theatre to vast comic effect. It was the same in the taxi with her

'She's no good!' It was an over-harsh statement, springing perhaps
from an exasperated heart, and something of which she would later
be a little ashamed, but for the moment she had amused herself,
knowing that her broadside had been delivered with a measure of wit.
I caught the edge of a smile as she settled herself more comfortably in
the cab, wrapping herself up against the chill air and giving a tweak
to her fawn-coloured Jaeger beret.

No small-part actor in the early thirties, and presumably even less
so in the twenties, would have dreamed of addressing the star of a
show he was in by her Christian name, or even speaking unless
spoken to. It was very much 'Yes, Miss Evans', 'Of course, Miss
Compton', 'After you, Miss Baddeley', 'Please, Miss Braithwaite',
'Sorry, Miss Ashcroft', 'Good evening, Miss Lawrence', or 'Allow
me, Miss Jeans'. When so many became Dames of the Order of the
British Empire it all sounded much cosier. 'Allow me, Dame Edith',
'Hello, Dame Peg', 'Can I help, Dame Lilian?' Now, of course, it's
the fiction of all pals together (and quite right too) and the achievements and applause of a lifetime are democratically ignored.

>   – to have done, is to hang
> Quite out of fashion, like a rusty mail
> In monumental mockery.

From the moment I first saw Edith Evans I became her ardent
admirer and rarely missed a new performance. For me she was
the greatest high-comedienne and probably the finest actress in the
English-speaking world. (I never saw Laurette Taylor.) When,
finally, I was in a production with her – playing the tiny part of the
Apothecary in Gielgud's *Romeo and Juliet* – I had the privilege of
watching her Nurse each night, but never a word was spoken to me.
I would hold open doors and not get even a nod let alone a thank-you.
It didn't worry me; I was proud enough to be ushering on to the
stage her tall, imperious presence. She did speak to me once though,
for the first time, during a night rehearsal of *The Seagull*, which
Komisarjevsky was directing. That was at the New Theatre in May
1936. I was understudying Stephen Haggard as Constantine and also
appearing as the workman (wordless) who operates the curtain to the
little outdoor stage in Act I. On this particular night, during a
rehearsal of the last act, I was sitting in the darkened stalls a few rows
behind Edith. Peggy Ashcroft and Stephen appeared to have got into
emotional difficulties with a scene and Komis was being belligerently

unhelpful. I could see the back of his bald head twitching. Edith decided she had spotted the trouble, wanted to voice her opinion without interfering with the rehearsal and strained from side to side seeking an audience. She spotted an unknown face in the darkness – mine – and said, 'You see, young man, it's all a great big glass tube and you blow down it.' She re-directed her attention to the stage, well satisfied with her perspicacity but leaving me totally in the dark. Later I worked out what she was getting at: that emotion must be channelled through some invisible technical achievement, which would direct it, shape it and lend it force. At least, I think that is what she meant.

She didn't address me again for several weeks and was most likely ignorant of my existence. The rehearsals of *The Seagull* were remarkable, with a shining cast for me to gawp at – Gielgud, Ashcroft, Haggard, Martita Hunt, Leo Quartermain, Freddy Lloyd, Ivor Barnard – and provided me with a vivid memory of a piece of stage history. We had been working on the play for about two weeks, the actors knew their lines, and we had a morning run-through of the first act. Komis had arranged for the spectators of the play-within-a-play to sit on a long bench with their backs to the audience proper. A moment came when it was Edith's cue to speak. Gielgud was sitting next to her and, after a moment's pause, he whispered, 'Edith, it's you.' From where I was standing in the wings I could see she hadn't dried up; she just had no intention of speaking. The stage-manager gave a prompt which was firmly ignored. Komis, in the stalls, sat still; a deep silence fell on the stage and no one moved. I glanced at my watch. After four minutes Edith gave a slight shiver with her shoulders, as if touched by a chill breeze, and then quietly said her line, 'Let's go in,' with infinite sadness and yet somehow callously. And that's the way it stayed, through the remainder of rehearsals and the run; a four-minute pause, an unheard-of length of time in the theatre, in which actors and audience seemed to hold their breath. It came of Edith's supreme daring, confidence and imagination.

It was during the rehearsals of *The Seagull* that I received, via Peggy Ashcroft, a sort of compliment that chuffed me no end. She returned early from a lunch break one day and found me, chewing an apple, in a corner of the stage. 'I've just had a squabble with Komis about you,' she said. My heart sunk a little. She went on, 'I said to him, "Isn't it clever how that young man who pulls the rope to open the curtain makes you manage to see it?" and Komis said, "Not

clever; he just pulls on a rope which hangs from the flies." When I
pointed out that there isn't a rope he refused to believe me.' She
looked at me almost doubtfully for a moment before adding, 'There
isn't a rope, is there?' 'Of course not,' I said. 'There's nothing.' 'That's
what I told him. He'll be furious.' She moved away smiling; leaving
me smiling too. Suddenly there was a new world hazily forming
before my eyes; a world of mime which could create illusion; a world
where props and scenery would be of minimum importance to the
actor, an area where the actor's use of his body, his eyes, and above
all his imagination, would create for an audience things they only
thought they saw and heard. I feel now that if I had been given a
further push of a similar sort, in those formative days, I might have
tried to move in this direction. I believe I had the ability, but I had
no means of making a livelihood except in the way I was already
doing.

About a year later this particular, unrealised talent came to the fore
when, while still working nightly in the theatre, I studied for a few
months as a part-time student under Michel St Denis. Michel had
rented, along with George Devine and others, Diaghilev's old rehearsal
rooms in Beak Street, off Regent Street, which became the initial
headquarters of the London Theatre Studio, later to move to Isling-
ton. It was by no means all mime and improvisation with Michel,
but I suspect that my own taste in mime was insufficiently serious
for the atmosphere of Beak Street. I longed to do absurd and clownish
things. My mime of an old man being blown off the end of a pier
while clinging to an open umbrella (not visible), or a youth catching
a large fish which he kept alive in a cardboard box because he loved
it so, were barely tolerated; perhaps because I found them too funny
myself. In my day-dreaming of such things the face was always dead
white and blank, the personality ridiculously single-minded. Buster
Keaton and Stan Laurel were my heroes rather than Charlie Chaplin.
While on this subject, there was an embarrassing afternoon in Beak
Street when Michel persuaded me, much against my will, to represent
Piccadilly Circus on a wet day. I set about the honking traffic,
hurrying shoppers, flurries of rain, Eros dripping wet, people coming
up from the Underground, etc., with fury in my heart. The result
was hailed as a triumph of revealing, artistic abandon over grave
discrimination. It took me weeks to live it down.

Gielgud left *The Seagull* after some weeks to go to New York and
the part of Trigorin was taken over by Ion Swinley, a handsome
actor of commanding presence, with a beautiful voice, whose career,

sadly, never caught up with his fine talent. Edith, who was clearly captivated by his tweediness and pipe-smoking, cheered up no end, and although saddened by John's departure for the States, I was in a small way a beneficiary. I was promoted to playing Yakov, the butler, when the young man who had been playing it joined the stage-management. There were only half a dozen lines to say but Komis, in his lazy way, had directed it amusingly, with a sure-fire laugh on an exit line. I had my eye on this, feeling I might be able to give it a little something extra. On my first night as Yakov I pulled it off and achieved not only a stunning laugh but also a good solid round of applause. I walked into the wings, quite nauseatingly pleased with myself, and my eye caught Edith's. She was sitting on a box, waiting to make her next entrance. I couldn't repress a bold smile. She returned the smile, in a rather enigmatic way, and bowed her head. My own head just swelled. The following night there was no laugh and certainly no applause. Edith was in her place in the wings but somehow avoided my look of puzzlement. It was depressingly the same again the next night. On the third evening she beckoned me to her and whispered, 'You've lost that laugh.' 'What am I doing wrong?' I whispered back. 'You're trying too hard. You didn't know how you got it in the first place. But it is natural to you, one day you will find it again. Take it lightly. Forget about it. But *when* it comes back make a note of what you were feeling *inside*.' I thanked her and turned away, but she called me back again. 'It will take about a week before you find it,' she said, in a very practical way, 'and once it is there you will never lose it.' She was dead right. A week later the laugh was there once more; I was happy again, relaxed and, strangely, not over-excited. Edith appeared not to see me but gazed moonily at the other actors on stage. What the lesson was she had taught me I am not quite sure – some inner mystery – and yet it *was* a lesson and I have to remind myself of it frequently. From then on we often exchanged a few words backstage; she learned my name and began to take more than a lofty, distant interest. It was the beginning of a pleasant, on the whole easy-going friendship – not of great intimacy, because I was far too young at twenty-one – but a rewarding relationship, from my point of view, which lasted to the final decade of her life when, unfortunately, I saw all too little of her.

When I think of her now, these few years after her death, my mind see-saws between gratitude for what she was, her enormous generosity in big things, and exasperation at her meanness in small ones, amusement at her egocentricity, reverence for her artistry, and total astonishment at her occasional lapses into artistic blindness, which almost amounted to dishonesty. If I think of, and record, a pettiness or silliness in Edith's behaviour, I can always cheerfully outweigh it with five times as many actions of human warmth, affection and wisdom. Like most actors, her personality changed subtly with each part she was preparing, unconsciously bringing into everyday life whiffs of what she was brewing in her theatrical imagination. (Just before she started rehearsals for *The Dark Is Light Enough* she came to dinner with Merula and me at St Peter's Square, wafting in with such smug piety and spiritual know-how that I could hardly swallow my food. She barely picked at what we put before her, smiling all the time like a penitential nun of some austere order presenting a face in which a queer attempt at melancholy was at odds with a smirk of satisfaction. Before *The Witch of Edmonton* she whined a good deal about her friends and life in general. With *Waters of the Moon* it was all gaiety, sophistication and snobbery. The end-products of these try-outs were, of course, modified, disciplined and made acceptable.)

Let me put two of her different sides back to back, so to speak, like bookends and then cap her large, generous action with the gesture of beautiful thoughtfulness and kindness she showed me.

When she was giving her superb, definitive Rosalind at the Old Vic in the latter half of 1936 (in a rather humdrum production by Esmé Church, all Watteau and cut-out backcloths) she often invited Michael Redgrave and sometimes myself for a weekend to Washenden Manor, her home in Kent. We would drive down after the performance on a Saturday night and wake up to a quiet, sunny, peaceful Sunday. Sometimes there would be another guest or two – an Australian actress friend of Edith's, or Michael Gough, who was then in his teens, studying agriculture but longing to get into the theatre. They were enjoyable times; except for the bitterly cold day when Edith decided that what she wanted most to do was have a bathe off the endless pebbles of Dungeness beach. There exists an unfortunate snapshot, taken by Edith's chauffeur, I think, of her, Redgrave and myself, teeth chattering but bravely smiling, arm-in-arm, in our old-fashioned wet, clinging and revealing bathing costumes. It stood for many years, to my acute embarrassment, on the over-mantel in her Albany flat. There was also a disastrous outing to Margate sands, where Edith was appalled to see how many people there were in the world and we beat a hasty retreat without so much as an ice-cream. On Sunday evenings, after an excellent cold meal of chicken, ham and apple pie, we drove back to London; there were rehearsals on Monday morning. Always, however many we were to dinner, there was an insufficiency of cream to go with the apple pie – just a thimbleful in a tiny white jug, not enough for one, let alone five or six. This eventually got me down and, rashly feeling I was more or less at home, I mentioned it. Unfortunately it was on the same day that I had sat, inadvertently, in her late husband's special chair. 'That's *Guy's* chair! *No one* is allowed to sit in Guy's chair!' Baleful looks had followed me for hours. By evening I assumed I had been forgiven and when the apple pie appeared I piped up, 'Edith, do you think we could have a drop more cream? We are six, and there's not enough for one.' 'No!' she snapped. 'This is a farm. I've got to make it pay.' We travelled back to London in silence.

Some years after that, in the first winter of the 1939–45 war, a theatre company was formed, rather grandly called the Actors Company, of which George Devine was the leading light. We had no very great view, other than creating much required work for ourselves and some others, and apart from Marius Goring, who was able to contribute something like fifty pounds to the common fund, we had no money. Merula and I were unable to fork out more than five pounds between us. We all decided that we couldn't get going with our first production (which only very incidentally happened to be the adaptation I had made of *Great Expectations*) unless we could raise £700, so our first task was to approach moneyed friends or acquaintances who might be sympathetic. We decided to avoid asking any actors, who as a tribe are nearly always too hard pressed. All replies were negative except for £10 sent me by Mr John Lewis, of the Oxford Street–Sloane Square Partnership. Mr Lewis, whom I didn't know, had taken me to lunch at Prunier's that summer to tell me his firm was going to buy three Shaftesbury Avenue theatres and he wished to put me in charge of them. I had declined the offer hastily, pointing out that I was no businessman and that, in any case, I hadn't the faintest idea about how to run a theatre. I only wanted to act. Well, the £10 paid for postage stamps and telephone calls. Eventually, George Devine and I said we would seek advice from Edith, who was on tour with *The Importance of Being Earnest*. There was no question of asking her for money; the object of our visit was, I suppose, to seek sympathy, encouragement and possibly a commonsense opinion. We called on her as soon as the curtain fell after a mid-week matinée and explained what we were trying to do. She sat at her dressing-table, in Lady Bracknell's wig and hat, listening to us very seriously. When George, who was the spokesman, had finished speaking a long silence fell. Her elderly dresser, who was called Potter, offered us tea. We shook our heads. Then Edith turned to Potter, saying, 'Potter, how much did I pay for the fur coat I bought last week?' 'Seven hundred pounds, Miss Evans.' 'Potter, bring me my cheque book.' George and I stood silently, a little apprehensive, certainly embarrassed. Edith wrote a cheque for £700 and handed it to us, saying, 'Can't have actors out of work for the sake of seven hundred pounds when I buy a coat for the same amount.' We must have expressed our gratitude but I think we were too overcome to do more than mumble. So the production of *Great Expectations* went ahead, got rather good notices (it was much championed by James Agate), played to fair though modest business and lost every penny. That was the end of the Actors Company. Edith never mentioned her loss, anyway in my presence; but I suspect she knew it was a write-off from the moment she unscrewed her fountain-pen. I don't think her bit of farming and economy with cream paid off either, but when she died she managed to leave something like £80,000 to the Actors' Charitable Trust. Actors were always close to her heart, even when she disapproved of them.

*

My first season at the Old Vic, under Guthrie's auspices, provided me with a variety of small parts: Boyet (which I disliked) in a lovely, gay production of *Love's Labours Lost* (starring Redgrave, Rachel Kempson, Alec Clunes, Margaretta Scott and Ernest Milton), Le Beau (which I loathed) and William (which I loved) in *As You Like It*, to be followed by Aguecheek, and Exeter in *Henry V*. My first big part ever was to be Mr Sparkish in *The Country Wife*, with Edith as Lady Fidget, Michael as Mr Horner and Ruth Gordon, imported from America, as Mrs Pinchwife. My contract for the season, at £7 a week, also included understudying Olivier as Hamlet and playing Osric (another part I had grown to dislike) and Reynaldo, which I mistakenly thought wasn't worth playing. It is probably salutary for every young actor to be given the sack sometime in his career. When it happened to me it seemed like the end of the world, but being removed from *The Country Wife* was as good for me as, later, the necessity of joining up in the Navy proved to be.

 The Country Wife was the most extravagant production the Old Vic had ever undertaken; it was expected to pull in West End audiences, usually indifferent to what was happening in the Waterloo

Road, and it did just that. Apart from a splendid cast, Guthrie persuaded Oliver Messel to design sets and costumes, which he did with his usual glorious flair. Lilian Baylis was still alive, hiding in her poky office with its low-wattage lamp, and no doubt frequently at her prayers, for she was a prophetess of doom once more than five pounds had been spent. ('There are *lots* of lovely costumes in the wardrobe, dear. What was good enough for dear Ben Greet should be good enough for you.')

On the third morning of rehearsals we reached the roughing out of the first scene I had with Miss Gordon; a duologue. Edith was not required that day and I can't recall any other actors being present. The time was 12.15 and we were to break for lunch at one o'clock, except that I was broken before then. The footlights were on – an extravagance to impress the visiting star. Suddenly Miss Gordon lowered her script, shielded her eyes from the light, and called to Guthrie in the stalls. 'Tony! Tony, I can't act with this young man. Would you get another actor for the part, please?' It was unlike Tony to knuckle under to such a statement or attitude, but he capitulated immediately. 'Ernest Thesiger would be marvellous,' she added. She was dead right of course; I was too young, too inexperienced and lacking in the flamboyance the part required. Tony was clearly embarrassed, was fearful I might have hysterics and promptly suggested an early lunch.

The play was to run for six weeks; as soon as *Love's Labours Lost* had closed I would be out of work. 'Anyway,' I thought, 'I have a contract and they will have to pay me £7 a week for doing nothing.' I had underestimated Miss Baylis. After much haggling she finally handed me three crumpled, dirty, one pound notes. 'Your compensation money, dear.' 'But Miss Baylis, it should be forty-two pounds.' 'Three pounds, dear. If it's no use to you we can use it on this thing that Tony Guthrie is doing – we need every penny, and more.' So I was left with my crumpled notes to last me six weeks. (In fact I picked up a rather boring job at the Arts Theatre almost immediately, which fitted in just nicely and provided me with food.)

When I got down to the theatre that evening, to give my wretched, humourless Boyet, I was astonished to find Edith at the stage door. I assumed she must have been to a costume-fitting, though it seemed an odd hour. I greeted her cheerfully enough, wondering if she knew of my dismissal. 'I've come down to see you, Alec. They told me you always get in early. Come outside.' She led me out to the

Waterloo Road. 'I've heard what happened this morning and I'm sorry. But you know, it's probably just as well. You are not quite right for the part. In another ten years perhaps, but not now. I came down to tell you that *I* believe in you; Tony believes in you – and I know Johnny Gielgud does. In ten years' time you won't be playing parts like Mr Sparkish, unless you want to. By then you should have your name in lights but, more importantly, you will be a good actor. That's all. Goodnight.' She kissed me and got into the taxi which was waiting for her. I couldn't even feel bitter about Ruth Gordon after that; at least not after a day or two; and certainly not after I had seen her as Mrs Pinchwife, and Thesiger in 'my' part. They were both superb.

Edith came to see me in Guthrie's full-length 'modern dress' *Hamlet* at the Vic in 1938 but I was unaware she had been in front until John Gielgud told me, no doubt displaying careful discretion (which is not always that good man's most evident quality). 'Edith said that what she liked about your performance was that you never attempted to do what you knew was beyond your reach, so you were always true to yourself.' It pleased me no end.

Edith was the first person I told, in the spring of 1938, that I was engaged to be married. We were playing in almost adjacent theatres and I dropped in on her, with some excitement, before her performance in *Robert's Wife*. I thought she would be delighted, but when I blurted out my news her face fell and she gave a dismal cry of, 'O-ah, – No-ah! You are an artist! You shouldn't marry!' Her wisdom wasn't *always* far-seeing. And she didn't know Merula, though she had seen and greatly admired her as one of St Denis's students. She sent us some hideous soup bowls as a wedding present, which didn't survive the war.

Michel St Denis cast me (not, I believe, with Binkie Beaumont's approval) as Trofimov, the student, in *The Cherry Orchard*; a production which never saw the light of day. And it was going to bring me in £28 a week, the largest salary I had been offered. The cast was spectacular and formidable, with Edith as Mme Ranevsky, Peggy Ashcroft as Anya, Cyril Cusack as Firs, the delightful Ronnie Squire as Gaev and a handful of other distinguished actors. I sensed from the beginning I was going to be bad in it, and I would have been. In retrospect, the performance I would like to have given was that of Ian Holm, in the same part, some years later at the Aldwych. I found difficulty getting to grips with it and certainly couldn't get to grips with Edith in the ballroom scene; or rather, not the sort of grips

Edith required. Mme Ranevsky and Trofimov briefly waltz together, and Edith was determined to swan around beautifully – she was an excellent ballroom dancer – and wished her partner to do the same. 'You must dance properly,' she kept saying. 'I *am* dancing properly,' I said, 'but Trofimov is not a good dancer. *You* have a line saying how clumsy I am.' She wouldn't have it. '*All* Russians are good dancers,' she said. 'It's in their blood.' It might have developed into an ugly situation if war hadn't broken out after only two weeks' rehearsing and the production was cancelled. On the morning of Saturday, September 2, 1939, Binkie assembled the cast at the theatre and told us it was a case of *force majeure*, he was sorry, but it couldn't be risked; theatres would be closed, London bombed, etc., etc. It was a beautiful sunny morning. We dispersed. Edith sat on the stage for a moment, looking very mournful. Turning round, she noticed me. 'Alec, take me for a walk.' So the two of us, having sadly said goodbye to all the others, walked slowly, arm-in-arm, along Piccadilly to Hyde Park. We didn't speak until we were near the Serpentine; then Edith hardly paused for breath. It was one long, sad wail of, 'What am I to *do*? I am an actress. I can't act with bombs falling! What shall I *do*?' There was not a single reference to what might be in store for young men and their wives, how the less privileged would manage or even, apparently, anxiety about the nation as such. There was nothing in her talk but self-pity. She chilled me – but it was a chilling day in spite of the warm sunshine and the sparkle on the water.

With the war came Merula's pregnancy, barrage balloons, no bombs and no money. The Actors Company did *Great Expectations* and disintegrated. In March 1940 there arrived a play by Clemence Dane, called *Cousin Muriel*, in which Edith was to play a lady kleptomaniac. Apparently Noël Coward, a great friend of Miss Dane's, had suggested she should write a play, not in the high-flown style of her *Will Shakespeare* but one in which someone said, 'Will you please pass the salt?' Miss Dane took his advice to the letter and Peggy Ashcroft was given the memorable line. Another of Peggy's memorable lines, while gazing with admiration at a vast bunch of paper delphiniums (which Tony Guthrie said Edith thoroughly bashed and punished while arranging them in their waterless vase), was: 'Oh, how paintable!' No, the dialogue was not high-flown this time. The whole production was a sort of tired trauma. The nice, solid, worthy Frederick Leister (who had been wonderful as the Emperor Franz Joseph in *White Horse Inn*) was the leading man,

Peggy his daughter, Edith his lady housekeeper, and I her advertising agent son, just back from the U.S.A., worried like hell to find mummy was doing quite a bit of shop-lifting on the quiet. Edith would never face the fact that she was portraying a thief. 'No, no, she just likes pretty things; she doesn't steal.' Which made nonsense of Miss Dane's drama and difficulties for her fellow actors.

The set was all sunny French windows with yellow curtains, striped Regency chairs, a small grand piano on which stood the paper delphiniums and silver-framed photographs, so presumably rarely played, and a good sofa from which to view the never very full auditorium. Winifred Dane attended nearly all the rehearsals, unwisely as it transpired, dressed from shoulder to shoes in vast flowing robes of black satin with here and there some gypsy-like chiffon. She made herself very friendly toward me, in an imperious way, and made me a present of a large wooden box of oil paints across which she had written, in quotation marks, 'Oh, how paintable!' The sight of it nearly made Peggy ill. Norman Marshall directed, not with much spirit, and rehearsals often verged on the disagreeable. I think Norman only made one suggestion to me, and that was negative. 'How would it be,' I asked, 'as I am alone on the stage with nothing to do but look worried, if I opened the piano and struck a note or two?' 'It would look very common,' he said; so I ceased to be creative. Binkie, who was presenting *Cousin Muriel*, was paying me £30 a week, which seemed pretty glorious to this juvenile lead (until Diana Wynyard told me it ought to be £70), and said he would also have made for me a lovely chalk-stripe grey flannel suit, brown brogue shoes and pay for a little toupee, as I was balding fast. All was put in hand; but when I went to try on my toupee I found a large wig with great wings of dark hair buttressing it on either side. I gasped at the wig-maker; there was obviously some very nasty mistake; it bore no resemblance to what we had agreed. 'I'm sorry, Mr Guinness, but it's Mr Beaumont's instructions. He says your ears stand out so much I must put in a lot of hair on each side, to disguise them.' 'But it emphasises them,' I protested, 'as well as making me look like Clemence Dane.' We compromised with some scissor-work; after all, his business greatly depended on Binkie's patronage.

There was a distressing incident, of some magnitude, during an afternoon rehearsal; much more dramatic than anything that happened in performance. We rehearsed at the Globe Theatre, with essential furniture in place. At one moment I used to sit on the sofa and Edith brought me a cocktail. She stood in front of me, smiling,

with the glass in her hand. When I took it from her I was so
profoundly struck by her total relaxation, even when fumbling for
words, that I couldn't resist putting out a hand and giving a little
push to her arm, which was hanging at her side. It swung lightly
away, as if blown by some wind. She hardly seemed to notice. I
apologised, explained, and we continued. She was quite clearly rather
pleased; I was a good, dear boy that day. Not so a day or two later,
when we came to do the scene again. I can't remember what the line
was I had to say but it was sharpish, because it had to do with
mummy's financial fiddles and kleptomania, and I said it sharply.
Edith stiffened. I thought she was acting. Suddenly, in a pained,
angry voice, she confronted me with, 'Do you intend saying that
line the way you did?' 'Well, yes; I think so; don't you? I mean, he's
very cross with her. He now knows about the stealing.' She stared
at me for a moment and then gave a great wail, which rent the
theatre. Her arms flung in the air as she screamed, 'Alec doesn't love
me any more! He doesn't love me! He *hates* me!' Then she flung
herself full-length on the stage, drummed with her feet and, taking
the corner of a small Persian rug in her teeth, worried it. It was some
performance. I sat rigid and appalled on the sofa, pressed back against
the chintz cushions. From the back of the stalls came Winifred
Dane's voice, booming, 'Edith, calm! Calm, Edith!' and slowly,
mountainously, a cloud of black drapery advanced down the stalls.
Peggy, who had been in the wings, flew like Juliet on to the stage
and with enormous, boisterous sympathy flung herself on top of
Edith, pinning her to the ground and removing the rug from her
mouth. Edith continued to wail. By now Winifred Dane had made
it to the brass rail of the orchestra pit and decided to climb over it.
She got halfway and stayed there, straddled, balanced between a
likely broken neck and the ignominy of withdrawal, but keeping up
her calming calls to Edith, which sounded like some vast pigeon in
distress. The stage management rescued her. I tiptoed into the wings,
where Freddie Leister was smoking his pipe and scanning an evening
paper. 'Trouble?' he asked. The stage-manager appeared, whispering,
'That will be all for today. We'll let you know your call for tomorrow
when we have located Mr Marshall.' Except for heavy breathing,
silence reigned on the stage.

The next day no reference was made to the incident. We were all
very quiet, polite, formal and perhaps a touch cool. It never occurred
to me to blame myself, and it still doesn't. I think it all stemmed
from Edith refusing to face an artistic truth which, in her heart of

hearts, she knew was there. Or perhaps she wasn't ready to face it yet, or in public.

It was a short, unsuccessful and not very happy run, only relieved for me on the matinée when my make-up flaked off (I was experimenting with water-colour) and I got uncontrollable giggles – for which I was rightly reprimanded.

I have often noticed that dedicated actors who work exclusively in the theatre are usually contemptuous of those who work in films – that is until they themselves are inveigled into a film and find that money can be just as satisfying as artistic integrity. I believe I had something of that attitude myself, and any time now may revert to it. One summer day, a few years after the war, I took Edith to lunch at the Mirabelle. She was in good form but rather anxious, on my behalf, at what the bill might come to. 'Not to worry,' I said, 'I'm filming.' Rather coyly, after a lot of looking at me sideways, she was bold enough to ask what I was being paid. It was *The Lavender Hill Mob* I was making and I told her I was getting £6,000 for the job. I might have stabbed her with a fish-fork. She fell back in her chair, agony written all over her face. 'Six *thousand* pounds?' I repeated it, thinking to myself, 'Oh Lord, perhaps I undersold myself; should have held out for ten.' But it was the vast size of the amount which had dumbfounded her. She became very grave. 'I must make a film,' she said. 'Or do you call them movies?' 'The money is the same, whatever you may call them.' 'And you enjoy it?' 'Quite,' I said, truthfully. A certain impatience was detectable in the rest of her meal; she got through her Bombe Surprise in a flash, anxious, I believe, to get to a telephone to call her agent. When she did start filming she loved it – and was as remarkable on the screen as on stage – bearing out what I have always maintained, that if you can be truthful in one medium you can be truthful in all (fighting your way, of course, through the tosh of some directors), and, as a corollary, that phoneyness will out on stage or screen. Good acting is pretty well indivisible, and for all her particular shades of colour, from black to white, grandeur and simplicity, egomania and warm generosity, Edith could not be divided. She nourished and protected her talent as if it was the most important thing in the world, and for her it was. For many of us, if not quite that, her artistry was very important also. She gave us definitive performances as Rosalind, Millamant, Lady Bracknell, the Nurse in *Romeo* and Lady Utterword in *Heartbreak House*. And to those extraordinary performances must be added the parts she played in *Evensong, The Late Christopher Bean, The Old Ladies, The*

Apple Cart, Daphne Laureola, Waters of the Moon and plays too numerous
to mention. She played something like a hundred and thirty parts
between 1912 and her death.

The last time I saw her was on some occasion, a reception I think,
at Equity's offices in Harley Street. She was quite old, a little frail,
smaller than I had remembered her, and very impatient with the
proceedings. She clutched at me during someone's speech and said,
far too loudly, 'Tell that man to be quiet.' She was immediately
shushed by a lot of people but remained undeterred. 'I don't want to
listen to that man,' she called out, 'I want to talk to Alec.' Horrified,
I hurried her out of the room. When we reached the landing I steadied
her and she became very quiet and sweet. 'Have you seen Bra-a-hn?'
she asked. I couldn't think whom she meant. 'Coral Browne?' I
ventured. 'No,' she said crossly. 'Bra-a-hn!' I still couldn't get it. She
lightly stamped a foot. '*You* know!' she said. 'He's a dear dear boy.'
She seemed distressed. I shot an arrow in the air, 'Bryan Forbes?'
'That's what I said,' she replied, obviously relieved. 'De-a-ah Bra-
a-hn.' I took her downstairs, to where her Rolls and diminutive
chauffeur were waiting, on the opposite side of the road. It was dark.
No traffic. The chauffeur opened the car door nearest us, took out
an embroidered foot-stool and placed it in the middle of the road.
Edith mounted it, and with a little trip fell among a heap of fur rugs
and coats. She was quite unhurt and hardly looked surprised.

The final glimpse I had of her, as the car slid away, was of her
attempt to wave at me, from a slowly heaving pile of bearskin rugs
and mink.

Since her death I have thought about her more often than most of
the great dead. Not always, perhaps, with total love; but always with
profound regard, personal gratitude, and gratitude that my footpath
should have zig-zagged across her broad highway.

CHAPTER TWELVE

The Words of Mercury

'Celia Johnson is Beelzebub!'

Ernest Milton munched on a piece of duck, sipped his wine and dabbed at his lips with a napkin. Merula and I and Robert Flemyng, who was our other guest, put down our knives and forks in astonished silence.

'Beelzeebub!' Ernest repeated, with malicious relish. Realising it wasn't some bizarre joke, but meant to be taken seriously, I felt an angry flush beginning to rise to my face.

'But, Ernest,' I said, 'Celia is one of the most loved women in the profession and profoundly admired by us all, both as an actress and as a person. What right have you to say something so monstrous?'

'I have my reasons,' he replied. (He pronounced the word as 'raisins'.) 'She went down the Grand Canal in a gondola,' he continued, 'doing the *Times* crossword puzzle and never once so much as glancing at the Venetian palaces.'

'She's as blind as a bat,' I said, 'and probably couldn't even see the canal. And, anyway, why shouldn't she do the *Times* crossword in a gondola? She has a passion for crosswords.'

'I say she is an evil woman.'

'Oh, come off it!' I said, trying to laugh a little. Perhaps his pre-dinner dry martini had been too strong; he was rather abstemious by nature.

'So I am a liar?' he shouted. He pushed his plate away vigorously, jumped up from the table, knocking over a chair, rushed in to the hall, seized his green pork-pie hat, slammed his way out of the house and disappeared into the gardens of St Peter's Square.

Bobby Flemyng, Merula and I looked at each other with a wild surmise, wondering what on earth could have caused such a sudden brain-storm. Celia and Ernest had recently returned from a European tour – Shakespeare, I believe – but no word of discontent or gossip had reached our ears, and Celia, being the most light-hearted, delightful and considerate companion, was unlikely to have quarrelled with anyone in the world. Perhaps she had giggled at something on stage, some minor mishap perhaps, and Ernest, who in later years was too often on the look-out for imagined slights, had taken it as a personal affront.

Five minutes later there was a wild knocking at the front door. Ernest still looked mad and furious but I put on a show of welcome, forgiveness and understanding.

'I haven't come to apologise,' he said. 'I've come to finish my duck.' With that he rushed back to the dining-room and sat himself down, while Merula recovered his plate from the kitchen. We made an effort at some light conversation but he said never a word. He was as greedy for his duck as Shylock for his bond. When he had cleaned the plate he rose, made a stately exit, put on his hat like a Spanish grandee, and again slammed the front door behind him. At this moment, so far as I was concerned, it could have been for good; and yet I knew I could never be angry with Ernest for long. He had a strong streak of genius in his make-up, more than any actor I have personally known, and, for all his affectations, egomania and persecution-mania, could be very endearing. He was witty and, when not on the absurd treadmill of how John Gielgud, Binkie Beaumont and a host of others had plotted all their lives to ruin his career, he was interesting and stimulating.

Ernest Milton was born in San Francisco in 1890; he was always proud of his American birth and Jewish blood. He first appeared in London in 1914, in a play called *Potash and Perlmutter* (a typical title for the sort of play that so often attracted him) at the Queen's Theatre, and he was back again a year later to give his Oswald, in *Ghosts*, and Marchbanks in *Candida*. 'I never played small parts,' he once said to me, 'I was always a star.' (Possibly he made a star performance out of the First Camel Driver in *Joseph and his Brethren* in New York, prior to coming to England.) From that time on he made England his home, joining the Old Vic Company in 1918 to play most of the major Shakespearean roles, repeating many of them – particularly Hamlet and Shylock – as the years rolled on. His first great personal success in the commercial theatre was in *Loyalties* in 1922, which he followed with Pirandello's *Henry IV*, and *Rope*.

In the spring of 1932 he entered management, briefly and disastrously, taking the St James's Theatre to present *Othello* and *The Merchant of Venice*. I saw the latter at an almost totally empty matinée. The only other Shylock I had seen was the late Henry Baynton, at the Pier Theatre, Eastbourne, when I was a schoolboy. Baynton was one of the tribe of actors who endlessly toured the provinces in tatty productions of Shakespeare, catering for the most part to bewildered children. (He was inclined to slip out of the theatre, in full costume and make-up, to have a quick pint at the local and, on one notorious occasion, misjudged the length of Lady Macbeth's sleep-walking scene. At the end of Lady M's effort no Macbeth could be found, so the lady stage-manager stepped forward and had the temerity to announce to the assembled scholars, who were studying the play for exams, 'That is where the play ends. You can go home now.' As they huddled against the rain, trotting down the pier, who should come lurching up but Macbeth himself, in Viking helmet, somewhat awry, and plaited red wig flying in the wind. Astonished to see his audience leaving he called out, 'Surely not going home so soon?' He got no reply as they were hustled on their way by terrified tutors.) Baynton was reputed to give a good imitation of Irving as Shylock, dressed like Holman Hunt's 'Light of the World', and making strange sinuous gestures whenever he greeted anyone; gestures which I learned to perfect in the cricket pavilion the whole of a summer term. Baynton may have been a poor, though striking, copy of Irving, with whom he had worked, but Milton was very much his own man. I can remember little of that afternoon except Athene Seyler's delicious Nerissa, the beautifully-painted McKnight Kauffer sets, and Ernest's hair-raising reading of the 'Hath not a Jew eyes' speech. And his interminable, insufferable final exit, which lost him all sympathy. Granville-Barker, in his *Prefaces to Shakespeare*, refers contemptuously to what he calls the 'gerrymandering' striving for effect of too many Shylocks as they finally leave the stage. He must have had Ernest in mind as a prime example; not only was Ernest loath to leave the stage but he managed to convey the idea that we would never see his like again and we had been over-privileged. If, as a youth, I missed much of the subtlety of his Shylock and was alienated by his actor's persona, I came round to him overwhelmingly when I saw him in *Rope*, which was revived by Robert Newton at the old 'Shilling Theatre' in Fulham. That was a performance of wit and urbanity which managed to combine decadence and moral fervour. It was also very dangerous.

Then, in 1933, at Sadler's Wells, there came a revival, for a few performances only, of his Hamlet. It has remained for me, as possibly for some others, the most thrilling performance I have ever seen. Someone like Sir John Clements, who saw the same performance, and whose taste often differs from mine, I suspect, shared my enthusiasm. I am not at all sure what 'great acting' is and yet, when seen, it is instantly recognisable. Alan Bennett said to me not long ago, 'I *hate* Great Acting' – and I know what he meant: the self-importance, the authoritative central stage position, the meaningless pregnant pause, the beautiful gesture which is quite out of character, the vocal pyrotechnics, the suppression of fellow actors into dummies who just feed, and the jealousy of areas where the light is brightest, and above all the whiff of, 'You have come to see me act, not to watch a play.'

Ernest could be guilty of all these attitudes, and even condone them in others, but when it came to Hamlet it was a different matter – he sought the truth and neither theatrical effect nor personal aggrandisement. He and Shakespeare seemed to be of one mind, presenting the Renaissance Prince *par excellence*, a man familiar with the ways of mankind – not unlike Montaigne – who could always see the two sides of a coin, tortured by conscience and burdened by duty, a man of sharp wit but exquisite manners. It was a performance which lifted the spectator away from the theatre and expanded the spirit. The voice, although pleasing, had tiresome affectations; particularly when he drawled out a vowel sound beyond human comprehension. Physically he was not important, except when his spirit charged his body with total concentration or a remarkable stillness. His Hamlet may have been a man 'bounded in a nutshell' but he was a prince whose horizons were far and wide. That particular performance was a rare diamond in a drab, work-a-day production by Ben Greet, the old Shakespearean touring actor and producer, much respected by an earlier generation than mine. It was a full-length version of the play, in black drapes and rather flat erratic lighting. The cast was full of distinguished names, including Sybil Thorndike, but none of them took fire, except for a very funny Osric from Robert Speaight; and the graveyard scene and duel at the end I remember as being ludicrous. It didn't matter. When I left the theatre I felt shattered. I returned to my bed-sitter in Bayswater, incapable of speaking for about twenty-four hours, knowing I had witnessed something I can only call both transcendental and very human, qualities which Ernest carried in the depth of his heart however absurdly he sometimes expressed them. He neither did Shakespeare a favour, as some of our actors manage to imply they do, nor kow-towed to him; he met him, in Hamlet, on mutual and loving ground.

In 1936 he played Don Armado in *Love's Labours Lost* at the Old Vic, which is when I first got to know him a little. He was not really at his best in the part, striving only too successfully for a somewhat

'camp' comic effect. 'Shall I *careen*, Tony, on the edge of the pool?'
he asked Guthrie during a rehearsal. 'Would *they* think it funny?'
Tony encouraged him, but with doubt in his mind, and the result
wasn't funny. Perhaps it is too late to save a performance from
indifference by the way you say the last lines of a play, but Ernest
managed to do just that, and gave us all a frisson. The last lines of
Love's Labours are:

> The words of Mercury
> Are harsh after the Songs of Apollo.
> You that way: we this way.

The small hairs on the back of my neck stirred: he had put, with
sweetness and regret, a great gulf between audience and players; a
gulf which would widen as the curtain fell, the lights went out and
auditorium and stage would be empty even of ghosts. Maybe he
didn't even intend it: like all great executant artists he often excelled
beyond his awareness. Edith Evans had the same capacity; she would
do something brilliantly by instinct but, if questioned, would ration-
alise what she had done almost idiotically. The difference between
them, I think, was that Ernest had irony and Edith none; however
wayward his interpretation of a line might be, he could justify it
intellectually. I have admired several actors 'this side of idolatry' but
only three have held quite the same fascination for me as Ernest
Milton – Pierre Fresnay, Charles Laughton and Cyril Cusack. When
not compelled to appear in boulevard comedies (in which he was
delightful) Fresnay was the most superbly austere, trim and intellectually challenging actor I have seen; Laughton, in latter days largely
dismissed by critics because he had done time in Hollywood, was
a genius who, like all geniuses, could misfire, though never without
interest. Ernest, I know, would always see himself centre stage and
up stage (it was part of his generation's star actor tradition) but
Fresnay, Laughton and Cusack would make their own centre-stage
wherever they were, even with their backs to the audience.

At the end of the war my loose, lopsided adaptation of *The Brothers
Karamazov* was directed by Peter Brook (who had his twenty-first
birthday during the production) at the Lyric, Hammersmith. The
fine Czech actor Frederick Valk, a bull of a man, simple and endearing, was enticed to play old Karamazov; James Donald, Pierre
Lefèvre, Raymond Jaquerello and I were the sons, and I was given
the most difficult task of all – to persuade Ernest to play the saintly

Father Zossima. Accordingly I visited him in a gloomy little flat in Charing Cross Road and, after an hour of intense flattery, succeeded. But it wasn't just the flattery that worked; I had the inspiration to tell him that if he did it he would be mercilessly attacked by the anti-clerical press. He suddenly saw himself as a holy martyr, being led on a trundle to an auto-da-fé on Hammersmith Broadway.

He was not particularly good as Father Zossima and he was acutely jealous of Freddie Valk – fortunately they didn't have any scenes together. Ernest and I shared a small white-washed dressing-room, which was a pleasure for me although I was always apprehensive about his fumbling make-up and the terrible tangle he frequently got into with his beard. 'But which way *round* should it go, Alec?' he would ask nightly. 'The pointed bit at the bottom,' I would reply, wearily, 'and the hairier bit in front.' There are some actors who behave like tiny-tots when it comes to making up, not knowing their elbow from a crimson-lake liner. I seem to remember that Ernest, like many old pros, kept an assortment of half-squashed grubby sticks of Leichner greasepaint, tattered powder puffs, broken pencils and a near-empty bottle of congealed spirit-gum in a filthy old cigar box. Everything in it looked as if it had been chewed for half a century. My own theatre dressing-table betrays my amateur streak, everything laid out spick-and-span as if for a sale of cosmetic goods.

The notices for *Karamazov* were indifferent, except for a glowing headline from James Agate for Freddie Valk and a quite dreadful one in the *New Statesman* for Ernest. The day the latter appeared I prayed he wouldn't see it; there was no hope of Agate's praise of Valk having escaped him. I was half made up and keeping a wary eye on the door when he slowly entered the dressing-room. He barely said 'good evening', put his old green pork-pie hat on a peg as if saying farewell to the world, sat disconsolately at his table and gazed forlornly into the mirror. 'He's seen it,' I said to myself, and quickly pretended to be very busy with an eyebrow. Quite suddenly there was a dramatic whisper from his side of the room. 'Have you *seen* the *New Statesman*?' Turning to him over-cheerfully I said, 'Yes! And you should be proud. Please remember that when I asked if you would be good enough, and brave enough, to play this part I warned you Zossima would be attacked by the anti-clerical press. It means you have brought it off.'

He got up, put on his hat and stalked out of the theatre. Thinking he would return in a few minutes I waited until the 'quarter hour' was called before reporting his absence. No one knew where he had gone; panic stations; his understudy was rushed into preparing himself – he had to open the play – and he had had no rehearsals; the box office put up a slip in their window reading, 'owing to the indisposition of Mr Milton, etc., etc.,' and an air of crisis and alarm seized the theatre. My own foolish fear was that he might at that very moment be throwing himself off Hammersmith Bridge. As the 'five minutes' was being called he reappeared, jaunty and humming. The hat was thrown like a quoit on to the peg, he ripped off his clothes and started to put on his beard – the right way round. I couldn't resist, after a few moments, saying, 'What has happened, Ernest? You have changed your tune.' 'I'll *tell* you, dear Alec,' he replied, doing wild things with a powder puff. 'There's a little Catholic Church round the corner.' (He always pronounced it Ca-ar-tholic.) 'I knelt before a statue of our Blessed Lady and I said, "*Dear* Mother of *God*, forgive that filthy *bugger* on the *New Statesman*," and immediately I felt better and here I am.' He became, for the evening, sprightliness itself; he even managed to make a near-complimentary remark about Valk – 'Full of blood, isn't he?'

During the war I had taken my ship a few times, in the Anzio beachhead days, between the mainland of Italy and the island of Ischia, but always at night. The beautiful, mysterious, romantic silhouette of Ischia beckoned me for the future and I promised myself, when the war was over, I would return to see it by daylight and have a holiday there. In the very early summer of 1948, an opportunity presenting itself, I booked Merula, Matthew and myself into a small hotel, practically on the beach, a mile or two up the coast from the crumbled fairy castle isthmus of Castel San Angelo. One evening in St Peter's Square, shortly before we were due to leave, I was showing maps of the Naples area to Ernest when he said, rather wistfully, and to my surprise, that he had never been to Italy. On an impulse, with insufficient reflection, I invited him to join us. After reassurance that there would be no financial difficulty, and a warning that it would be a very simple sort of holiday, he accepted. 'But clothes!' he said, with horror. 'I have no clothes!' I sent him the next day to Lilly-white's, where he bought a beige cotton suit, a panama hat and white shoes. He envisaged the holiday, I fear, as a kind of *Death in Venice* situation, strolling on Lido-like beaches, sipping long cool drinks and eyeing the jeunesse dorée. 'And Rome, Alec?' he half-suggested. 'I couldn't go to Italy and not see Rome. It would be so disloyal.' So I added a couple of nights in Rome to our itinerary, rather against my will. Perhaps I have made him sound as if he was cadging; if so, it is a wrong impression. He never sought anything for himself except work. If he hinted at Rome it was because he would have been genuinely distressed, having gone so far south, not to have a chance to glimpse the power-house of his religion.

It never occurred to me that Ernest might not be able to swim. As our holiday was spent mostly on the beach, beside an inviting, calm, bright blue sea, it was somewhat embarrassing when Matthew, who had only just learned to swim, would constantly call out, 'Come on in, Mr Milton, it's lovely out here!' Ernest managed to suggest, to save his face before the very young, that he could swim really, if he wanted to; but the most he would allow himself was some bobbing and splashing in about three feet of water. Matthew was clearly not convinced. All went well, in a childishly happy way, until the day Ernest spilled a whole bottle of sun-tan oil on the Lillywhite suit. 'Ruin! Ruin!' he howled. Timon of Athens had nothing on him for rage at his own folly, contempt for an island that had no dry-cleaning facilities, and the desire to exile himself far from the sight of men. He suggested, when he had calmed down, after about three days, that we should make an expedition to Naples to get the wretched suit cleaned but I wouldn't allow it. The incident might have spoiled the holiday had we not stumbled across Peter Glenville and William Hardy-Smith, also holidaying on Ischia. Peter and I had met briefly a couple of times before but William was unknown to me; their bright good humour and their ability to soothe Ernest out of his tragic attitudinising saved our remaining days on Ischia from pursed-lip exasperation. Also it heralded, for me, the commencement of a long, close friendship with both of them.

Matthew found a pleasing companion, a personable young fisherman called Salvatore, who inhabited a ramshackle hut on the beach; the two of them spent happy hours each day playing in the sand with Matthew's dinky cars and trucks, which accompanied him everywhere. I envied Salvatore's ability to be so completely absorbed in infantile games and detected a trace of jealousy in myself (always fearful of being thought a rotten father) and Ernest was quick to notice and comment on it. 'When are you going to learn wisdom, Alec?' he asked. I answered without a thought, 'When I'm sixty-four.' Then I began to torture myself with the number sixty-four – what, if anything, did it mean? At first I decided I was going to die at the age of sixty-four; later, that perhaps it meant that I would die in the year 1964. Ernest reminded me, over the years, of this small aberration with, 'You're still far from sixty-four,' whenever he heard me express some ill-considered opinion or saw me upset by a triviality.

We left Ischia for Rome. Ernest's first pilgrimage was to the great basilica of S. Maria Maggiore where, no sooner had we pushed our way through the huge leather draught-excluders, than he stood stock still in horror. Sniffing the slightly incensed air he let out a loud petulant hiss, 'The Real Presence isn't here!' Nothing quite satisfied him, neither the Forum – where he saw himself as Julius Caesar – not St Peter's nor S. Clemente. But he was greatly taken by an all-female band which played song hits of the thirties outside a café, and even more enraptured by the mildly erotic fountains at Tivoli. He envisaged himself, I believe, in the smarter costumes of all centuries from 70 BC onwards – sometimes in a purple toga, sometimes in parti-coloured tights with a cheeky feather in his hat, sometimes in a Cardinal's silk, and always with delightful pages in attendance. I watched his sad eyes scour the Roman hills, as if they might house his true home if only he could find it, a spiritual home which San Francisco, London and the twentieth century had in many ways denied him.

We went to see Keats's grave in the Protestant Cemetery. I had visited it in early 1939, when it was well cared for, and again after the fall of Rome, when I found it overgrown and, buried in the long wet grass, a few withered stems of flowers, black with decay, stuck in a small, muddy jar for meat paste – the only offering to a great poet since war had broken out. Now it was tidy again but, as always, a sad spot. Ernest turned it immediately into a vale of uncontrollable tears, with screams of grief, and he had to be dragged away to a taxi. Keats combined with Rome does strange things to rare spirits. (Iris Tree was greatly given to reading the 'Ode to a Grecian Urn' from the Spanish Steps, with Lord Butler sitting at her feet weeping.) I kept a sharp eye on Ernest that evening, as he pushed the tagliatelli around his plate in a desultory way, indifferent to the gaieties of the Piazza Navona and deaf to our chatter.

The following winter, back in London, Ernest came to dinner one evening; sensing he was desperate to act something I asked him if he would read some *Macbeth* to us as I had never seen him in the part. He only had Merula and myself for audience and our sitting-room for theatre but he seemed pleased by the idea. After sipping a glass of port he took a small edition of the play – he felt he knew the lines but needed a safeguard – and said he would prefer to act a scene rather than read. Moving across the room when he felt inclined but mostly standing stock still he gave us Macbeth and Lady Macbeth in the scenes immediately prior to and following the murder of Duncan. He presented a haunted man in whom you felt the poison of evil rising, something supercharged from a mysterious black world and, in some strange alchemical way, he changed the atmosphere of our shabby room for days to come. It was almost as if blood had been dripped on the carpet. We were enormously impressed and told him so. I also thought it sad that a younger generation of actors had never witnessed his particular magic, so I suggested that he should sing for his supper again the following week, when I would find two or three actors who would appreciate him to make more of an audience. He agreed and said that the following week he would give us Lear rather than Macbeth. I invited Richard Burton and Richard Leech with whom I had recently become friendly. Both were young, bright, perceptive, comparatively unknown contract players of small parts to H. M. Tennent.

It proved a lamentable, rather embarrassing evening, during which we had at times to gulp back our suppressed laughter. Ernest was self-conscious in an 'actory' way, his reading was false, and he could scarcely take his eyes from the beauty of Burton's head; in short, for Lear, he presented an ingratiating old queen who was about to have the vapours. He complained of a headache, of not being in the mood, and left early. The next day he telephoned and by way of apology said, 'I was *distracted* by such beauty. Ah, the breasts' (pronounced braasts') 'and the eyes of the young men are *damning*,' and he rang off abruptly.

Not long after this his wife, Naomi Royde Smith, died. His life became accident-prone, embittered and querulous; he suffered dreadfully from the actor's disease of persecution mania. He never told me of Naomi's death and barely referred to it in later years, but one day when I visited him at a small hotel in Hampstead he showed me a few keepsakes of hers and very tenderly said, 'I loved her.' And he meant it, though it had the theatrical tone of Hamlet's 'I loved Ophelia'. Within an hour, after some food, he reverted to an area of his marriage, saying, 'It will surprise you, dear Alec, when I tell you that only one woman really aroused me physically. Guess who!' I couldn't even guess at one. Triumphantly he came out with, 'Lilian Baylis!' It certainly did surprise me and I asked, impertinently, for details, which he declined to provide, but he gave me a lubricious leer and somehow I believed him. But then I always believed him.

He took me one Sunday morning to Mass at St Etheldreda's in Holborn, a favourite haunt of his, and explained what was going on seriously, beautifully, tactfully and with great simplicity. I returned the compliment a few days later by giving him a revolting, pretentious dinner at a new restaurant in Covent Garden where, unfortunately, he worked himself up to an un-Christian frenzy at another actor's Hamlet, which he had seen forty years previously. 'He stole all his best readings from me,' he said, thumping the table. 'You remember the way I said, "The potent poison quite o'crows my spirit?" ' He rose from the table and gave the line a full Drury Lane treatment, bawling out, 'the potent POISON', to the consternation of the other diners, who dropped their forks with horror, wondering if they were eating the same dish. There were furtive looks towards his plate. I had to hurry him away past the scowls of the pompous waiters, never to darken their doors again. Not long afterwards the restaurant closed its doors for good. Perhaps Ernest had put a curse on it. I certainly did; but Ernest's would have been more potent.

Later on he became a resident of Denville Hall, a pleasant home for retired actors in North London, where I visited him a few times (too infrequently, I fear) but always bearing a box of soft-centred chocolates, for which he had an unaccountable passion. Fay Compton spotted me one afternoon loaded with flowers, chocolates and a bottle of wine. 'Who's that for?' she demanded. I told her. 'Take care he doesn't bite you,' she snapped. 'He's an asp when he's roused.' Turning down a corridor I ran into a dear old actor I knew, his neck in a plaster halter, hobbling on two sticks but exuding, as always, his considerable charm. 'Who are all the goodies for?' he asked. When I told him they were for Ernest Milton he said, 'My dear fellow, you are a very, very brave man. Just give me time to get away before you open his door.' Fay's acidulous nature I was used to and could be amused by, but this second warning alarmed me. I wondered if Ernest had gone crazy and I knocked on his door with some trepidation. I found him in a wheelchair, very pale, frail and melancholic. My gifts were accepted in silence and conversation proved almost impossible.

'They tell me,' I said, 'that you are being taken to Lourdes next week.'

'Am I?'

'Well, aren't you?'

'So they say.'

'That's nice. Do you know where you will be staying?'

'No.'

'Well, I hope it's somewhere pleasant, that doesn't smell of Irish stew. And I suppose someone will take you down to the grotto.'

'What grotto?'

'You know – the grotto at Lourdes where Our Lady is reputed to have appeared to St Bernadette.'

'Bernie who?'

'St Bernadette. The peasant girl. Eighteen-fortyish.'

'I don't know what the hell you are talking about.'

He closed his eyes and either fell asleep or pretended to sleep. Quietly I let myself out of the room. I never saw him again. Not long after, death took him gently away.

There was a memorial service for him at the Catholic church in Maiden Lane, not very far from some of the theatres he had graced, at which Albert Finney (always ready with a sympathetic hand for actors in distress) and I read the unintelligible lessons in boring translations. We were, I believe, the only actors present; the very sparse congregation had no idea whose requiem they were attending and made no enquiries. The whole service had an air of indifference, though Albert and I were genuine mourners. Ernest should have been sent to his rest to the sound of a full choir, with boys' treble voices, clouds of incense and surrounded by dozens of beeswax candles.

CHAPTER THIRTEEN

The Prime Minister Has It In Mind

The tall, angular lady in a severe blue felt hat, who met me at Mexico City airport, was not too pleased at having to be up and about at 2 a.m. and being required to see some actor-chappie through immigration and customs. 'Your plane is over an hour late,' she said accusingly, as if I had been responsible for the head winds. I felt sorry for her and said, 'You shouldn't have waited.' 'Ambassador's orders,' she replied, implying duty encompassed the most unpleasant tasks. We drove to my hotel through the moonlight and mostly in silence. A hundred or so Mexican peons, squatting on their haunches, wearing white pyjamas and vast straw hats, were wearily chipping away at the stone paving of a great plaza we passed through. 'Do they work all night?' I asked. 'They are not the only ones,' she said meaningfully. When we reached my small, elegant, modern hotel she gave me my instructions. 'The Ambassador will see you at ten in the morning. Don't be late. A car will pick you up here at twenty to ten. The driver's name is Miguel. Remember Mexico City is very high up; new arrivals sometimes find difficulty in breathing.' She said goodnight without a smile and, duty done, sped away into the beauty of the early hours with obvious relief. It was my first visit to Mexico and I found myself excited, entranced, jet-lagged and, indeed, breathless.

Two weeks before going to Mexico – this was in the summer of 1958 – I was on a short holiday in Venice, together with my wife, son and Peter Bull. Those were the days when the travel allowance was £200 a year and I was slightly anxious as how we would manage, staying, as we intended, at the Grand Hotel. Shortly before leaving London David Lean telephoned to say he would be passing through Venice but would probably miss us; he asked if I was all right for cash. I said I was doubtful, and very kindly he offered to leave £200 worth of lire with the concierge at the Grand, and more if we wanted it. I said £200 would be fine, and this I collected immediately on arrival. A few days later the telephone rang in our room early in the morning and a lady's voice said, 'The Consul wishes to see you at four o'clock this afternoon. It's very important.' 'Oh, God!' I thought. 'I'm going to be accused of violating currency restrictions.'

It was a great nuisance, interfering with a holiday afternoon, but I turned up at the British Consulate as commanded and was welcomed affably enough. The Consul's wife, a Scots lady, provided tea and Dundee cake while we pursued a rather aimless conversation. Tea finished, she said with a knowing look, 'I am sure you gentlemen have something to talk about,' and withdrew. There was a long pause before the Consul spoke. Finally he said, 'I had a call from the Foreign Office this morning. They want you to go to Mexico next week. Apparently there is to be a Film Festival of some sort and they think it important an English actor should be present. They want someone they can be sure will behave himself. You may not know it but we have been supplying arms to Batista in Cuba and as a result we British are very unpopular in Mexico at the moment; particularly as it looks certain that Castro will take over in Cuba before long.'

'How on earth would my presence make the slightest difference?' I asked.

'Heaven knows!' he replied. 'Of course your fare and hotel expenses will be taken care of by the Foreign Office. They would like you to go for a week.' I was so relieved at not being accused of a minor piece of financial fiddling that I felt bold enough to make further comment.

'That's all very well,' I said, 'but it's very humiliating for British subjects abroad not being able to return hospitality, for instance. Being in Venice, in a very private capacity, is bad enough; I'm nearly through my meagre allowance already: I assume I shall be allowed to renew my allowance or even take more.' 'I am afraid not,' he said. 'Anyway,' he continued, with what I interpreted as a touch of slyness, 'actors always have the means of picking up an extra couple of hundred pounds when they want it, don't they?'

'I'll go,' I said. And so I found myself in Mexico City, moving slowly for lack of oxygen, and not having a clue as to what was required of me.

Standing at the window of my Mexican hotel in the morning, taking in great gulps of air, I gazed at the dazzling view.

> I stood where Popacatapetl
> In the sunlight gleams.

Miguel was on the dot at 9.40 with a black limousine and we drove sedately through the residential part of the city; there wasn't a soul about.

'Where is everyone?' I asked. 'It can't be siesta time yet.'

'Troubles,' Miguel replied. 'You can see down the side-roads there are barricades.'

'What for?' I asked.

'Troubles,' he said again. 'It is expected many peoples will storm your British Embassy. You will see.'

When we arrived at the Embassy I saw what he meant; the entire building was boarded up, as if for a siege, and the gates boarded and chained; there were a few eye-holes and presumably gun-slits. After a hurried unchaining and unbolting of the gates I was hustled into a small front garden. The lady who had met me at the airport stood on the Embassy steps looking at her watch. 'Just ten o'clock,' she said by way of good morning, 'Follow me.' I followed her to a small study where His Excellency was reading the newspapers. He was a small elderly man and from an ear dangled wires to a hearing-aid apparatus.

'Guinness?'

'Yes, sir,' I said.

'Do sit down. Well, you see the fix we are in.' He adjusted his wires. 'It is not a pleasant situation. Have you been to Mexico before?'

I told him I hadn't.

'Speak Spanish?'

I told him I didn't.

'Pity,' he said.

I told him I had once had to make quite a long speech in Spanish, for a film, that I had learned it phonetically and understood that my accent was reasonably acceptable, but of course I couldn't very well just go around repeating that.

'Come again,' he said, agitating some knobs.

'No, I don't speak Spanish,' I said, and decided to abandon any attempt at facetious jokes.

'I heard you the first time.' The Ambassador looked a little put out.

'What am I expected to do?' I asked.

'I have no idea,' he replied. 'There is some sort of Film Festival on. More your province than mine. Make yourself agreeable. Let them know you are British. We are not at all popular, I should warn you. Well, do your best. Good luck. Thank you for dropping in. Goodbye.' He shook hands and returned to his daily papers. The blue-hatted lady was waiting for me outside the study door.

'They are showing a film you are in tomorrow night and we want you to be there.'

'*The Bridge on the River Kwai?*'

'No, it's not called that. Something about a horse. The Festival opens tonight but you needn't attend. And please wear this badge on the lapel of your coat.' She handed me a small, circular, cardboard Union Jack.

'Won't I get shot on sight if I do?' I asked. She closed her eyes in pained disapproval of the remark, not at the prospect. I pinned the badge to my coat.

Going back to the hotel, past the barricades, I wondered if on the following evening I would be expected to say a few words; I had forgotten to ask. At the concierge's desk I scribbled a very short speech – just in case – saying how marvellous it was to be in Mexico City, how I hoped the Festival would be an annual event and, quite untruly, that I brought fraternal greetings, etc., etc., from all the actors in England. This I handed to the reception desk asking for it to be translated into Spanish. When it was done I spent the rest of the day wandering through the streets of the city learning it. It is my habit to copy out lines I have to learn on small cards, like visiting cards, and keep them in a pocket so that I can take a look at them during odd moments, and I did the same on this occasion; but I learned the beginning and the end first, leaving out the padding in the middle, in case I found the whole thing too difficult. In any case, I reflected, I had twenty-four hours in which to get it under my belt.

While I was sampling a very fierce tequila in the hotel bar that evening, screwing up my face at the lime and salt, I was summoned to the telephone. It was the lady from the Embassy. 'You are to go to the Festival tonight. Miguel will pick you up in half an hour. Wear your badge.' Luckily I had made no other plans.

The Festival was held in a vast hall, not unlike Earls Court, and must have housed at least seven thousand people. I was given a seat far back in the ramped auditorium and noticed there were several people wearing their national badges – Spanish, Mexican, Argentinian, Japanese, French, German, North American and Russian – but no other person I could see sported a Union Jack. I felt very lonely. Someone made a speech, presumably of welcome, from the stage and then called on various delegates to stand and say a few words. 'Our delegate from Russia!' he called out, and a spotlight pierced its way to a large, grizzled-haired gentleman who appeared to me to be impeccably dressed in what looked like a Lanvin suit. A microphone was thrust at him and he growled a short speech in Russian, which was not understood by anyone, and sat down to polite applause. The same thing happened with the Italians, Scandinavians and all the others who were called upon although naturally the Spanish and South Americans were understood. Finally the man on stage announced, 'And now, our representative from Great Britain.' There was silence, followed by a low, prolonged hiss. I took a quick look at the cards in my pocket and rose, very unsurely, to my feet. The audience was astonished at being addressed in Spanish by a foreigner and broke out in tumultuous applause. Flushed and astonished by my sudden success I sat down; and was immediately tapped on the shoulder by the Embassy lady. She was all smiles. 'Jolly good show,' she said.

The following evening there was a screening of *The Horse's Mouth*; not a really suitable film, I thought, for such a large non-English-speaking audience; *The Bridge on the River Kwai* would have been better fare, but at that time was not permitted to be shown in Mexico, for reasons that I forget.

The British Ambassador and his wife and entourage came to the film and we sat together. There had been reports in the papers about my little speech in Spanish and there was a growing feeling that a Union Jack badge was not quite such an unpopular emblem. The film ended to wild cheering (it had not been enthusiastically received in England) and as I followed His Excellency along the red carpet to the exit he pushed me ahead of him, saying, 'It's your evening. Go ahead.' He was either very wise, if not slightly cunning, or he can have had no idea of the shambles that awaited us. Hundreds of poor people, none of whom can have been at the showing, were trying to get on to the carpet to shake my hand or even just touch me. A vast cordon of police was broken and they drew their truncheons to bash the crowd. Some were knocked to the ground but the crowd kept on yelling, 'Alecco Guins!' I tried protesting to the police but was brushed aside. The Ambassador disappeared in the mêlée, while I was shoved unceremoniously into a waiting car. That was not the end of it; the car was picked up by about twenty enthusiasts and carried down the road. 'Where is the Ambassador?' asked the flabbergasted Miguel as we bobbed on our way. 'Lost in the crowd,' I told him. 'But this is *his* car!' he said. 'You must be in the one behind.' Our sweating, puffing, grinning escort finally put us down and I saw the other car, with its diplomatic load, slowly drive up behind us. The Ambassador opened a window and shouted, 'You go on. I'll go back to the Embassy in this.' I tried to get out but it was impossible; but I did manage to call out, 'I am so sorry,' – but he couldn't hear me.

The next day all barricades were taken down and the Embassy unchained. I attended a small press luncheon and was photographed sitting on British farm machinery and trying on Scottish knitwear. In the evening I was entertained to dinner by a Mexican millionaire of immense charm who presented me with a beautiful little, valuable, pre-Colombian figurine – later to be smashed by my Abyssinian cat. The following day I managed to get out to the great Aztec pyramid – Popacatapetl always in the distance, gleaming – and to see over the University: but always pursued by a genial press who wanted to photograph me wearing vast, highly-decorated sombreros or take up attitudes as if doing a flamenco dance. None of this is my style but I submitted as cheerfully as I could, almost dying of embarrassment in the service of my country. On my last day I attended a slap-up luncheon, sitting next to an extremely elegant lady who spoke perfect English who said, 'Don't go back to Europe. Come down to Yucatan for the weekend. I have a nice little place. We will shoot the cat.' 'These delightful people,' I thought momentarily, 'are really not to be trusted. They eat tiny birds, talk of feathered serpents, worship the sun, kill each other with obsidian knives and now invite me to shoot cats.' I eyed her warily before saying, with some horror, 'Cats?' 'Yes,' she said, firmly. 'The jaguar, of course. You don't shoot?' 'Not jaguars,' I replied, 'or tigers, or lions, or anything of that ilk.' Her mouth twisted with contempt and I thought she might be capable of arranging for the barricades to be put up again. 'Ah, yes,' she said, 'you are English.'

In the evening the lady from the Embassy saw me off at the airport. She proved very genial but in saying goodbye she extended her arm straight out from her shoulder (as if pulling a longbow) and I did the same. We were, I reckoned, yards apart. 'So long,' she said. 'Hasta luego,' I replied. I have always meant to return to Mexico; Chimborazo, Cotopaxi . . . magic names for me, always.

A week after I returned home, sorting through a few letters at the breakfast table, I spotted one from 10 Downing Street. I slit it open, rather puzzled, and read the short letter twice, to make sure I wasn't imagining things, before saying to Merula, 'What am I to do? It's from 10 Downing Street and it says I am to reply by return of post.'

'What's it about?' Merula asked.

'About?' I said – and I was genuinely astonished and rather fearful.

'It says, and I quote, "The Prime Minister has it in mind to rec-ommend to The Queen, etc., etc., – that I should receive a knight-hood. But I am to say immediately if I would be a willing recipient, etc." It is signed by Mr Macmillan's Private Secretary.'

'What are you going to say?' Merula asked, spreading more marma-lade.

'What do you think I should say?' I rejoined.

'Would you like it?' she asked.

'Well, yes; I'd like it all right. But it's a bit strange.'

We finished breakfast in silence, both of us ruminating. Then I wrote to the Private Secretary, happily accepting the honour if it was finally approved of. When I had stamped and sealed the envelope I returned to Merula.

'Do you think shop prices will shoot up for us?' I asked.

'Not for some months,' she replied.

I remained in a daze for most of the day, shamefacedly going over memories of the past forty-odd years, and picking out particularly Venice and Mexico City.

> Chimborazo, Cotopaxi –
> they had stolen my soul away.

CHAPTER FOURTEEN

Sneck Up

Over the years Ralph Richardson, always generous to a fault, gave me a number of presents which I greatly treasure, including a finely-bound set of Sheridan, an exquisite malacca cane with a rhinoceros-horn handle and a beautifully-carved walking stick, late seventeenth-century, made from a narwhal's tooth. All I ever gave him, I think, was a classic work on parrots when he bought José, a highly-coloured bird, in Spain, and a white azalea on his seventieth birthday.

Some time ago, three days after an operation for a hernia and sitting up in a hospital bed, the door to my room was pushed slowly open. It was a Sunday afternoon and all was very quiet and dreary. I looked at the door expecting to see someone at eye level but the figure that entered was on the ground. Pushing a pile of books before him Ralph crawled in on all fours.

'Who,' he asked immediately, 'is Miss Mackenzie?'

'Never heard of her,' I replied.

'She is your next-door neighbour. Shall we have her in?'

'Don't be ridiculous,' I said, 'she's probably just had an operation. Like I have.'

Ralph deposited the books on my bed and went to the adjoining wall and thumped on it.

'Miss Mackenzie? This is Ralph Richardson. I am in Alec Guinness's room. We would like you to visit us. Do you hear me, Miss Mackenzie?'

There was an ominous silence, but Ralph continued in spite of my protests.

'Are you lonely, Miss Mackenzie? Guinness is lonely too. He would appreciate your company.'

He sat on my bed, chatting for ten minutes, explaining how eyes were first formed by sea-worms rubbing against rocks, and then left the room, again on all fours. He must have had a very good lunch. I forgot about his visit until the floor sister woke me the following morning.

'Wasn't it awful about Miss Mackenzie!' she said cheerfully.

'What's happened?' I asked with some apprehension.

'Apparently she thought she heard strange voices and in the night she got up – she is very ill – and ran out of the hospital in her nightgown and went screaming round Bryanston Square before she was caught. Now she is heavily sedated.'

'Poor thing,' I said, and opened one of Ralph's books.

Such times as I visited him in his dressing-room he always poured me half a pint of champagne into a silver tankard; he appeared to knock back half a pint of gin himself with just a splash of water. On one occasion he rose to his feet, stood at attention and raised his beaker in a military-style toast. 'To Jesus Christ. What a splendid chap!' – and gulped it all down. He often made references to his Catholic and Quaker upbringing but I never heard him discuss religious matters or politics. He seemed happiest, socially, when talking about books, his ferret, his rat, his parrot, painting, or his boyhood in East Sussex or his love of Northern England. He rarely talked of theatre or films and I never heard him mention one of his own performances.

We only appeared together in three plays, two films and one television. The television (*Twelfth Night*) was unfortunate; very uncharacteristically Ralph took a great dislike, and expressed it, to a young actor playing a small part whom he referred to, *sotto voce*, as 'Bright Eyes'.

'What about Bright Eyes?' he asked me one day early on in rehearsals.

'What about him?'

'I don't go much on Bright Eyes,' he said.

'Well, he's not very experienced.'

A day or two later Ralph enlarged on his displeasure.

'Bright Eyes,' he said. 'Have you noticed? He wears a bracelet.'

'It's only a plain gold bangle. Probably some sort of identification. A lot of young persons wear them nowadays.'

Ralph looked suspicious and a few days later cornered me again.

'Bright Eyes,' he said.

'Well?'

After a long pause he said, 'Not right for the part.'

He never mentioned Bright Eyes again or, as far as I know, ever spoke to him. He remained dejected throughout the remainder of the production but managed to be comforting to me. Joan Plowright was the Viola and Larry Olivier was invited to watch the final run-through of the play. Having quite a long gap with nothing to do I went up to the viewing box to see some of it. Larry caught me by the arm, saying, 'Fascinating, old dear. I never realised before that Malvolio could be played as a bore.' It was my fault for taking a peek and I was a little put out; I would hear the word 'bore' running through the rest of my performance. When I told Ralph he shrugged it off with, 'He's wrong, old cock. He *can* be wrong, you know. I think your performance is fine.' I was grateful to him for not adding, 'I can be wrong too.' It was generous of him, particularly as he was going through agonies with his own performance.

One night in Madrid, where we were filming *Dr Zhivago*, I took him and his delightful wife, Mu, to a rather precious little restaurant I had been told about in the old quarter of the city. The food turned out to be not particularly good but the clientèle was amusingly odd, largely consisting of aged Spanish grandees sitting at little rickety tables communicating with each other through enamelled ear-trumpets. Ralph, well-wined, got on to the subject of his beloved ferret, describing how it had chased a white-coated house-painter through his house. The ferret, Ralph insisted, had thought the painter was a rival rodent and was determined to get him by the throat. To tell his story Ralph acted it out, rising from his chair, hiding behind it, making a dash for another table and squatting on the floor beside some astonished old Marquesa, rising on tip-toe with a hiss and finally dashing round the room pretending to be the painter on the run. Ear-trumpets followed him like Triffids, napkins were flicked in his direction and old voices croaked in horror. Out in the street, no taxis being available, Mu and I marched him for what seemed miles through the damp and cold. He was extremely cheerful and insisted we go to some very impoverished-looking bar which was just about to close. There were no other customers and the sweet, tired-looking woman who ran the bar poured us hefty brandies. Language was a difficulty but Ralph expressed great admiration for a highly-coloured oleograph of the Blessed Virgin, framed in sea-shells, which stood among the bottles on a shelf. 'You like?' asked the woman. 'I show you better. Please come.' So we followed her up steep, creaking stairs to her bedroom. There, among a muddle of knick-knacks, powder puffs, mantillas, fans, dolls and Spanish flags, stood a large statue of the Sacred Heart exposing his viscera, wearing a blue ribbon and surrounded by red and yellow feathers.

'You like?' she asked proudly.

'She's lovely,' said Ralph.

'Not she! He!' Mu said sharply.

'Ah!' Ralph sounded surprised. 'I hadn't noticed the beard.'

As we left the premises Ralph pushed a handful of high-denomination banknotes towards the woman – probably about £20-worth. Her mouth fell open with astonishment, tears filled her eyes, and as we went out of the door I saw her turn with gratitude towards the sea-shelled Madonna.

A few days later Ralph and Mu left for a fortnight in England and I felt excessively lonely. On the day they were due back in Madrid I telephoned and asked them to dinner again but they declined, although Mu said I would be welcome to an omelette if I came round to their hotel fairly early; an invitation I jumped at.

A waiter with a menu opened the door for me to the luxurious Richardson suite.

'Who can one hit,' said Ralph, 'if not one's friends?'

As he advanced across the hall I assumed it was to shake my hand; but there I was wrong. A fist landed unexpectedly on my jaw and I slumped to the carpet. The waiter, who had come to take an order for dinner, fled in panic. Mu, who had seen it all from the sitting-room, called out, by way of explanation, 'He's very tired.'

'What was all that about?' I asked rather peevishly as I picked myself up. But Ralph had already sunk into a deep armchair and was apparently fast asleep; and he remained that way for an hour or so.

It wasn't typical of him to welcome guests in that way, but it is a fair example of how unpredictable such a steady, kindly and courteous man could be if the mood seized him. You were always on the alert for some possible eccentricity and yet you were always taken by surprise. His timing was impeccable, though individual. He was decisive, practical and very aware even when he seemed to be dreaming. His motives were always honourable and I never heard him make a derogatory remark about anyone – except, by implication, about 'Bright Eyes' and an excessively camp understudy who had to go on at short notice at the Old Vic. Ralph watched the understudy for a while from the wings, wincing, and then turned to me, whispering under his breath, 'Oh dear! Oh no!' Then he strode on stage and pulled everything together.

The first time I met him must have been in about 1936, at a small party given by Peggy Ashcroft at her house on Campden Hill. We all were glancing anxiously towards a stout, middle-aged gentleman who looked as if he might be sick on the carpet; but Ralph frustrated him, picking him up like a child, running downstairs and depositing

him in the gutter outside. Ralph made no comment when he rejoined
the party except to apologise, with old-world gallantry, to John
Gielgud's mother for having trodden on her feet.

As an actor he was compelling and could be wonderful to the point
of greatness. His early Toby Belch (though not the performance
in the television *Twelfth Night* in which we found both ourselves
floundering), his Cyrano, Peer Gynt and Bottom were superb; as
were many of his modern parts (particularly in *For Services Rendered,
Sheppey* and *Home*), but it was his Falstaff which was definitive and
truly great – witty, cunning, bombastic and rather sad – a man
regretfully saying goodbye to the pleasures of the flesh and cocking
a quizzical eye at the foolishness of all men, including his own.
Whatever Ralph touched he imbued with nobility; even his famous
motorbike seemed like some splendid, black, mediaeval steed champ-
ing for its knightly rider to charge, though the targets were sometimes
only windmills in the head. Of all the actors of repute in our time
he was, I think, the most interesting as a man; original, shrewd,
knowledgeable, commonsensical and yet visionary, with a great love
of animals, a respect for inanimate objects and a passion for books.
He was pained that I couldn't share his enthusiasm for Conrad and
could only meet him halfway over Henry James (preferring, as I
do in that area, Edith Wharton). But he introduced me to many
contemporary books which I could read with confidence and pleasure.

Dozens of actors imitate him well and amusingly (the best, in my
experience, being Anthony Quayle and Michael Jayston) and in the
past twenty years or so Ralph 'stories' have multiplied prodigiously
and become theatrical legend. Most of them I believe to be true,
which is rare in theatrical gossip.

When I was with him in Priestley's *An Inspector Calls* he came to
my dressing-room one evening and said, 'Your patent leather shoes
squeak horribly. Do something about it.' I explained that I had tried
oil and vaseline but nothing seemed to help. 'Try water,' he said.
The following evening when I went to put them on, during a fairly
quick change of clothes, I found the shoes standing in a bucket of
water. I squelched noisily through the last act and then missed two
performances through near pneumonia. When I returned to the
theatre I called on him to apologise for my absence. 'Oh, have you
been off, cocky? I didn't notice.' The shoes were never mentioned.

A story I have always liked, told me many years ago by Beatrix
Lehmann, concerned a fast car and a tiny aeroplane. Ralph invited
her one Sunday to go for 'a little spin in the air' as he had hired a

plane for the day. He drove her through London, with small regard to traffic lights or other cars, at eighty miles an hour with Bea screaming, 'Slow down!' and punching him hard on the arm. When they arrived at the airfield she got out, shakily, and shouted, '*Never* do that to me again! *Much* too fast!' They climbed into the plane and took off. The plane lolloped through the air desperately slowly with Bea now screaming, 'For God's sake *go faster!*' But no, they remained just airborne until they slumped in a field.

Beautiful cars were a joy to him but he objected to the ostentatious. He told me once, with a lot of chuckling laughter, of an outing he had with Jack Priestley who was at the wheel of his brand new and flashy car. Priestley, appreciating Ralph's knowledge and love of cars, was seeking his approval and suggested a 'jaunt to Brighton'. After several miles of driving in silence Priestley turned to him and said in his broadest Yorkshire accent, 'Well, what do you think of the bus, eh?' Ralph hesitated before taking the bull by the horns. 'I'm sorry, Jack. I'm *really* sorry. I don't like it.'

'Why not?' snapped Jack.

'It's all very fine – but this dashboard! It's hellish! All these little bits of glass that look like fake diamonds and emeralds! And all this gilt work. I'm sorry, but it's *vulgar!*'

There was a horrible pause before Priestley said, 'I asked you out to enjoy yourself, not to criticise.'

They turned round and drove home. Ralph said it was months before Jack would forgive him.

A few years ago, after Ralph and Mu had given me dinner at a smart London hotel, we walked slowly across the road to his car while he fumbled in a pocket for a pound note. An obsequious commissionaire, with a sharp eye for a good tip, followed us, raising his top-hat and saying, 'Good night, Sir Alec. Nice to see you, sir. And good night to you, too, Sir John.' 'Bastard!' Ralph muttered, putting away the money. However, as we reached the car I noticed him surreptitiously take out the note again and slip it to the man. Ralph was lost in a dream and drove at a steady four miles an hour down Oxford Street leading a long line of exasperated buses.

The last time I was with him was on a summer day when he, Larry Olivier and I were to be photographed for a Christmas issue of *Vogue*. (Gielgud and John Mills were unavailable.) In the morning I telephoned to ask if he and Mu would dine with me at the Connaught that night, and when they accepted I called Larry to invite him and Joan Plowright as well but Larry said he wasn't feeling well enough and Joan had a prior engagement. It was arranged that a car should pick up Larry in mid-afternoon from his Chelsea address, collect me from my hotel and that we would then go to Chester Terrace to gather up Ralph. When Larry arrived I thought he looked dreadfully frail, and when he said, 'It's one of my bad days,' I tried to persuade him to go home but he wouldn't hear of it. His sense of duty, which seemed unnecessary on this occasion, has always been of paramount consideration with him, and his courage ever undaunted. We found Ralph, in a brown suit, with bowler hat and yellow gloves, leaning on a silver-knobbed cane on the steps to his house. I got out and whispered to him that Larry was feeling far from well. 'Oh, poor Laurence,' he said, obviously deeply concerned. Ralph got in the car and, sitting next to Larry, took his hand and held it. There was something very touching in the sight of those two elderly great actors sitting side by side; Ralph comforting Larry and Larry dismissing his illness lightly and with wit.

Arriving at the *Vogue* studio, somewhere in the area of Theobald's Road, Ralph bounded up the stairs with alacrity but it was a slower and more painful climb for Larry. At the top of the stairs stood a lovely *Vogue* lady who made, in my opinion, a tactical error; she was holding a tray of bottles of gin, vodka and whisky. 'Welcome!' she said. 'Welcome indeed,' said Ralph, following the tray into the studio.

The bottles were opened and large drinks were poured into outsize tumblers. I declined, rather prissily, saying I couldn't drink in the middle of a hot afternoon without falling asleep. Ralph, in antic disposition, struck a vast number of poses for the photographer while keeping up a soaring, fantastic and wildly funny monologue which was designed, I am sure, to cheer up his old friend; rather like an uncle pulling mad faces to enchant a sad child. Larry began to blossom again and by the end of our session had shed ten years. Going down the stairs again it was Larry who led, almost jauntily, and Ralph who had to be more cautious. Outside the building Ralph refused a lift in the car, saying he intended to walk the two miles home. Bowler-hatted, elegantly accoutred, he waved his cane in a wild valediction and strode off in the wrong direction. 'I'll see you and Mu at eight,' I called after him. Secretly I thought that at about seven Mu would telephone to say they couldn't make it.

Sharp on eight o'clock the swivel doors of the Connaught swung round at speed, propelling Mu and a stately Ralph into the lobby. 'A drink before we go in to dinner?' I queried. 'Perhaps a dry martini,' Ralph said very gravely. Mu rolled her eyes. We sat rather silently

before our drinks while ordering our meal. Ralph only wanted a
Spanish omelette. 'He *always* has a Spanish omelette,' Mu explained
when I protested that it was a dull idea. We eased our way into the
crowded dining-room, which appeared to be full of Americans,
including a bevy of elderly Southern Belles who sat at a round table
near ours. Ralph complained that he couldn't hear anything because
of the loud chatter all about us but he heard when Mu said, 'José bit
Ralph's finger this evening,' because he held up a sore forefinger.
'You remember José?' asked Mu. José was the parrot, which had
been bought in the flea-market in Madrid during the making of *Dr
Zhivago* and had been brought back to England, not exactly in a
diplomatic bag but with all sorts of government certificates obtained
from the British Embassy. I think Ralph had fallen for my South
African Grey which I had for nearly thirty years and talked about
endlessly. (Percy, for that was his name, had on one occasion flown
off across a cornfield and was missing for three days. Breakfasting
out of doors on a bright morning Merula and I suddenly heard,
coming from a distance, Percy sweetly whistling, 'Speed bonny boat
from over the sea to Skye'. Following the sound we found him
perched on a small branch over a fox's lair. When I picked him up
he fainted with relief on my chest.) Ralph was entranced by the story
and immediately wanted to add a parrot to his entourage of rodents.
José, spotted on an afternoon walk, was the answer. He was brought
to the Palace Hotel in Madrid by two small boys who had been his
owners. No cage, no perch; so the parrot sat on the back of a gilded
chair in the Richardson suite, swiftly demolishing most things around
him. According to Ralph the two boys produced a camera and said
they wanted a photograph, so Ralph obligingly posed. 'No, no!' they
chorused, outraged. 'Fotografia of José!'

Mu, always beautiful, elegant and equal to any social occasion, did
her best to pull the three of us together towards some animation but
nothing could displace Ralph's gloom as he stared at his Spanish
omelette. Finally, he said, 'Would you forgive me, old fellow, if I
went home now?'

'Of course,' I said. 'Are you unwell?'

'No. Bored. I'd rather go home.'

He rose from the table and I followed him. As he passed the
Southern Belles he caught his foot in a chair and fell flat on his face.
The Belles all turned round and squealed with excitement, 'Why, if
it isn't Sir Rafe Richardson!' I went to help him but he managed to
pull me down on top of him. '*And* Sir Alex Gwines,' a blue-rinsed

matron added. As waiters got us to our feet Ralph gave me a wicked
look. 'Sneck up!' he said, quoting a line of Toby Belch's to Malvolio.

I offered to get him a taxi but he said he would prefer to walk. I
watched him amble away across Carlos Place, day-dreaming and
looking forlorn. He must have day-dreamed a lot as a boy, and
continued to do so through a long life, for I often thought that the
things he said were not always invented on the spur of the moment
but were dredged up from years of contemplation. A day or two
after our non-dinner at the Connaught he telephoned me.

'Did you walk all the way home?' I asked.

'Yes,' he replied. 'But I sat for a while on a bench in Oxford Street.
It was very nice until a chap on a bicycle stopped by me. "I know
you," he said. "Oh, yes?" I said. "Yes," he said. "You're Sir John
Gielgud," he said. "Fuck off!" I said. Then I walked home. It was a
lovely night for walking. So many stars.'

CHAPTER FIFTEEN

Full Moon in Connemara

Whether it was the intensely bright moonlight that woke me in the early hours of the morning or a desperate attempt to escape from a nightmare I cannot tell. Merula and I were staying in a charming small hotel in Connemara, on a long arm of the sea which reached in from the Atlantic a mile to the west. We had a ground floor semi-suite which faced a vivid green lawn surrounded by bushes of battered October roses, yet the wind only seemed to reach the tops of the trees that enclosed us. The moonlight so disturbed me that, reluctant to shut the curtains, I put on a dressing-gown to sit by the window, and for an hour contemplated the shadows on the now milky-blue grass, the fading globes of pale hydrangeas, and a few leggy, pastel-coloured geraniums. The fir trees had become silent and only the tall eucalyptus behind them swayed furiously. Sitting here at a round table I comforted myself with the beauty of the night and tried to shake off my foolish dream.

In my dream I was eighty years old; ten years older than I am at the time of writing. I was in Hollywood to play a very small part, for which I was being paid handsomely, in a movie directed by David Lean. If I was eighty he must have been getting on for eighty-seven, but he was as lithe and handsome as ever. He appeared to be riding on some giant camera which resembled a combine-harvester. On this strange apparatus were various seats, canvas chairs, slings and steel bars on which were perched a dozen assistant directors I have known in the past, together with camera crews, continuity girls, producers and press representatives. I was heavily made up, with a very black beard, curly black wig, and dressed as some sort of tramp. My part consisted of a few lines, mostly gibberish, and required me to be killed in a train crash. The huge camera was facing a railway truck tilted on its side, about fifteen feet up in the air, and David, wearing his smart blue collarless jacket, had his eye glued to a lens. 'When he arrives,' he said, 'put him in the truck but don't let it fall until we do a take.' 'I suppose we are properly insured,' said a producer I didn't recognise, 'should anything happen.' 'For God's sake,' piped up someone else, 'he's eighty, so what's it matter?' Maggie Unsworth, a delightful continuity girl who always smoothed over awkward situations with great tact, whispered to David, 'Alec is here.' David unfocussed his eye from the lens and re-focussed on me. 'Where have you been?' he asked irritably. 'Crossing the Atlantic and the United States. I got in two hours ago. As you see, I am made up. But I don't appear to have a dressing-room. I changed in a passage.' All the assistant directors jumped off the camera. 'No dressing-room?' they chorused. 'The last time I was at M.G.M. Studios,' I said over-modestly, 'I was given Spencer Tracy's room. Of course I wouldn't expect anything like that now: that was forty years ago and I was starring with Grace Kelly.' 'Oh, we know, we know!' David said. It struck me that no one else knew: the press representatives were feeling for their notebooks. 'Well, climb in the truck,' David said, 'and we'll have a go. When you've said your speech – blah, blah, blah – the camera eases in and the truck falls over. End of you.' 'How do I get in?' I asked. The assistants ran in circles, David thumped his head with his fists and everyone left the set to have coffee. 'I think I'll go home now,' I said to no one in particular. At that moment the truck fell over, doing a lot of damage. Looking at the wreckage I realised that had I been in the truck I would have been crushed to death. 'What a fucking way to die!' I said. Then I saw my doppel-ganger, spread-eagled on the railway-line, its head separate from its body. 'Is the make-up okay?' the head asked. 'The beard is too black,' I replied to the head. I turned to look for David, to ask his opinion, but by now they were all making another film, in a different location, and were no longer concerned with me. I woke, shielding my eyes from the arc-lamp of the moon.

I don't think I have ever had a dream with a film background before; the theatre, yes, regularly, when nearly always the dreams have been nightmares of inadequacy – going on stage not knowing a line, thinking I could cover up some obvious mistake by executing an amateurish little dance, realising my fly isn't zipped, even appear-ing in the wrong theatre before an outraged audience and nonplussed cast. Films have never provided any similar horrors in my sleeping life, though heaven knows they have provided enough angst by day. Tucked into my foolish dream I can detect little touches of the mild paranoia which occasionally assailed me in my late forties and early fifties; a nervous tension and lack of confidence which has taken me years to overcome, or at any rate disguise.

Grainy moving pictures of my film life began to super-impose on

BEFORE AND AFTER MAKE-UP.

Two cartoons by A.G.

LAWRENCE OF — WHERE?

Making up for *Dylan*. Photo: S. Schapiro, *Life* Magazine

With Peter Ustinov. Photo: John Timbers

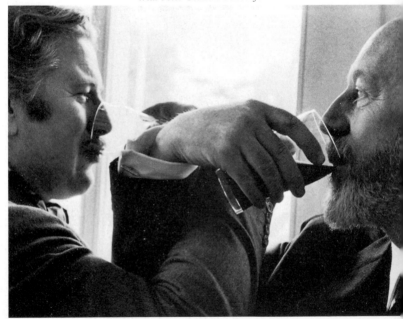

David Lean

Graham Greene

Merula

Matthew

the moonlit view, and then on my closed eyelids when I climbed back to bed. A composite figure of smart lady journalists, writing for glossy magazines, formed itself which, sitting at the bed end, surreptitiously angled a tape-recorder towards me.

'What makes you tick, Sir Alec Guinness?'

'I wasn't aware I ticked.'

'Have you any funny stories about filming which you could tell our readers?'

'Such as the day my toupee blew off?'

'Oh, yes! That's the sort of thing. Were you embarrassed?'

'Why should I have been embarrassed? I hadn't stuck it on myself or made the wind.'

'What is the most embarrassing thing that has ever happened to you?'

'Madam, your clichés are beginning to show.'

In my mind I made her instinctively fumble at her cleavage. She faded to nothing.

Haphazard memories intrude – of Robert Hamer, for instance, who looked and sounded like an endearing but scornful frog. I did four films for him, one of which (*Kind Hearts and Coronets*) was brilliant, one passable, one rather awful, and one quite dreadful. Robert and I spoke the same language and laughed at the same things. He was finely-tuned, full of wicked glee, and was marvellous to actors – appreciative and encouraging. Sadly, with the years, he succumbed increasingly to alcoholism and became a burden to himself and his devoted friends. His loss to the British film industry was a severe blow.

Ealing Studios, although I am eternally grateful to Michael Balcon for the comedies he put in my way, frequently tried to kill me – or so it seemed to me during moments of paranoia. Of course I knew they weren't really trying to kill me; it struck me only that they were rather casual about my safety.

During *Kind Hearts and Coronets* I was required to make a balloon ascent dressed as Lady Agatha D'Ascoigne, in Edwardian clothes. It was to take place on an afternoon from a field near Pinewood Studios. The weather was sunny, with a warm westerly breeze and I was enchanted at the idea of going up in a balloon. The only anxiety I had was about insurance, which I guessed would be inadequate to support my wife and young son should there be an accident. Accordingly I spoke to the producers about it. 'You're well covered,' they said, and when I asked for how much I think they told me

£10,000. I decided it wasn't nearly enough and informed them I wouldn't go up more than fifteen feet in the air unless they raised the insurance to £50,000. They were very huffy and said, 'You will have Belgium's greatest balloonist concealed in the basket with you so you can't possibly come to any harm.' They refused to increase the insurance so when we came to do the shot I insisted on being let down shortly after we had risen from the ground. Contempt was written on all faces. Belgium's greatest balloonist was dressed and be-wigged as Lady Agatha and sailed away. And away. At speed. And then out of sight. The wind took over and the poor man was found some fifty miles away, floundering in a long skirt in the Thames estuary where he had been forced to ditch. Smugly at home I sat down to a hot dinner.

'This is piano-wire,' I said, looking at the thread that was to support me when I did a fifty-foot climb down the side of a house in *The Man in the White Suit*. 'Nothing stronger; it can carry tons,' the property department said. 'Unless it has a kink, in which case it's useless,' I said. 'This wire has no kink. Please don't teach us our business.' My naval training jumped to the fore. 'It should be a right-handed flexible steel wire of about an eighth of an inch,' I explained. Sandy Mackendrick, the brilliant and amiable director stuttered out, reassuringly, 'I'm sure it's all right. Do give it a try.' So I did. As I walked, horizontal to the ground, down the side of the house, suspended by the piano-wire from a belt round my waist, the wire snapped when I was about four feet from the ground and I landed flat on my back. A kink, of course. No one apologised; they rarely do in films, as very few people care to take responsibility. During the making of *The Lady Killers*, again with Mackendrick, I had to stand on the edge of a sixty-foot-high wall and I took hold of what looked like a solid iron rail for support. 'Is this secure?' I called down, when I realised the rail was in fact only wood. 'Perfectly!' they called from below. Whereupon it snapped and I had the good fortune to fall backwards. I have never been physically reckless and now I am cannily over-cautious, skimming through scripts for possible hazards. Recently I declined an admirable script when I spotted that the character I had been asked to play was required to scramble up the side of some giant, jungle waterfall clinging to overhanging ferns. A slippery way to go, I thought, having survived three score and ten.

'A touch more wind on Grace's hair,' they said one afternoon at M.G.M. as Grace Kelly and I, hand in hand, stood at a plaster balustrade apparently gazing out over a non-existent lake. They turned up the wind machine slightly and it blew dust in Grace's eyes, so she had to retire for an hour to be re-made up. When she returned, the director, Charles Vidor, said, 'More wind, fellas, but without the dust.' It came with a whoosh and blew off my toupee. Grace cried with laughter and had to be repaired again by the make-up artist. Another idle hour. In the end they resorted to wafting a gentle breeze by waving a small board at us.

I must have fallen happily asleep before dawn. When I woke it was to be greeted by a dear, bouncing Irish maid bringing in our breakfast. She looked out of the window at the grey sky and heavy drizzle saying, 'It's a fine lovely day, and no mistake.' The day before, Merula and I had hired bicycles and ridden for miles along bumpy tracks across the bog-land, and intended to repeat the exercise that morning but the weather confined us. It seemed a good opportunity for me to follow up my moon-gazing with day-dreaming and scribbling about the peripheries of my film life.

Before the start of Carol Reed's *Our Man in Havana* (script by Graham Greene from his own novel) Noël Coward kindly invited Merula and me to spend ten days with him at his Jamaican home; the idea being that we should get to know each other better before starting work and that then the three of us would fly on together to Havana. Naturally he chose the dates for our visit so I found it a little odd to come across a reference to us in his published diaries (a book I suggested to my favourite bookshop would be more suitable on the fiction tables than the non-fiction) saying, just before our arrival, that he hoped we wouldn't stay too long. Noël was a wonderful and thoughtful host and the other guests, apart from his constant companions Cole Lesley and Graham Payn, were Anton Dolin and John Gilpin. Gilpin was to dance at the end of the year in a ballet devised by Noël; he and Dolin were there to discuss costumes, setting and other balletic matters. The evening we arrived – hours late because of a delayed flight, which Noël took quite well – we were shown around the grounds before going to our guest bungalow near the swimming-pool. 'One marvellous thing about Jamaica,' Noël said, wagging his instructive finger, 'is that there are absolutely no insects and nothing poisonous on the island.' I pointed to something at the side of the pool. 'What's that?' I asked. He gazed at it without seeing before saying, 'I haven't the foggiest.' It was a scorpion. But then his eyes, mostly very observant, were shut to many things he didn't wish to face, or were shut for him. A few days after our arrival

Merula and I were robbed while bathing – our watches, my shaving
gear, fountain pen and a few odds and ends were lifted from our
bedroom. When I told Cole he nearly had a fit – not about our very
minor losses but for fear we might tell Noël. 'The master mustn't
know! Promise you'll never tell him!' We didn't greatly mind but it
was a nuisance not being able to claim insurance; also we knew
perfectly well who had taken the things and I would like to have got
my pen back, but Cole pointed out that any attempt at recovery
would cause trouble in the village and there was Noël's reputation
as a kindly and tolerant employer to be considered. We knuckled
under and from then on I had to keep asking the time.

One evening Noël invited us to dinner up in his eyrie, where he
slept and worked (rather rashly far from any assistance, we thought)
and on the narrow road, surrounded by banana plantations, he ran
over and killed a small goat. He burst into tears, handed over the
driving to someone else, and remained greatly dejected for the next
few hours. Ten shillings was sent down to the goat's owner. 'Give
them ten shillings for a goat,' one of the guests said, 'and they'll stand
in the road throwing their children under the wheel of the car.' 'I
shall never, never drive again!' Noël said, which brought an audible
sigh of relief all round.

We were taken on a tour of his anaemic paintings and found it
difficult to make suitably appreciative noises, but tucked in a dark
corner we spotted a small painting which was really excellent. 'This
is lovely,' we said. We had made a blunder – the painting was not
by Noël but by Cole. On another day we were taken on a raft
down a jungle river, during which we were rewarded, if somewhat
sickened, by the sight of two giant crabs snapping off each other's
claws to impress a big female crab who stood with her back to a tree
and just screamed, a damsel in medieval distress. Our days were very
happy, with swimming, beach picnics, visits to rich neighbours in
their lovely houses and a splendid variety of great rum drinks and
superb bullshots. Once or twice the evenings were tricky. Noël,
nearly always good-humoured and witty, could be severe about the
ill manners of the younger generation so we were astonished, not to
say put out, when he flared up in a shouting rage with Gilpin during
dinner. In the ballet Noël was concocting Gilpin wanted to be dressed
as a Midshipman in reefer jacket and trousers when he did his solo
dance before a backcloth of Buckingham Palace but Noël insisted he
should appear as an Able-Bodied Seaman in bell-bottoms. 'There is
nothing lovelier than bell-bottoms!' he shouted. We left the table

in loud and flushed disarray (Merula and I kept our mouths shut throughout the storm) and took our coffees to different parts of the verandah. There was a long silence before Noël broke the ice. Thumbing through a smart social magazine he suddenly read aloud, 'Mrs So-and-So, a well-known figure in Café Society.' Pause. 'Nes-café Society.' We all laughed and the trouble was over. Dolin, looking relieved, whispered to Gilpin, 'Apologise and make it up with him in the morning.' When we eventually saw the ballet at the Festival Hall as Noël's guests, Gilpin was wearing, as I recollect, his Midshipman outfit.

Merula, Noël and I flew to Cuba together to join up with Carol Reed (who was directing *Our Man in Havana*), Graham Greene and the rest of the film unit. We were put in a very gilded hotel and given vast over-decorated suites: Noël's suitably furnished as a Mandarin's palace, ours looking like an ante-chamber at the court of Louis XVI. Merula had difficulty getting a hair-do in the hotel salon as it was always crowded with Castro's officers having their shoulder-length hair permed and their beards curled while they sat, with sub-machine guns across their knees, being flattered and cosseted by adoring Cuban hand-maidens. It was only two or three weeks after Castro's forces had taken Havana and the city was full of excitement and chaos. Rich American businessmen were withdrawing rapidly and there were no tourists. What looked like tumbrils made their slow way through the streets; they were in fact farm carts or battered lorries with cages of chicken-wire imprisoning shocked and puzzled peasants on their way to be interrogated. Men in the streets would often stop us, pull up a trouser leg to show scars from electric shock torture inflicted by Batista's police, and then laugh, saying, 'Viva Fidel!'

On our first evening there, before going in to dinner, I pushed open one of those doors painted with a top-hat and cane to indicate the 'gents' and nearly knocked over a rotund man who was loading his revolver. All his bullets were spilled on the floor and rolled to the pissoir, where they came to rest. I waited to see if he would retrieve them before I made use of the place, but after hesitating a moment he thought better of it. When I left he was still hovering near the door, thinking again perhaps. Shortly afterwards I came across Kenneth Tynan at the bar. I had known him on and off for a few years and liked him; he had been in my disastrous 1951 *Hamlet* which gave him his start as a professional drama critic, though not as an actor. On this occasion he took my breath away. Sipping elegantly at his daiquiri and drawing deeply on a cigarette he looked pale and urgent. His speech impediment became very pronounced when he said to me, 'I have t-two t-tickets for the fort tonight. One o'clock. Care to join me?'

'What's on?' I asked.

'They are shooting a couple of sixteen-year-olds. A boy and a girl. I thought you might like to see it. One should see everything, if one's an actor.' I declined. Ken, usually so liberal-minded, could be fierce and very dogmatic in certain moods but he was undoubtedly the finest dramatic critic we have had since James Agate.

One morning, early on in the filming of *Our Man in Havana*, Carol Reed, Graham Greene, Noël Coward and I were summoned, while shooting in the streets of the city, to go by car to meet Castro at a beach bungalow some twelve miles off. It was far from convenient but Carol thought it expedient for us to go. When we arrived at the place we were shown up to the first floor sitting-room of an apartment from which Castro and his advisers could be seen through the slatted blinds of the bungalow below, all bearded, long-haired, forage-capped and gesticulating to each other in a cloud of cigar smoke. Every ten minutes or so a henchman appeared and announced, 'Fidel will be here in a minute.' Ninety minutes passed and no Fidel came. We were all getting impatient when Carol firmly said, 'This is a bloody waste of time. Let's go.' Even Graham, an ardent admirer of Castro and a personal friend of his, thought it proper to leave; which we promptly did. The distressed henchman wrung his hands in despair but we pushed him aside. It was Noël, I think, who gave the fellow a reassuring smile and mouthed 'mañana' at him.

There were two great and unexpected pleasures in making that film; one was getting to know Ernie Kovacs, who played the Chief of Police (he was tragically killed in a car accident in Beverly Hills some years ago), and the other was spending an evening with Ernest Hemingway. Hemingway I admired as a writer but would not have classed him as a comfortable man to be with or looked on him as a possible friend and yet I found him most companionable and, given time, I believe we would have formed a firm friendship. Distance, work, and then death intervened. The fact that his death was self-inflicted, sad though that is, did not take me entirely by surprise. Kovacs was as different as could be; outrageously extrovert, wild, rash, gipsy-like and, in a Goonish way, just about the funniest man I have ever met.

The first day Ernie and I worked together he deliberately got his head stuck in the clapper-board, kept up a hilarious, foul-mouthed commentary on all who were watching, and I thought, 'Oh, hell! This is going to be an endless music-hall turn and we shall never complete the film.' And it was exhausting. Carol was tolerantly amused, which is more than some directors would have been. It was not the sort of behaviour to have gone down well on *Dr Zhivago*. As the days went by and Ernie grew slightly less frenetic I grew very fond of him. We went for walks in Havana, dropping in on numerous bars, and one evening I was touched when he suddenly said, 'You know something? I was dreading working with all you toffee-nosed Brits; *Sir* Carol Reed, *the* Noël Coward, *Sir* Guinness. There'll never be a laugh, I thought; but you're the ones who laugh with me – not all those American broads and clapped-out bores.'

Ernie Kovacs and I had rooms on the same floor of our hotel and I had to pass his to get to my own. One afternoon, on a day when neither of us were working, I walked down the corridor and saw his door was wide open. He was sitting at a desk typing furiously, a vast cigar jammed in his face. (He was often very busy writing sketches and commercials for T.V.) He spotted me and waved in a 'I'm terribly busy' way but somehow I sensed it wasn't quite real. Then I noticed there were about half a dozen lovely girls, all totally naked, sprawled about the room reading magazines. 'Shall I shut your door?' I asked him.

'No! For heaven's sakes!' he replied. 'What would people say? They'd say Kovacs is in that room with a bunch of naked broads. And they'd think the worst. With the door open they can see for themselves it's all perfectly innocent.'

One of the girls gave me a languid smile, licked her finger and turned a page of *Playboy*. Later Ernie said, 'I asked one of them to go to your room and ask for a bar of soap, but she refused. Shy, I suppose.' The last time I saw him was at a small party he gave at his Beverly Hills house for Marilyn Monroe and the voluble American poet Carl Sandburg. Poet and superstar sat opposite each other at a small table, gazing at each other open-mouthed; that is, Monroe's lips were parted and her eyes adoring and Sandburg never closed his mouth to cease talking.

'Don't disturb them,' Ernie said. 'They are either on another planet or playing footsy under the table. You never can tell with poets and broads.'

'But he's in a wheelchair,' I protested.

'Maybe they like it that way. Give him a push and take his place.'
I funked it.

Hemingway I first met in a Havana bar, where I was having a rum
with Graham Greene, and he invited us, together with Noël, Carol
and Merula, to dinner the following evening at his lovely, tree-
smothered house. He and his bright, amusing, tough and little wife
were fine hosts but I thought, during dinner, that he was beginning
to look a little morose and when we eventually left the table he
beckoned to me. 'Come in here,' he growled, 'away from the others.'
He led the way into his study. 'I can't bear another minute of Noël's
inane chatter. Who's interested in a bunch of old English actresses
he's picked up from the gutter? Not me. If he wags that silly finger
once more I may hit him.' He glowered at some severed heads of
African game mounted on the walls. 'Lovely creatures,' he said,
softening. 'You love what you kill. I wouldn't kill Noël – just dust
him up a bit. Am I pissed?' 'A little,' I said. He laughed and gave me
a hug.

He took greatly to Merula and they chatted about animals and as
we left he whispered, 'Come again with your wife. We won't ask
the others. Except Graham of course. He's great.' But to my regret
no opportunity occurred. He wrote once or twice and sent Matthew
an inscribed copy of *The Old Man and the Sea*, and me a signed
photograph.

Carol wanted me to play the part of Wormold in *Our Man in Havana*
quite differently from the way I envisaged it. I had seen, partly suggested by the name, an untidy, shambling, middle-aged man with
worn shoes, who might have bits of string in his pocket, and perhaps
the *New Statesman* under his arm, exuding an air of innocence, defeat
and general inefficiency. When I explained this Carol said, 'We don't
want any of your character acting. Play it straight. Don't act.' That
might be okay for some wooden dish perhaps but was disastrous for
me. 'Mustn't act, mustn't act,' I kept repeating to myself; and didn't.
The director, particularly a world-famous one like Carol, is always
right. Or often so. When the film was released we both received a
well-deserved poor press. On the morning the critics flayed us Carol
invited me round to his Chelsea home for a drink. We stood side by
side rather despondently, looking out of a window at small children
scampering in the Kings Road. 'At least *they* can't read,' Carol said. We
shrugged the whole thing off. The only person I felt sorry for was
Graham, who had been lucky with Carol in the past but was to continue
to be unlucky with me.

To go back a little: on my last night of filming, in the old quarter of Havana, we broke at midnight for a meal and I took the continuity girl, who was sweet-natured, to a little café for bean soup and coffee. Just as we were finishing an over-excited man rushed in, shouted, 'Fidel is here! In the Plaza Mayor,' and rushed out again. The café emptied immediately but I continued to sip my bitter black coffee. A few moments later a Castro aide entered, pointed at me and said, 'Fidel is asking for you.' I thought of our ninety-minute abortive wait at the beach house and decided that *another* coffee would please me. The continuity girl bit her lips with anxiety. The aide returned and sternly announced, 'Fidel waits.' We followed him out under the black starless sky to the dimly-lit plaza. It was deserted except for a knot of about fifty people crowded around a tall, central figure, easily identified, who stood head and shoulders above the others. The plaza has steps along one side and I stood on them to look down while the aide kept beckoning me. 'In a minute,' I said. The continuity girl was breathless with admiration, saying, 'Oh, isn't he wonderful! So brave! There must be dozens of people who'd take a pot shot at him, given the chance, and here he is walking about without any bodyguard.' 'Hm!' I muttered. 'Yes, brave. But there is something not quite right and I can't make it out. Now let's go down and see.' I was led to Castro, who shook hands at a distance. He was completely surrounded by small boys – unobservable from the perimeter of the crowd – dressed rather like boy scouts and each carried a dagger pointing outwards. The tips of daggers touched me, one in the chest, one in the side and one in the stomach. I cannot remember the conversation we had but I know it was brief and that Castro did say, 'Why you no speak me in Spanish?' to which I replied, 'Your English is far better than my poor efforts at Spanish.' We left it at that.

*

Irish rain, because it is expected and well catered for with appropriate clothing, is less exasperating than rain elsewhere and when, in mid-afternoon, it eased a little I decided I would stretch my legs and take a ten-minute walk down to the local church, which is more pleasing than most Irish churches, being uncluttered and supremely quiet except for a loudly ticking clock perpetually telling the wrong time. Where else, I wondered as I strode along the road, had I been able in a matter of minutes to reach a church after the frustrations of work? Segovia, in central Spain, came to mind. When, in the winter of 1962–63, I embarked on an epic called *The Fall of the Roman Empire*

Tony Quayle, who was also in the film, rented a lovely sixteenth-century farmhouse a mile or two outside the town and invited me to share it with him. It faced a small turbulent river and the high walls of the Alcazar – where in 1623 the future Charles I, before he sat on his unfortunate throne and lost his head, went unsuccessfully to seek a bride. Only a few hundred yards away stood the beautiful Hieronymite Monastery del Parral, still in the process of restoration from the effects of the Civil War, and close by on the other side of the house was the hideous and bleak Convento de Carmelitas Descalzos, where the great mystic St John of the Cross is buried in a large, flamboyant tomb of lapis lazuli and bronze. On the floor at the side of the tomb is an empty hole, not bigger than a dog kennel, where the saint was originally laid to rest. Almost every day during my few weeks in Segovia I visited one or other of these churches to rid myself of the despondency or near-feuds of the film world. Occasionally I would walk further along the river, through crunchy snow and past icicles sixteen foot long hanging from the Alcazar, to the famous Vera Cruz where Crusaders to the Holy Land had so often kept night-long vigil. It was bitterly cold but the farmhouse, which had two great log fires always blazing in the living-room, was welcomingly warm; and the dear old cook-housekeeper provided just about the best omelettes in the world. Tony was looked on as the Lord of the Manor and whenever a new, huge barrel of sherry was to be broached in the village it was rolled down the icy street by stalwart men in black berets, eased into the house, and with much ceremony the first cup drawn and handed to him. It was all very feudal and delightfully far off from *The Fall of the Roman Empire*. I never saw more than twenty minutes of the finished film.

While flying out to Spain I sat gazing forlornly at the script and jotting down a few notes. A tall American came to sit beside me and asked if I was studying my lines. 'Well, re-writing them, where possible,' I said. 'What do you think of the script?' he asked. 'Not much,' I replied. 'For instance, I can't possibly say, as Marcus Aurelius, "Look after my Meditations when I'm dead." It would bring the house down.' (In the film the 'Meditations' looked like rolls of unwanted wallpaper stuck in a basket.) It was tactless of me; I didn't realise until I met him later that my companion was the scriptwriter. The saving grace – apart from Anthony Mann, who was a friendly director and well-disposed towards actors – was Sophia Loren, whose company I enjoyed enormously. An hour or two after we first met she said, 'I have just telephoned Ponti. He wanted to know what you are like. I told him, "He's a Neapolitan." ' Which I must say surprised me a good deal and I have spent a lot of time trying to puzzle it out.

There was a lot to like and admire in Sophia but the evening I took her to dinner in Madrid is outstanding in my memory. It was lashing with rain driven by a high wind; I hired a grand limousine to collect her from her luxurious film-star apartment. She came down the stairs in a shimmering, long, white dress, of which she was justly proud. 'New!' she said. 'First time I wear. For you.' She looked several million dollars. I put up an umbrella to escort her across the wide muddy pavement. Halfway across she slipped and fell full length in a big puddle, ruining her dress, bruising her hands and grazing her face. I picked her up. For a moment she was shocked, but then said, 'I'll put on another dress.' When I got her back in the building I tried to dissuade her from going out at all on such a night but she wouldn't hear of it. 'No, no,' she said, 'I want to come. Give me five minutes please.' And within ten minutes she reappeared in another dazzling outfit, hair rearranged, washed, scented and with a small piece of sticking plaster on her chin. 'You like this dress, too?' she asked. When I said that indeed I did she shrugged happily, saying, 'I think it is more prettier than the other. But I have lots of dresses; all pretty.' We dined alone but I got her back to her apartment early, thinking the combination of the accident and my company might have been too much for her.

A film which suffered from entirely different sorts of accident – a rather sinister one – was *The Comedians*, directed by my dear friend Peter Glenville. The first weeks of this were shot at Cotonou, the capital of Dahomey, in West Africa. Dahomey was standing in, so to speak, for Papa Doc's Haiti in the novel by Graham Greene. (There is a fascinating account of the country by Richard Burton, the nineteenth-century explorer, in his *A Mission to Gelele, King of Dahome*.) The leading parts were played by Elizabeth Taylor, Richard Burton (*not* the explorer), Peter Ustinov and Lillian Gish. There was an ugly rumour that Papa Doc, who bitterly resented Greene's account of his country and its politics, had sent a voodoo priest to Dahomey to disrupt the film. Apparently voodoo spells cannot travel over water and have to be operated close at hand. All great nonsense, I am sure, but, whether the rumour was true or not, on the first day of filming one of the unit stumbled on the beach, possibly from a heart attack, and drowned in a foot of water before anyone could assist him. Several people complained of difficulty in breathing, suffering from acute headaches and deep depression; one or two had to be sent home. (When it came to my turn to leave I thought I would be driven mad by the endless red-tape delays at the airport and, when finally released, I stood impatiently on the tarmac waiting to board the plane; I almost believed that another twenty-four hours in that part of Africa would cause my death.) The weather was hot and excessively humid although it was only January and the sky, which we had been led to believe would be a clear blue, was nearly always a milky grey. In spite of the bright smiles in black faces of the local population there was something a little sinister in the atmosphere. The Cotonou markets were wonderfully colourful and the oil-lit back streets – little more than wide dirt tracks – full of noisy night life. French domination over several decades had left its civilising landmarks, particularly in little coffee shops and two hotels where a very good dinner could be obtained. Lillian Gish and I resorted to one of them on several evenings, eating out of doors by candle-light and doing our best to rescue suicidal moths.

Peter Glenville invited me to share his little house, which was in a compound built by the Chinese a few years previously, about a mile outside the town. The Chinese had shown a political interest in Dahomey, apparently, but were no longer in evidence. Bill Smith, whom I had got to know well since we first met in Ischia, also shared the house. Another house in the white-washed compound was occupied by the Burtons, and the third by Lillian and the American comedian Paul Ford and his wife. We formed a small enclave facing the long straight road, a sort of promenade empty of people, which ran along the steep sandy beach and its sullen sea, fringed on the land side by coconut palms and pineapple groves. Behind these, as far as we could make out, were square miles of scrub and swamp.

Leaving the house one morning I was spotted by Mrs Ford, who was sitting in a rocking-chair at her porch, knitting. It suggested an idyllic picture of rural life in the Mid-West, except that Mrs Ford was surrounded by several black youths displaying a long white table-cloth. 'Come right over here, Sir Alex,' she called, 'and tell me how much these fellas want for it. I can't understand their lingo.' The table-cloth was of cheap cotton, crudely painted in water-colour with a few palm trees. The youths were in a giggly state but, in pidgin French, I managed to work out the Dahomean francs they were demanding, which didn't satisfy Mrs Ford, so I translated these in to French francs, the francs to sterling and the sterling to dollars.

It all took time and was mathematically very rough and very exhausting.

'About twenty-five dollars,' I informed her.

'Too much. Beat 'em down,' Mrs Ford instructed me. I started again.

'Call it nineteen dollars,' I said.

'Beat 'em down some more.' I had another go.

'Fifteen dollars and that's it,' I said.

'Tell 'em I'll ask Pauly when he gets back tonight. They can come again in the morning.'

The youths ran away, hysterical with mirth. That evening I had a drink with the French Consul, a stern young Marxist, and idly told him about the table-cloth. He looked very serious.

'They were probably laughing at the idea of cooking this lady and then eating her off the cloth,' he said.

'Are you serious?' I asked.

'Perfectly,' he replied. 'Twenty kilometres from here are many cannibals and please do not be so foolish to believe those people who tell you not so. I hope this lady is not by herself all day.'

Mrs Ford was persuaded to come down to watch the shooting on the pier for the next few days and the young men didn't turn up again.

Bill Smith had been ill on arrival in Dahomey with near pneumonia and was still in a rather weak condition. On one of our days off I went for a splash in the surf and when I returned to the house he said he might do the same. So he and Peter set off across the road for the beach and I said I would join them shortly but that I had had enough bathing for one day. We had all been warned about the treachery of the sea locally and advised never to go more than knee deep because of the fierce under-tow and the likelihood of sharks close inshore. A quarter of an hour later, taking a book and then, for some odd reason, slipping a rosary into my pocket, I strolled down to the beach and perched myself on a sand dune, where I thought I might read and at the same time keep half an eye on both of them. The wind was blowing quite strongly but the water was only choppy, with a few larger waves beginning to appear in the distance. Peter was swimming in the surf, some five or six yards from the shore, and I could see Bill's head bobbing a few yards farther out. I opened my book and brushed away the grains of fine sand which blew everywhere.

The wind grew increasingly noisy and above it I thought I heard Peter shout something. Looking up I saw his arm waving so I waved back and returned to my book. Then, unmistakably, came the word, 'Help!' He was not waving but near drowning. I rushed down to the water and waded in the surf up to my knees to within about four yards of where he was struggling. 'For God's sake get back!' he shouted. 'But get help.' Peter is a strong swimmer but within seconds he was being carried along and out by the tide. Nearby on the beach was a tiny half-tumbled-down hut. I ran to that and tried to dislodge a plank of wood but was unable to shift it. A young man and his girl stood watching not far off; there was no one else about. I shouted to them to run to the hotel and telephone the pier, which was about two miles away, to put out a boat. We had been told that should we ever get caught by the current the best thing was to let yourself be swept down to the pier, sharks or no sharks. The young couple laughed loudly, shrugged off the imminent drowning of two white folk and sauntered away. I returned to as near as I could get to where Peter was still making valiant efforts and called to him to just float before he was too exhausted, and I gabbled a prayer to myself. Bill was now quite a distance off and his movements looked feeble. Suddenly a large wave roared towards the beach, picked up Peter and rolled him to the very edge of the water. He was flat out and I had to drag him an extra yard or two to safety. A short distance from where Bill was I could see broken water on what was probably a sandbank and I made wild gestures to him to try to make for it, as I was confident that if he could reach it he might be able to stand up or at any rate get a foothold. Either he couldn't see me, or didn't understand, but more likely he had resigned himself to death. Then the second miracle wave appeared, picked him up and landed him near the spot where Peter had been washed up. Neither of them could speak for some time, choking, breathless and totally exhausted. Bill's face, remarkably enough, looked perfectly serene, as if he had rid himself of all anxiety; and even his habitual diffidence had disappeared. I felt awful, knowing I had been useless, accusing myself of cowardice in listening to Peter's warning shouts not to follow him in, and wondering exactly what I should have done.

When they were sufficiently recovered to stand up they limped back to the house and I insisted they should go to bed for a few hours. Later in the evening the three of us walked silently to the nearest Catholic church, which turned out to be locked but we could easily see inside, and we knelt outside for ten minutes in thanksgiving. That night we treated ourselves to a champagne dinner at the better of the hotels, Peter and Bill going over and over their feelings when they had thought all was lost.

Early the following morning I stood stripped to the waist before the steamy mirror in my humid little shower-room, shaving. Wiping the mirror dry for the umpteenth time I suddenly noticed a curious marking on my chest. My first thought was that it was a rash from an insect bite – but when I looked more closely I saw it was a map of Africa, outlined in pale pink and what looked like lead pencil, measuring about eight inches by ten. You could almost have used it as a navigational chart to sail from Tripoli to Mombasa. When I showed it to Peter and Bill during breakfast they were too absorbed in reliving their horrid experience to pay much attention. 'Probably a rash,' Peter said, pouring himself more tea. Within a day or two it began to fade, although I was still impressed by it, and there were light traces of North and West Africa when I finally got back to England and could show Merula. It left me with a superstitious feeling that I had received a sinister message never to go to Africa again. Since then I have worked in Tunisia and have every intention of going one day to Kenya and hope to re-visit Egypt and the coast of Algeria, but I am sure I would refuse to go anywhere between Senegal and Nigeria.

Two days after the sea adventure the Archbishop of Cotonou invited me to call on him. He was a very tall, extremely beautiful, black, youngish man dressed in white with a cyclamen-coloured sash which became him well. He stood shyly in his little, unepiscopal study in the Cathedral not knowing what to say. He had charm and a dazzling smile but there was a touch of weakness in his personality. I asked him if he was troubled by voodooism in the area. He almost paled. 'There is some, I think,' he said. 'I don't know. Perhaps in the villages. In the interior. Far away. Here we are Catholic.' 'And what about cannibalism?' I asked. He tried to look reassuring. 'Cannibalism? Oh, no. What a strange idea! Not for many years. Here we are Catholics. We do not eat each other.' He looked happy when the brief visit came to an end.

The Comedians was not a particularly successful film but it contained one beautiful performance, unfortunately not properly appreciated by the critics, and that was given by Peter Ustinov. It was a serious, wise and sensitive portrayal of a sad diplomat, full of feeling and superbly well judged. Also I was immensely impressed by Richard Burton's generosity as an actor; he gave of himself and his talent in the most unselfish way I have ever encountered in a great star.

Blessings in Disguise

Without his sympathetic attitude and relaxed concentration my own performance, which was negligible, would have been totally down the drain. Too often Richard's performances were wrongly dismissed by those who are supposed to know about these things. Some weeks after the film was released Merula and I received an invitation to spend Christmas in Haiti as Papa Doc's guests, so that we could see for ourselves what the country was *really* like. I had a notion that if we were rash enough to accept we might end up as zombies, turning spits in the kitchen of some Haitian palace; so we declined, with flowery politeness.

*

After an excellent dinner at our Connemara hotel, topped up with a couple of strong Irish coffees, I was ready for bed. As soon as the light was out the spooky lady journalist of my imagination began to materialise again.

'Is it true that you . . .' she started, but I didn't give her time to finish.

'Probably,' I said.

'But you don't know what I was going to ask,' she went on.

'I can easily guess half a dozen of your questions,' I replied, 'and I am weary of them.'

'Are you a rich man? My readers have to be satisfied,' she said sternly.

'No, not rich. Compared to striking miners and workless actors *very* rich; compared to successful stockbrokers and businessmen I expect I would be considered nearly poor.'

'But *Star Wars* must have made you a fortune.'

'Yes. Blessed be *Star Wars*. But two thirds of that went to the Inland Revenue and a sizeable lump on VAT No complaints. Let me leave it by saying I can live for the rest of my life in the reasonably modest way I am now used to; that I have no debts and I can afford to refuse work that doesn't appeal to me.' I hoped she was about to fade.

'Grace Kelly and the tomahawk,' she prompted me.

'Ah, well, yes. Briefly then; it has been told too many times. While we were making *The Swan*, on location in North Carolina, a troop of North American Indians came to town. One of the company bought a tomahawk and gave it to me. The day I flew off for a week's holiday in New Orleans I decided it was too heavy to pack, so I gave the hall porter at the hotel a dollar, asking him to have it slipped into

Grace's bed. For the next few years it became a sort of running gag between Grace and myself, although neither of us ever mentioned it. A few years after she had married Prince Rainier I returned home from an evening performance in London and, getting into bed, found the identical tomahawk between the sheets. My wife knew nothing about it. I waited two or three years and then, hearing by chance that Grace was going to do a tour of poetry readings in the USA with the English actor John Westbrook, whom I had never met, I telephoned him to ask if he would be prepared to help me with a little scheme. Sportingly he agreed, so I got the tomahawk to him through a third party so that we could remain unknown to each other. The mission was successfully accomplished, in Michigan I believe, when he managed to get the thing placed in Grace's bed. He told me on the telephone that when they met the next day Grace casually brought my name into the conversation, asking if he knew me. When he replied, quite truthfully, that we had never met Grace apparently looked puzzled and fell silent. I had almost forgotten all about it until I went to Hollywood in 1979 to receive an honorary Oscar. Grace was safely in Monaco, but after the ceremony I found the tomahawk in my bed at the Beverly Wilshire Hotel. Time passed and then Grace came to Chichester to give a reading, again with Westbrook. She had told friends with whom she was staying that she would like an afternoon nap before going down to the theatre. Westbrook, who had been armed with the tomahawk – again through the services of a third party – got it into the bed she would occupy, but when Grace came down for tea it was clear she hadn't discovered it. He slipped upstairs and saw that she must have been lying on the bed instead of in it, so he placed the tomahawk among her lingerie in an open suitcase. Before setting off for Chichester she said she had to go upstairs to finish a little packing. Then there came the satisfying scream. The tomahawk was still in her court, so to speak, when she returned to Monaco. A short time later she met her tragic end. Some fool, who had heard the story, wrote to me suggesting the silly thing should be buried with her. As if one would want to be buried with a joke.

'Now,' I said to my spook, 'that's more than enough of my film life. You really must go.'

'Just one more question.' It crops up like one more river to cross.

'Too late,' I said. 'I am now counting sheep.'

'Is it true,' she persisted, 'that you quarrelled with David Lean?'

'Yes and no,' I replied. 'I have worked for him in six films; on three we got along swimmingly and on three we had our differences. I suppose we are both strong-willed and his will is the stronger. Let me make it clear that I am very fond of David, admire his work enormously, know him to be extravagantly generous, and all is well between us. Or so I hope. I owe him my film career; and I shall always be grateful for his courage in letting me play Fagin. The fact that he didn't particularly want me for *The Bridge on the River Kwai* is understandable but of no consequence. And the fact that my bizarre Hindu song and dance were cut from *A Passage to India* was probably good judgment on his part, even if it left me presenting Professor Godbole as a comic-cuts character without the necessary oriental mystery. It matters very little. David is a man of genius cocooned with outrageous charm. Any skill in front of the camera that is still left me is entirely due to his early guidance.'

'Who is your favourite actor?'

'I would never dare answer that one. But I'll tell you who my favourite performer is. Ronnie Barker. Surprised? You shouldn't be. He's really great. It is now time you took your commercial break. Goodnight. I'm asleep.'

She had gone.

CHAPTER SIXTEEN

Ophidia and Others

Across the lawn of a house on the outskirts of New Delhi tripped a small, cherubic-faced Hindu lady, in sari, sandals and rimless spectacles. She carried a plate from which she was elegantly eating some orange-coloured substance. Merula and I had been invited to lunch by General Gurbux Singh and his wife – very cultured and sophisticated Sikhs – to whom Peggy Ashcroft had given us an introduction. (She had become friends with them during the making of *The Jewel in the Crown*.) There were about fifteen guests, mostly Sikhs, and after jugs of Bloody Marys had been downed, a splendid meal was served in the garden. The Hindu lady, plate tucked under her chin and full of smiles, faced me squarely.

'I do hope,' she said, 'you like the cobra snake.'

I looked somewhat aghast at whatever it was she was eating. (I had once sent Peter Bull, from Canada, a can of rattlesnake meat from which he had made sandwiches, passing them off to his guest, Frith Banbury, as chicken. Frith, who had pronounced them 'scrumptious', slumped to the floor when he discovered what they really were.) So I was rather suspicious about what was on the lady's plate.

'No, no!' she said, following my look. 'I am Hindu. This is carrot cake. Very good. I only meant, I hope you admire the cobra.'

'Well,' I said dubiously, 'I once had to stroke a cobra, in Sri Lanka, and I have felt a little differently about them since then.' I didn't think it politic to tell her that snakes scare me and also have a horrible fascination which I find quite disturbing.

'Oh, I'm so glad,' she said, misinterpreting my words as enthusiasm. 'You see, I worship the cobra.' For a moment I assumed she meant she found cobras 'divinely' elegant, but she meant far more than that.

'They are *divine*,' she announced, flashing her spectacles at me in the bright sun. 'I live with them, you see. In the rainy season, my house is swarming with them; under the sofas, on the chairs, in the kitchen. They like their saucers of milk. When the maids sweep the house they just push them around with the broom, saying, "Get out of my way you silly things!'' They are very patient, the snakes. They would never harm anyone. Not in the daytime. At night, perhaps, it is a different story. When it begins to get dark I tell them to go out to the garden, which is their proper place at night. Sometimes we sit in the dark in the garden, but always under a strong lamp, sipping our drinks. I tell my friends not to step outside the circle of light; that would be dangerous. Pythons now; they are sluggish, nasty things; not noble like my cobras. Never, good sir, let a python get more than two coils round you.'

'What do I do after two coils?' I asked.

'Unwind him, of course. The poor dears! All of them! The wicked snake charmers pull out their teeth. *What* I could do to those snake charmers! Boiling would be too good. But please, the next time you are in Delhi come to my house.'

I thanked her but made a mental note that my diary would be very full of engagements for the foreseeable future. Which was sad, because I liked her very much.

'Tell me,' she said, getting rid of the carrot cake, 'have you met a king cobra?'

'I've only seen one in the London zoo,' I told her.

'Ah, that *is* a snake! You know, when the king cobra rears up his eyes are on a level with yours, and when he looks you in the eye, well, this is truly a spiritual experience.'

I bet, I thought.

Feeling a bit queasy I helped myself to carrot cake (which was delicious) and a glass of cold beer. A tall, handsome young Sikh, turbaned and bearded, came to my side. It turned out he was a director of documentary films, specialising in wildlife.

'Do you like tigers?' he asked.

I told him I had no experience of them except from behind bars, but admired their beauty.

'Then perhaps you would like to come with me to see some in the wild, about two hundred miles west of Delhi. I go with only my driver, in an open jeep. I allow no guns or sticks as I wish the tigers to know we are friendly. For two years I have been visiting the same place and they recognise me and pay very little attention. But there is one tigress who doesn't like me – perhaps my turban upsets her – and she always charges. Fortunately she stops about six feet away. It is just to try to frighten me off. Will you come next Thursday?'

'I am afraid I have to be in Bangalore as from tomorrow,' I said.

'Then when you come back?'

'I'll try,' and oddly enough I meant it. He inspired more confidence in me than the lady ophidia-fancier. I didn't have an opportunity of taking him up on his invitation, but I keep his address handy for the day I feel sufficiently foolhardy.

In the three months I was in India I never saw a snake, except the tremendous python which lives half in and half out of a sack, alongside his pipe-playing master, on the steps of an hotel in Agra, and looks very browned off. A tourist non-attraction so far as I am concerned. But the Hindu attitude to all animals, which of course I had heard about, was a revelation when witnessed in reality. The beautiful white cows wandering the streets in the midst of screaming traffic, munching at vegetable stalls without reprimand; mares and their foals, sows with their litters, all confidently picking their way through buses, taxis and bicycles which seemed to threaten instant death to human-kind, touched me greatly. It struck me as never before that the world is the possession of all living creatures, with a right equal to ours to inhabit it peacefully, however dangerous they may be to us; and the Hindus have quietly and joyfully accepted the fact. The whole Indian experience was something of a reawakening for me, and I understand people who seize every opportunity of returning to the subcontinent to refresh themselves.

Ophidia again. Sessue Haiakawa, who was a most courteous man and had been a very glamorous Hollywood film star in the silent era, was wrongly hauled over the coals by the Japanese authorities when we were making *The Bridge on the River Kwai* in Sri Lanka, and it was this that resulted in my having to caress a cobra. It was reported in the British press that Sessue had struck me in the mouth and drawn blood. That may have appeared so on film but was not so in fact; he had been required in one scene to hit me in the face with a pamphlet, which he did very lightly, and at the same time I crushed a capsule of what looked like blood held in my mouth. As a result of the press report Sessue was reprimanded from Tokyo for bringing the Japanese into ill repute and, to make amends, or dispel any bad feeling (of which there was none) the Japanese ambassador in Colombo gave a dinner party for Sessue and the higher echelon of the *River Kwai* contingent. This was held at the ambassador's private residence on the outskirts of the city. Lovely doll-like ladies in flowery kimonos served us under the starlight, and, for our entertainment, an Indian fakir was brought in who appeared to make a small mulberry tree grow from a nut in a matter of minutes.

He also had with him, in a circular basket, a female cobra which must have been about eight feet long. When the snake reared up the

Japanese ladies ran as fast as their little hobbled steps could take them, screaming and tittering, to the safety of the house; and the gents, left to their sake and cigars, found themselves facing a deadly still creature, which sat up with its hood extended, eyeing them beadily. The fakir was a grubby creature whom I judged to be neither likeable nor trustworthy.

Suddenly he picked up the snake – she was quite a weight – and, saying 'Good luck to touch,' deposited her across my lap and arms. I found her warm and very dry to the touch but kept the experience as brief as possible before handing her over to Bill Holden, who promptly slung her around his neck. He would have kept her, I think, for the rest of the evening had not the snake spotted a chicken's egg which had been placed on the ground. The cobra disentangled herself from Bill, and, very slowly, set about swallowing the egg. No doubt the egg was a reward for doing her act. As she eased her way back into the basket the shape of the egg could be seen always at the rim, until she flipped her tail in and settled down, neatly coiled, to digest it.

Taking a look at the mulberry bush I reckoned it was about fifteen inches in diameter, its roots clearly part of the nut (if it was the same nut), but my suspicions were aroused by noticing that one of its young leaves was burned. No explanation. The fakir had manipulated the nut with his hands and his arms had been bared to the elbow. (Trickery of some sort, no doubt, but brilliant trickery; such as I witnessed last year in Delhi when a man lay on the grass, covered himself with a light cloth, and levitated to about four feet off the ground, hovered for a quarter of a minute and then slowly subsided.) Sessue was happy again, the ambassador satisfied – East and West were amicably reconciled – and when we finally left there was much bowing and Japanese hissing.

While making *The Bridge on the River Kwai* I was allocated a personal servant, a small, wiry Sinhalese of indeterminate age but probably in his fifties, called Fernando. He was solicitous, charming and hard to fault – or nearly so. When I arrived at the mock-Tudor-type house of lath and plaster (in a jungle clearing), which, together with Sam Spiegel, Bill Holden and others, was to be my home for several weeks, Fernando showed me to my room. He opened the bedroom door and pointed to a washstand in the corner; then, with prudish delicacy, he drew aside a little green curtain under it to reveal a flowered chamber pot. I told him I wouldn't be needing that as there was a perfectly good lavatory down the corridor. A day or two later I thought Fernando looked worried, and when I returned to the house in the evening after work he followed me to the bedroom and pointed, rather sternly, to the pot which he had now placed in the middle of the room. Again I explained I did not need it. The next day, on my return, I found it in the same position but standing on a large paper doily. The following day it was the same story but the chamber was now filled with mothballs. After that Fernando gave up and the thing remained for ever curtained. But he took a great fancy to my alarm clock.

'Master give Fernando clock?' he asked one day.

'Perhaps,' I said, 'but not before I leave.'

'Fernando like clock for wedding present for his daughter. Fernando want it now.'

'Not now,' I insisted. 'In a few weeks. When I go.'

From then on I noticed that the clock travelled round the room at about a yard a day, going from the bedside to a table near the door. We had been advised that if we noticed belongings on the move we should replace them immediately in their proper position, otherwise it would be considered that we had no interest in them and they would finally make a swift exit. I replaced my clock, in Fernando's presence, on a day when I spotted it had done quite a walk, but he was not totally defeated; he immediately started some violent dusting and managed to knock it to the floor where it fell to pieces. He shrugged, in a mock-apologetic way, and picked up the bits to show me.

'Master not want clock now,' he said triumphantly. 'So I can have for my daughter wedding present?'

'It will be no use to her,' I said, rather crossly.

'My daughter like.'

And he went away happily, jangling spring, screws and broken glass in the palm of his hand.

The next day he showed his gratitude. I was lunching at a rickety table under a bamboo awning on the edge of the jungle and Fernando was acting as waiter. Suddenly he dived under the table waving a paper napkin and shouting angrily. While trying to steady the table and stop the cutlery from falling I called out, 'What the hell are you doing, Fernando?' He emerged from the far side of the table looking quite unperturbed.

'Bad snake, Master. Cobra snake, sitting under table. Fernando frighten away.'

I had already lifted my knees to my chin and blanched. I don't know if there was a snake there or not; I never saw it, and I couldn't tell from Fernando's expression whether he had been fooling or rashly brave.

Tik-Polonga is an unpleasant little creature, dirty-white in colour with dark brown freckles, getting on for a foot in length and about the

thickness of a finger. It is reputed always to attack when disturbed, can
spring at least three yards, and its bite is deadly. It is greatly attracted
to milk jugs and small bowls; it is, needless to say, the bane of the
Sinhalese housewife in jungle areas.

Mr and Mrs Da Silva (many people in Sri Lanka bear Portuguese or
Dutch names) owned a modern, circular, concrete house which stood
at the top of a round hill a few miles from our mock-Tudor residence
and, although I had never met them, they kindly invited me up for a
coffee one Sunday morning. When I arrived I realised that things
circular had gone to their heads; apart from the house, which was
largely composed of circular rooms, the garden was oval and the
flower beds looked like vast coloured plates scattered on the grass.
Entering the round entrance hall I noticed a child's pushcart and dolls
and heard, from a distant room, a small girl's chatter. As I was shown
into the drawing room my eye went immediately to a round coffee
table in the centre, which was bare except for a sealed jam jar. Coiled
in the jar was a Tik-Polonga; dead and pickled, as it turned out, in
formaldehyde. I stopped in my tracks. 'Why the Tik-Polonga?' I
asked. Already I was off the idea of coffee in that room.

'It is nothing,' said Mr Da Silva, frowning. Mrs Da Silva was much
more forthcoming and, when coffee was brought, she settled comfortably in an orange and black velour armchair and embarked on her
story.

'Last week our little daughter, Maria – she is just four years old –
was playing in the garden when I heard her scream. I ran out to her and
found a small bite on her hand. Tik-Polonga, I said to myself.'

She looked admiringly at the dead snake but her husband kept his
gaze on his cup and saucer.

'Maria was already very ill. Sometimes, with Tik-Polonga, you
have only five minutes to live. I carried her to her room and my
husband jumped in his car and rushed down to the village to find the
snake doctor. Fortunately he was in. He came immediately but would
not come by car; he insisted on bicycling up the hill. He is very proud
of his bicycle. When he got here he looked at Maria, who was by now
in a coma, and then went into the garden where he began to whistle
softly. Soon the Tik-Polonga came to him and he picked it up very
gently; then he asked for a jam jar, which I gave him – that very one.
He put the snake in the jar and carried it to our daughter. All the time
he talked to the snake and he talked to Maria, who was unconscious,
and as he talked the snake began to die and the roses came back to
Maria's cheeks. In half an hour the snake was dead and Maria was

sitting up on her bed chatting. We put the Tik-Polonga in fluid and we keep it here as a reminder of how Maria's life was saved.'

I looked across at Mr Da Silva, who was flushed and angry.

'You don't seem to like this story,' I said to him. 'Why not, if it is true?'

'Oh, it is true enough,' he said. 'But it need not have happened. We are very modern here, as you see. We have a big refrigerator and we have all the snake serums. But it so happened that the idiot johnnies at the waterworks were on strike last week and, in consequence, we had no electricity. So I did not dare to use the serum and we had to fall back on these old-fashioned peasant ideas and fetch a snake doctor. It is not at all modern. I like things to be modern.'

The mystery of the snake doctor and his methods held no interest for a rich man with a circular house, furnished and equipped from a Tottenham Court Road store.

Back at the *Kwai* camp I told the Da Silva story to Lt. General Lance Perowne, who was military adviser on the film and with whom I had struck up a friendship.

'True, I have no doubt,' he said. 'These jungle wallahs know a thing or two. But personally I'd rather have a couple of Rikki-Tikki-Tavis around.'

We were casually watching Sessue Haiakawa, dressed in his midnight-blue kimono, slicing innumerable golf balls into a net. Two very pretty Thai girls set up the balls for him on the tee after every shot. Sessue was absorbed with his form and also enjoying, in a serious way, the tiny patter of polite applause and admiring *oeillades* of the girls.

'They know how to live, the Japs,' Lance observed, removing his monocle and putting it in a sock as we moved away. 'Don't much care for them but they are good fighters. In Burma I had a severed Jap's head boiled down and strapped on the back of my knapsack – facing outwards – when trekking through the jungle. It worked wonders. Never any trouble with snipers after that.'

Major General Orde Wingate was a tall, fair-haired man, with a straggly moustache, a ready laugh and a passion for engineering and the English language. He was undoubtedly something of an eccentric, with a soaring imagination, and full of unorthodox schemes for righting the world. At the end of the '39–'45 war he put forward proposals for marching home from India, through the Middle East, across southern Russia and Europe – which he reckoned would take six months – the victorious army which was listlessly awaiting transport ships. Not only, he felt, would it revive the

morale of the troops and be a remarkable experience for them, but
it would make the world conscious of the victory of democracy. He
was, of course, turned down: the politicians and statesmen were
already back at play. When Lance Perowne relieved Wingate in Burma
the first thing he did was to inspect the military hospital – ramshackle,
open-sided bamboo huts. He walked between the makeshift beds,
where a few dozen wounded and ill men lay, and when he reached the
end he turned to the medical officer and said, 'Fine. Now I'm going
away for half an hour; when I come back I want to see that every man
here has had a shave.' (They were all bearded, Wingate-style.) When
he returned he found all the men feeling their faces. 'Good,' he said. 'I
am going away for another half-hour and while I'm gone each man is
to have had his nails cut.' When he returned they were all examining
their fingers. 'After all,' he said to me, 'a man's hands should be his
pride; they should be taken care of, like good tools. Then I told the
MO that when I next visited them, in half an hour, every man was to
be standing at the foot of his bed. Of course he said it was impossible;
some of them were in a pitiful condition. But they made the effort and
I marched them out of there. Not Horse Guards' Parade stuff, you
understand. If I hadn't done so I think most of them would have died.'
    'Lance, tell me,' I said, 'why do you keep your monocle in your
sock?'
    'I used to wear glasses,' he replied, 'and during a long leave I hiked
to Tibet. I had a mule, a sack of flour and, carefully concealed, so as not
to give offence, a side of lamb. Took a few books, a map and my
reading glasses. I stayed in a Buddhist monastery for a month. They
were most hospitable and when I left I asked if there was anything I
could do for them. "Yes," they said. "Our old abbot is getting very
blind. Please give him your spectacles." Well, I couldn't very well
refuse. I thought, I'll be damned if I ever let that happen to me again; so
when I got back to Delhi I got myself a monocle and I keep it tucked
away. Socks are the best place.'
    Lance's presence was a great social asset to the *Kwai* film unit, which
boasted of course Sam Spiegel, Bill Holden and Jack Hawkins. Jack
and I had worked happily together in various plays and films. One of
the minor but daily amusements I had was in the make-up area, where
Bill Holden – by nature I believe a rather hirsute man – would shave
his chest because American ladies were reputed to be averse to seeing
body hair, and Jack, who was fairly smooth-skinned, stuck on
quantities of crêpe hair to please the English ladies. For my part, I was
gumming a wig over my bald pate; the three of us, each seriously

tackling our vanity, must have presented a rare sight to the many inquisitive eyes.

The coolest spot in Sri Lanka was the little corrugated iron hut in which, as Colonel Nicholson, I was confined for one sequence; it was cramped and uncomfortable but the heat of the sun on the roof attracted a welcome breeze inside and I remained there fairly happily for hours at a stretch. However, James Donald, who played the sympathetic doctor so admirably, was required to get in the hut as well and feed me coconuts. This wouldn't have been so bad if James and David Lean hadn't come to loggerheads as to how the scene should be played. Each time I got to the end of a coconut James queried something or protested in some way, and the whole thing had to be done again. 'Don't dare speak to the director like that!' the continuity girl snapped at him, when James said David Lean knew nothing about acting; but James was not one to be put down easily and the result was that I had to get through, wearily, a dozen coconuts and was doubled up for days. (I regret to say that in *Great Expectations*, because I kept fluffing, I had obliged John Mills to eat about fifteen boiled potatoes; little does the public know what film stars suffer for their 'art'.)

In 1954 Merula and I rented for six weeks, from the late Martın Coleman, an enchanting small house in Venice, facing the Grand Canal and a stone's throw from the Accademia Bridge. We had one or two friends to stay, including Irene Browne, of whom we had become most fond. Coleman called us one morning to tell us that Dame (as she was to be) Freya Stark would be pleased to give us lunch at her villa in Asolo the following day. We accepted happily and Coleman said he would drive us up to her hillside eyrie. Freya Stark was a friend of my old guide and mentor Sydney Cockerell and I had met her a couple of times in Paris, where she had been most kind to me. Also I admired her writing, so the pleasure of seeing her again was something to look forward to. (Cockerell gave me, when it was first published, a remarkable slim volume called *An Italian Diary* by Freya Stark's mother, Flora Stark, which I still treasure.)

Before we reached Asolo Coleman said, 'Do be careful. Freya has brought back from her recent travels in the Near East a snake poison which she is very keen about. She has a reputation for experimenting with snake poison.' As we entered the beautifully decorated villa Miss Stark greeted us with strange words. 'I made a wonderful discovery in Bessarabia; a truly splendid venom from a black snake there. Not at all lethal, I'm told, but it lays people out for twenty-four hours. I brought back two little bottles. Very precious.' And she showed them to us: a colourless liquid in small medicine bottles. Irene Browne's eyes rolled, indicating a preference for elegant and expensive little bottles from a Parisian perfumery. 'How lovely to be an actor,' said Miss Stark. 'If I were an actor I would play in nothing but Shakespeare. All those glorious words!' (Quaffing my pre-lunch aperitif I muttered to myself, '"Drink off this potion: is thy union here?"')

'And you, Miss Browne? You love to act Shakespeare?' Irene had played Ophelia to H. B. Irving's Hamlet before the Great War and was not too keen on pursuing the Shakespeare stakes further, her real enthusiasm being reserved for bridge. Unlike her usual, somewhat acerbic self, she was at a loss for immediate words and fumbled.

'I think,' I said, 'that Miss Browne feels much the same as I do. Acting Shakespeare can be all very fine, but it can lead you into wild self-indulgence, listening to your own voice and so on.'

'I wouldn't have dared to say that,' Irene whispered, and choked on her drink. Miss Stark looked surprised and disappointed and strode into the kitchen, with some determination, saying she would tell the cook we were ready for lunch. I forgot to look to see if she had taken the bottles with her. I don't think she was gone for more than a minute.

We sat down to roast chicken, potatoes and spinach *en branche*. Embedded in my spinach I found three burnt matches which, thinking they were probably a careless oversight of the cook's while busy at her Calor gas stove, I discreetly extracted, and hid under my plate. I didn't give it another thought for about an hour. Then, while taking coffee in the drawing room, it hit me. A violent sweat broke out, convulsive shivers, a horrible nausea and the room revolved. I fled on a zig-zag path for the lavatory. No vomiting relieved my stomach cramps and, to Miss Stark's chagrin, we bade a hasty farewell. Back in Venice, after a car journey which was interrupted every few miles by my nausea, a doctor was called who announced sagely, 'You have been poisoned.' I was very ill for two days. I believe the matchsticks had been dipped in the little bottles before being inserted in my spinach. Irene, Merula and Martin Coleman suffered no bad effects, so I came to the conclusion that burnt matches with spinach should not appear in any cook-book. I can only hope that I wrote a polite bread-'n'-butter-'n'-poison letter; but I can't remember.

CHAPTER SEVENTEEN

Towards the Pebbled Shore

Like as waves make towards the pebbled shore,
So do our minutes hasten to their end.

Shakespeare. Sonnet 60.

Late in 1939 Merula became pregnant and we spent a few comfortable weeks with my parents-in-law, Michel and Chattie Salaman, at their home near Ockley, in Surrey. It was a handsome old farm house which had been considerably enlarged, standing in about eighty acres, called Ruckmans. Gas masks, in their absurd cardboard boxes which looked as if they might contain Easter eggs, hung on strings alongside over-coats, scarves and tweedy hats in the downstairs cloakroom. Ruck-mans was always full, mostly with people as young as, or even younger than, ourselves leavened with a chain-smoking aunt or two; and Merula's father carved daily for between eight to twenty at the big dining-room table. We were a noisy lot. Food was still plentiful, the house was warm, but there were no longer great cups of early-morning Earl Grey tea or maids to light crackling little fires in the bedrooms. The breakfast sideboard boasted a vast ham, chafing dishes of sausages and bacon, cereals with jugs of cream, and the smell of methylated spirit burners for those who wished to boil an egg pervaded the room. There was a grand music-room, designed by Lutyens, where you could nearly always find someone doing ballet bar-practice, or singing Irish folk songs, or possibly a small group of would-be actors rehearsing a scene from a play. The heartier members of the household would be out riding, chopping wood or, with shotguns under their arms, be searching the woods for suspected spies or German parachutists who didn't exist. These were the days of Dad's Army.

Ruckmans had long been a haven for refugees, political or econ-omic; the Spanish Civil War and the Jewish pogroms had provided shelter for temporary or semi-permanent residents, and there was always a flux of the lost, the lonely or the broken-hearted. The refugees were now mostly perplexed people like ourselves. My brothers-in-law were either in the Fire Service or doing ambulance work in London prior to joining the Navy or Army; I felt guiltily indecisive, spending most of my days in an unoccupied attic I had discovered, filling it with rank pipe-tobacco smoke while I wrote my stage adaptation of *Great Expectations*. The household was eventually dragooned into hearing me read it aloud, all of us sitting round the dining-room table. The drawing-room, although crowded and full of chatter after dinner, was a holy of holies for the radio, which was never turned off for fear of missing a news bulletin; but, in spite of that, death and disaster seemed very far away.

B.B.C. Radio, through the kind offices of Barbara Birnham, provided me with a few short jobs, mostly of a semi-highbrow nature, for which I received fees ranging from twelve to twenty pounds, but in spite of these money was always very short. The strain of indecision as to when and where to offer my services, the ugliness of the future and, above all, the worry as to how to stave off my mother's petty debts, eventually took their toll physically – though only for twenty-four hours. (Two years before my marriage my mother had somehow got into my bed-sitter at Notting Hill Gate while I was on tour and removed such clothes and small possessions as I had; in their place I had found a little stack of pawnbroker tickets, which I suppose was not unwitty of her but very inconvenient for me. My great fear was that Merula or her family would be saddled with this trashy, constant muddle and minor dishonesty should I get killed.) Then there came the evening when I announced, quite cheerfully, that I was feeling rather ill. I went to bed with a temperature of 105 degrees – no pain, no vomiting, just sweat and delirium. Throughout the night I saw myself at the far end of the bedroom, but I wasn't a human being; I was a small submarine washed up broadside on the shingle beach at Eastbourne, where I had spent four years of my schooling. The submarine lay inert in the darkness, jolted now and then by little whispering grey waves. There was no sign of life on board and I knew the ship was empty and yet at the same time it was me – a sort of feeble metallic slug. No lights could be seen anywhere and the war was a silent, static affair which existed, if at all, only in the imagination. Perhaps my half-conscious mind was feeling its way round 'The eternal note of sadness' struck by Matthew Arnold's 'Dover Beach'.

> Swept with confused alarms of struggle and flight
> Where ignorant armies clash by night.

Merula came continuously to my bedside and I expect I made reassuring sounds, but as soon as her back was turned I reverted to contemplating my vision of submarine/me and its/my predicament. With hindsight, after so many years, my fever seems like a clip from an old black and white film, discarded on the cutting-room floor, giving me a preview of my own ship, broadside on the rocks, in the Adriatic. When I woke in the morning my temperature was normal and I got up with resolution, intending that when my call-up came I would try to make sure it was for the Navy.

So many friends have died in the past forty years that my address book begins to look like an old English country churchyard, with RIP engraved on lichen-covered stones; people who helped me when young, people whom I knew I could always turn to when worried, actor friends, wise and witty people who could make me laugh at myself when I was taking things too seriously. And so many to whom I wish I had shown more openly, while they were still alive, the affection I felt in my heart. But the Feast of All Souls is a consolation. And the greatest, the best and most loving is still, thank God, at my side. I cannot imagine life without her or what it would have been like had I never known her or had not had the courage to suggest marriage. What sort of life would it be if I couldn't grumble about the missing coffee pot, the dangerously exposed electrical appliances, the burned potatoes, the oil paint on the door knob, the barking of *her* dog, or the forgotten arrival time of my train from London?

Merula, on her mother's side, was a Wake – a proud descendant from Hereward the Wake (surely a mythological rather than an historical character) and on her father's from the Salomon who was Haydn's impresario in London. The name had been changed to Salaman at the end of the eighteenth century by a member of the family who thought it would make it easier for him to get into the Navy, and indeed he succeeded at being at the Battle of Trafalgar. Or so they say. Merula's maternal aunts were totally Edwardian in attitudes, true blue and inclined to speak of 'common people', but her mother considered herself a communist while at the same time being an ardent supporter of Haile Selassie of Abyssinia. She was a beautiful woman of great charm, a skilful gardener (her flower arrangements were always breathtaking, in a very English way), but was not above hurling the best china cups and saucers at her husband when in a rage. At the time Merula and I announced our engagement she said, 'And the cook's given notice!' before slumping to the floor in a faint. When Merula told Chattie of her pregnancy she was rounded on with a storm of indignation; 'How dare you bring a child into this filthy world! At a time like this! With a war on!' (She had six children herself.) I have a picture in my mind of her, in later years, stooped in her garden, behind in air, planting or weeding and sprinkling herself with violent insecticides to keep off midges. She had the same capacity as Merula for doing too much, too strenuously and for too long. She had little or no idea of the theatre and when she announced that she had written a play I guessed we were in for some embarrassment and my wildest fears were not exaggerated – she handed me a huge bundle of hand-written foolscap which turned out to be a word for word copy of the novel *The Gay Lord Quex*.

Humbert Wolfe, the poet and man of letters, once said to me of my father-in-law, 'You can't be an artist, a country gentleman *and* a Jew,' and yet Michel appeared to succeed well enough on all three levels. Although the house was often alarmingly hearty for a rather intimidated stranger, with its horsy and huntin' talk, there was often good conversation – or at any rate shouted disagreements – about literature and painting. Books were everywhere and also fine works by Augustus John, Gwen John, Orpen and Steer, as well as Rowlandson and etchings by Goya. It was an education for someone like myself, who had encountered such things only in galleries. Michel had a memory for classical poetry which must have rivalled Lord Wavell's and it was among books that he and I found our mutual, though usually uneasy, ground. As I set off to join the Navy he handed me a pocket edition of Thucydides, saying, 'This will help you keep things in perspective.' Inside the book he had scribbled, 'Plus ça change plus c'est la même chose.' It was a more acceptable gift than the vast unplucked turkey which he dumped, on Christmas Eve, in the kitchen of our tiny cottage. Seizing the duck we were going to have he said, 'That's just what I want; an extra duck,' and made off with it. The turkey wouldn't go in our oven anyway and Merula burst into tears.

Not only had I found a wife; I had acquired a family.

Since quite early years, and certainly from the time it dawned on me that I was illegitimate, I had assumed, but without any good reason, that my father must have been Andrew Geddes: a managing director of the Anglo-South American Bank, who had been born, I discovered later, in 1860. The Guinness on my birth certificate was a mystery and still is. Approaching my mother on these matters was worse than useless, like facing a catatonic blank. Michel Salaman explained to me that many Edwardians would ask their best friend to give his name to an illegitimate child so that it was on the cards that Guinness was a close friend of Geddes, if Geddes was my father

that is. One day at Ruckmans I had cause to speak on the telephone
to the old and very reliable nanny who was with a family who were
intimate with the Salamans. She told Merula, when they saw each
other a short time afterwards, that she was amazed at hearing my
voice because it was so typically Guinness; and that she had worked
before the 1914–18 war for a family where a Guinness and a Geddes
were frequent weekend guests. She totally dismissed the idea of my
being related to the Geddes she had known, saying that the voice
was quite different and that he had been a dour Scot. This information
fascinated but did not convince me; I stuck to the Geddes idea.

Andrew Geddes cropped up in my childhood only two or three
times, as far as I know, and then only very briefly. The last time I
saw him was when I was eight years old, prior to going to my
preparatory school in Southbourne. He came one afternoon to
Bournemouth to visit my mother; I was scrubbed, polished and
persuaded into my best grey-flannel suit. He arrived, top-hatted and
white-haired, sitting very upright in an open carriage outside our
ground floor flat. The neighbours, no doubt, must have been impressed by such a sight, tweaking at their lace curtains, which usually
revealed little of interest. Half an hour later he left and I was told to
get myself ready to accompany 'uncle' back to the station. He must
have heard my protests from another room and most likely he
deciphered my thoughts when I appeared before him in my straw
boater, smiling sheepishly. I had remembered, in the nick of time as
it seemed to me, that on the last occasion he had said goodbye he
had slipped me a sovereign. There was nothing as familiar as a kiss of
course. My mother and I drove with him in silence to Bournemouth
Central station and saw him settle comfortably in his compartment.
No sign of the sovereign. However, just before the train started, he
unstrapped the carriage window and, fingering in his waistcoat
pocket, said, 'I almost forgot.' His smile was somewhat cynical as
he handed me half-a-crown. That was the Andrew Geddes personality
I remember, and I have seen in myself, I fear, something very similar
when I have felt hurt or taken advantage of. He died when I was
sixteen. *The Times* printed a fairly long, dull obituary, representing
him, if I remember correctly, as an industrious, worthy and conscien-
tious man. When I became stage-struck, in my early teens, I thought
of him as looking remarkably like Henry Irving.

Shortly after my twenty-first birthday I went to see the solicitor,
a Mr Morris, who had been in charge of my minuscule financial
affairs for the previous seven years and had paid out my school fees

and sent my allowance, while it lasted. He was a large, fleshy, bald man and sat at a highly-polished desk behind a green baize door in a Dickensian sort of room in the City, surrounded by documents tied with pink ribbon and black japanned tin boxes. On several of the boxes I saw the name 'A. Geddes' painted in sloping white lettering, now turning yellow. Mr Morris seemed mockingly puzzled as to why I had come to see him. I told him I wanted to know who my father was and if by any chance he had been Andrew Geddes.

'What on earth makes you think he could have been Geddes?' he asked. 'Why not Stiven? After all, your mother married David Stiven and you were known as Alec Stiven until you left your prep school.'

'Stiven could not have been my father,' I replied. 'He once held me upside down from a bridge, threatening to drop me in the river below; and another time he held a loaded revolver at my head, threatening to kill me and himself to get whatever it was he wanted out of my mother; he made life a terrifying hell for about three years. And Geddes doled out the cash, or so I have always understood.'

'That doesn't mean it was him,' Mr Morris said.

'And what about the name Guinness, which after all is on my birth certificate?'

'It's no use asking me,' he said. 'I know nothing about that. Before my time.'

Shyly, and in a small voice, I asked, 'Is there anything for me? I mean, I was told when I was twenty-one there would be something coming to me.'

'Such as?'

'I'm not sure. A gold watch, perhaps.'

'A gold watch? Never heard of it. Some delusion of your mother's I'd guess. I am sorry, but there is nothing. Money gave out, as you know, more than a year ago. There are a few shares in a company in Tierra del Fuego, which we are selling and when they are realised you may get about £700. And that's it.'

I left him, none the wiser, without the watch I had dreamed of, or even a letter of explanation from someone; but I could look forward to a bit of cash one day. When it materialised I would buy a gold watch I decided.

Many years later, leaving the stage door of the Theatre Royal, Brighton, and accompanied by Binkie Beaumont, who was present-ing the play I was in, a rather frail lady stopped me.

'Does the name Andrew Geddes mean anything to you?' she asked.

I assured her it did.

'I am his youngest daughter,' she said. She must have been about twenty years older than me. I explained I couldn't talk then or in the street so we arranged to meet later.

Her name was Kate Weldon; she was a gentle quiet creature but talked freely when we sat down in my dressing-room at the theatre. She told me that she had often wanted to write or speak to me but had been sworn by her elder sisters to keep silent and never approach me; now that they were dead she felt free to make contact. She said she felt sure she was my half-sister because when in Paris with her father, in 1913, he had confessed to her, in great distress, that someone he knew in England was expecting a child which he thought must be his. When that child was born he informed the family and they were so outraged they strictly forbade the subject ever to be mentioned in their presence again. Apparently he had one confidante in the household whom he trusted implicitly; a maid or nanny who had been in his service for several years. It was she who told Kate Weldon that after a day visit he had made to Eastbourne, shortly before he died, he had said to her, 'I think I saw the boy.' He became melancholic, wept a great deal and maintained long periods of silence. She also told Kate that he had written a letter, to be given to me after his death, which he kept locked in his desk. It was, she knew, in a bulky envelope, as she had seen it. Mr Morris, according to Kate, had gone immediately to the Geddes house when he heard of her father's death and shut himself in the study for several hours. When he left there was no letter to me to be found. As she told the story I began to feel I was playing some minor character part in *Bleak House* or *Dombey and Son*.

Two years later Kate Weldon died of cancer. We lunched together two or three times in London but she had no more information to give. During her last illness I visited her in a nursing home in Eastbourne run by fierce and unamiable nuns (very rare in my experience) who were reluctant to let me see her. A dragon nun took me to her bedside, stood glowering impatiently at me for a minute and, when Kate opened her eyes, hissed in my ear, 'She doesn't recognise you. Come away.' When I remonstrated about such a brief visit she curtly said, 'We are very busy here,' and, with a swish of her black skirt, a clatter of rosary beads and a flagging of starched head-gear, pulled open the door to shoo me out.

There the question of Andrew Geddes being my father would have rested, more or less to my satisfaction, had I not crossed the Atlantic in the *Queen Mary*, from New York to Southampton, during November

1959. As I was dining alone in the Verandah Grill, reading a book propped up on the table, a scrap of paper was brought me by a steward. On it was written, 'I would like to meet my cousin. Will he join us for coffee?' It was signed Honor Svejdar née Guinness. I sent back a note saying I would be delighted to join them but, alas, I was no cousin. Honor (who was Lord Iveagh's daughter) and her husband Frankie were sitting by themselves a few tables away, looking amused. They were most welcoming and we became good friends very quickly; my friendship with Honor deepening with the years. Over coffee I told them as much as I knew about my parentage and Honor kept saying, 'I *still* think you are my cousin.' When I said I knew my mother had been living in Cowes, on the Isle of Wight, when I was conceived, she said, 'That practically clinches it. Our yacht was there in the summer of 1913.' She and Frankie then embarked on a game of speculation as to who were likely dark horses among her uncles and near relations. Lord Iveagh was automatically ruled out, naturally, as were one or two other members of her family; but she had her suspicions, she said, and would get to the bottom of it. She never did, of course, because it is my belief there was no bottom to get to. Poor Honor; she thought a bastard in her grand family might be fun.

From time to time Honor would send me a snapshot of one or other of her uncles leaning on the rails of a yacht or skiing, with comments such as, 'He stands the way you do,' or, 'The shape of the eyes is very you,' or, 'What about the mouth?' I could detect none of the resemblances she thought she saw. In Ireland I was taken to be vetted by Lord Iveagh, who was most polite but noncommittal, and others of her family were keen to get a look at me; but after a few years the subject ceased to interest me much and I'm sure must have bored them. The one thing which might have tied it all together, and which I was never able to unravel, was whether Andrew Geddes was in Cowes in 1913 and whether he had been a guest on the Guinness yacht that summer. My guess is that my father-in-law was right in his suggestion that Geddes may have asked a Guinness to lend his name to an unwanted child.

I have to admit that the search for a father has been my constant, though fairly minor, speculation for fifty years. With my first week's salary from Eliot's *The Cocktail Party* I bought myself the gold vest-pocket watch that had never materialised and always wore it during the play. On the inside I had engraved, 'The readiness is all.' Not that I have ever felt really ready for anything; but in an obscure way I suppose I felt I had arrived – somewhere, somehow, and from God knows where.

Perhaps I should have chosen a quotation from Tom Eliot who, Shakespeare and Milton excepted, is my best loved poet. 'In my beginning is my end' or 'A condition of complete simplicity / Costing not less than everything' from 'Little Gidding'. My favourite quotation, from the same poem, would have been too long:

> We shall not cease from exploration
> And the end of all our exploring
> Will be to arrive where we started
> And know the place for the first time.

At the risk of pretention I have to say that, for me, the great adventure could be yet to come, had I only the courage and strength of will to embark on it: a spiritual journey, all foibles, silliness and ill-will mastered and thrown overboard and a genuine attempt made at achieving total simplicity. A day-dream only, I fear. I lack sufficient humility and it is so warm and cosy on shore. The seas look wide and dark; storms quickly arise, great waves can mount threateningly; and there are probably monsters in the deep. To leave friends behind must be sad and bitter, even when we know so many who have gone triumphantly before us, but we remain in touch, I believe, in some mysterious way. Of one thing I can boast; I am unaware of ever having lost a friend.

Re-reading that last sentence in 1996, eleven years after it was written, I am saddened to say I can no longer make such a boast. *Mea culpa. Mea culpa. Mea maxima culpa.*

Index